"An inspiring work, full of insights on the life ot a beloved of God. It reveals his pursuit of the divine will through his spirit of purity of heart, simplicity, humility, and perseverance. He knows that God loves him and all he wants to do is to love Jesus. This is a spiritual treasury for our faith journey."

—Br. William Chng, OCSO, New Clairvaux Abbey

"Is it possible to produce saints in the mold of the desert fathers in the midst of a modern secular culture? Rafael Arnaiz Barón, a Cistercian oblate living in the middle of the twentieth century during Spain's civil war, proves that it is. O'Keefe and Gonzalo-García distill materials from sources that confirm the authenticity of Brother Rafael's spiritual life, including letters and journal entries. A few full sources allow us to see that the cited portions are consistent with his entire body of writings."

—Martha Fessler Krieg, lay Cistercian associate and independent scholar

"What the Spanish have known for decades about Saint Rafael now comes in English thanks to O'Keefe and Gonzalo-García: a person who encountered God in the mundane of everyday life. This is a well-rounded biography of a man who is like us; a man seeking God in fits and starts, not in a continuous, uninterrupted journey. A good, interesting read."

—Deacon Mark Plaiss, Oblate, Saint Meinrad Archabbey

MONASTIC WISDOM SERIES: NUMBER SIXTY-EIGHT

To Live for God Alone

The Life and Spirit of Saint Rafael Arnaiz

Mark O'Keefe, OSB,
and Sr. María Gonzalo-García, OCSO

α

Cistercian Publications
www.cistercianpublications.org

LITURGICAL PRESS
Collegeville, Minnesota
www.litpress.org

A Cistercian Publications title published by Liturgical Press

Cistercian Publications
Editorial Offices
161 Grosvenor Street
Athens, Ohio 45701
www.cistercianpublications.org

1   2   3   4   5   6   7   8   9

Library of Congress Cataloging-in-Publication Data

Names: O'Keefe, Mark, 1956- author. | Gonzalo-García, Maria, author.
Title: To live for God alone : the life and spirit of Saint Rafael Arnaiz / by
    Mark O'Keefe and María Gonzalo-García.
Description: Collegeville, Minnesota : Cistercian Publications, [2023] |
    Series: Monastic wisdom series ; sixty-eight | Includes bibliographical
    references. | Summary: "A biography of Saint Rafael Arnaiz including
    excerpts from his writings"— Provided by publisher.
Identifiers: LCCN 2022027123 (print) | LCCN 2022027124 (ebook) | ISBN
    9780879072919 (trade paperback) | ISBN 9780879075910 (epub) | ISBN
    9780879075910 (pdf) | ISBN 9780879075682 (pdf)
Subjects: LCSH: Arnáiz Barón, Rafael, Saint, 1911-1938. |
    Trappists—Spain—Biography.
Classification: LCC BX4705.A727 O34 2023 (print) | LCC BX4705.A727
    (ebook) | DDC 271/.1202—dc23/eng/20220906
LC record available at https://lccn.loc.gov/2022027123
LC ebook record available at https://lccn.loc.gov/2022027124

Contents

Abbreviations

CF   Cistercian Fathers series, Cistercian Publications

Conf   Conference. In John Cassian. *The Conferences.* Trans. Boniface Ramsey. Ancient Writers Series 57. New York: Paulist Press, 1997.

CW   Saint Rafael Arnaiz. *The Collected Works.* Ed. María Gonzalo-García. Trans. Catherine Addington. MW 162. Collegeville, MN: Cistercian Publications, 2022.

MW   Monastic Wisdom series, Cistercian Publications

OC   *San Rafael Arnaiz: Obras completas.* Ed. Alberico Feliz Carbajal. 7th ed. Burgos, Spain: Editorial Monte Carmelo, 2017.

OCSO   Cistercian Order of the Strict Observance

RB   The Rule of Saint Benedict. From *RB 1980: The Rule of St. Benedict.* Ed. Timothy Fry. Collegeville, MN: Liturgical Press, 1981.

S   Sermon

Usages of 1926   *Regulations of the Order of Cistercians of the Strict Observance.* Published by the General Chapter of 1926. Dublin: M. H. Gill and Son, 1926.

Introduction

Perhaps for many of us today it would be difficult on the face of it to identify with Rafael Arnaiz. He was a young man of early twentieth-century Spain with its distinct historical, cultural, and religious events and perspectives. Although he grew up in a wealthy family, connected with Spanish nobility, Rafael entered an austere Trappist monastery. There his monastic vocation unfolded in an unusual way. Rafael's spirituality was particularly intense, with a passionate focus on the cross of Jesus. As was true of Saint Thérèse of Lisieux, his was a spirituality formed by the free embrace of suffering. Like her, he died young—barely twenty-seven years old. But in his brief life, Rafael Arnaiz attained a human and spiritual wisdom that few can attain in this life. His is a timeless, straightforward spirituality lived with great intensity, and even fire.

But at the same time, Rafael is hard to resist. Reading his life story—but especially reading his writings—one almost inevitably feels the attraction of his warmth and sincerity, of his deep but simple faith, of his profound insight into the meaning of the Christian life and into the cross, and his intense love and single-hearted pursuit of God. His was a heart on fire for God, and he invites his readers to let God set their hearts aflame together with his. Despite the distinctiveness of the particular unfolding of his life, his readers can quickly gain a sense that in watching his journey unfold they recognize it as somehow the common journey of a true disciple of Jesus. His experience reveals a life path that must for all of us inevitably pass through suffering and the cross. In a particularly intense way, Rafael teaches us to respond with trust and surrender to what seems to be the divine will and thus to arrive at that purification that leads to a true freedom to love God and to give ourselves in response to God's gratuitous self-giving.

It is no surprise that Rafael's complete works are now in their seventh Spanish edition since their first publication in 1988. What a blessing to the English reader that Cistercian Publications has recently published a slightly edited translation of his works in English.[1] Books and articles about Saint Rafael ("Hermano Rafael") are proliferating in Spanish.[2] Modern readers—despite the many ways that Rafael's life was a distinctive one—are separated from him by less than a hundred years. Having died in 1938 and been canonized in 2011, he is a truly modern saint. His writings are easily accessible for a contemporary reader. In Rafael's writings, we encounter a Christian spirituality every bit as profound as that of many of the spiritual classics of our Christian tradition but expressed in a language, style, and freshness that can be easily grasped by a modern reader.

Rafael's writings—particularly because they are not treatises and essays, but personal letters and journals—are profoundly human, personal, and—in that sense—simple. They reveal Rafael as a richly attractive personality—sincere, earnest, fervent, young, humorous, humble, common. His writings draw the reader in by his simple power of expressing his deep feelings, his effort to understand himself, and to explain the depth of his experience. Without formal theological education, in an amazing way he absorbed and brought together what he had been taught and what he had read, especially from traditional Roman Catholic spirituality, to arrive at a theological understanding of his journey—and

1. Saint Rafael Arnaiz, *The Collected Works*, ed. María Gonzalo-García, trans. Catherine Addington, MW 61 (Collegeville, MN: Cistercian Publications, 2022).
2. See the Bibliography for many such titles about Rafael in Spanish.

especially of suffering and the cross. We can all be deeply enriched by walking with him and allowing his life and writings to offer us a simple but profound wisdom for the journey.

A SPIRITUALITY OF THE CROSS

Marriage, parenting, and the monastic life—they are all, at their best, meant to be paths of increasing self-giving, of other-directedness. For most of us, this process unfolds through the daily and ordinary challenge to become generous, forgiving, and patient as we live, work, and interact with our fellow sinners in the midst of the ups and downs of daily life. In this way, slowly freed of our own selfishness and self-focus, we can arrive at a true freedom to love God and to love our neighbor. But, like a time-lapse video, Rafael's journey allows us to see in a telescoped form the path that all of us are meant to walk. His path is like our own—only compressed, condensed—so that we can see in him the path that we must all walk, whatever our vocation in life. And it was especially Rafael's experience of the cross in his life that accelerated the journey that we share with him.

Rafael offers us a model of dealing with the suffering that every human life entails—not, of course, exactly like his, but inevitable for all of us. And it is usually suffering, difficulties, trials, and contrarieties that bring every Christian (really, every human being) to the foot of the cross. It is there, as people of Christian faith, that we, like Rafael, must choose over and over again—even if with a trembling and shaky faith—to embrace the cross and to unite ourselves with Jesus crucified (or, really, to allow him to unite us to his cross). Our life too must be formed by the cross—by surrender and by trust. Thomas à Kempis's *The Imitation of Christ* was a great favorite of Rafael's.[3] In his classic work, Thomas notes that Christians can easily say that they want to follow Jesus—until his way leads to the cross—and that it inevitably leads to the cross.

3. Thomas à Kempis, *The Imitation of Christ*, trans. Ronald Knox and Michael Oakley (South Bend, IN: Greenlawn Press, 1990).

Suddenly, many Christians fall silent or turn away. But the way of the cross is the path that Jesus our Savior walked. And it is the way that he taught to his disciples. Rafael recognized and embraced this profound truth. He lived it. He reflected on it—meditated on it—and we are privileged to listen to his musings and to his praying, to his surrendering and his trusting.

Different legitimate Christian spiritualities place different levels of emphasis on the cross of Jesus. Some have a particular focus on Jesus in his humanity or in his glory—Jesus crucified or Christ glorified—but there is no authentic Christian spirituality without the cross. There is no Christian faith without the cross of Jesus, and there is no Christian discipleship that does not involve our embrace of our own distinctive cross. In fact, there is no human life that does not involve difficulty, trial, and suffering. It is no accident that the cross is the central image of our faith. It is the only path to a mature Christian faith, the principal doorway to that truly self-giving love and to the trusting abandonment into God's hands that Jesus himself modeled for us. And it is what Rafael modeled, refusing to become bitter or angry in the face of the unwanted turns that his life took. Instead, he looked to Jesus crucified and humbly tried to unite himself with him, finding comfort in being united with Jesus in trusting self-surrender and self-offering. Ultimately, united with Jesus, Rafael learned not simply a personal, individual self-giving but, in union with the crucified Jesus, a self-giving love for others.

Perhaps today especially we live in an age when many who choose to embrace Christianity want it in a cross-less form. Many Christians say that they have chosen to attend or belong to this or that church because they leave its Sunday worship feeling uplifted and happy. The preaching makes them feel good and affirmed in themselves. And all of that is good, as far as it goes. But on its own, it suggests that religion is a useful distraction, a coping mechanism, a shot of adrenalin or serotonin. But life is not just sunshine and happiness. Even a superficial reading of the Gospel—of the life and teaching of Jesus—makes it clear that we cannot reduce the message of Jesus to the pursuit of a superficial happiness that seeks to make us forget, for a time, the clouds and storms. Life just simply is not that way. There are trials and difficulties, loss and grief, frustrations and obstacles, failures and downturns. We need more than distractions and coping mechanisms. We need the cross: that is, we need to see our lives and embrace our responses in light of, under the shadow of, the cross of Jesus. It is profoundly true that there is no cross without the resurrection, but arriving at the resurrection requires passing through the cross, just as new life is found only on the other side of the dying. Rafael embraced this most fundamental truth. Thus he can teach us to suffer well. Trying to resist suffering that cannot be changed or trying to numb ourselves against it often only increases the pain over the long run. Rafael teaches us that freely taking up our cross with Jesus can bring us peace and even joy—a profound solace that comes not from eliminating the suffering but from learning to love and hope in every circumstance.

A Monastic Heart

Rafael Arnaiz was a monk. He never formally professed vows. He was forced by bad health to leave the monastery several times within a few years. But Rafael was profoundly a monk. He embraced the monastic life and its practices immediately and generously. He reveled in the monastic liturgy. He loved the rhythm of daily prayer and work in the monastery. He learned to embrace the daily challenges of living with his brother monks just as he found them. He discerned the presence of God in the midst of the ordinary. He was a model of humility, obedience, and prayer. He understood the value of silence and solitude even in the cenobitic life. And he loved his particular monastery—the place, its rhythms, its community, its church, and its tabernacle.

Rafael lived in a time in which the classic writings of monastic or Cistercian spirituality were not the object of formal study for young monks. His coming and goings from the monastery did not allow for a prolonged formal monastic formation. But he was a monk through and through. He had the heart of a mature monk, as if he had lived the monastic life for decades. And he had a profound monastic intuition (or what Cardinal Basil Hume referred to as a "monastic instinct"),[4] as if he had studied and prayed over commentaries on the Rule and the works of Saint Bernard and other early Cistercian authors. And so just as he reveals in condensed form the journey that every Christian must walk, each in his or her own distinct way, so too he reveals the monastic journey for those who have professed it and for those who wish to learn from its wisdom for life outside a monastery's walls.

A Look into the Life and Spirit of Saint Rafael

In the pages that follow, we hope to introduce Saint Rafael and his rich spirituality to our readers. We begin in the first chapter by reviewing his life and the unfolding of his vocation. In the second chapter, we examine his writings, his motivations for writing, and the influences on his thought. In the third chapter, we introduce the monastic ideal of purity of heart as a virtual synonym for what was a kind of motto for him: "God alone" (*Sólo Dios*). We suggest that this singlehearted focus on God provides a lens or window for understanding his journey and his deeply monastic instincts. In the fourth chapter, we consider Rafael's discernment of his vocation in the midst of unexpected and often undesired turns, suggesting that he offers wisdom for the work of discernment for us today. Since Rafael was never professed as a monk and was forced to leave his beloved monastery three times in only a few years, we devote the fifth chapter to a study of the authenticity and depth of his vocation as a monk. In the sixth chapter, we look at desire and yearning—tempered with a spirit of hope and waiting—as key characteristics of his spirituality. And in the sev-

4. Basil Hume, *Searching for God* (Wilton, CT: Morehouse-Barlow, 1978), 23–26.

enth and final chapter, we examine the place of suffering and the cross in his life and thought. Like few others, Saint Rafael can teach us to accept, embrace, and deepen our faith through the reality of suffering.

We hope that reading this book will invite our readers to turn to Rafael's own writings and to discover there the true riches of what he has to offer us today. In a brief appendix to this work, we offer several excerpts from his works to amplify points that we have made in the text but also to whet the readers' appetite for reading more. Finally, we offer a bibliography that can direct the reader to other resources, though unfortunately most of these are currently available only in Spanish. It is our hope that this book, together with the recently published English translation of his works, will invite others to study and share Saint Rafael's life and spirit.

Chapter 1

Life

Rafael Arnaiz Barón was born in his family home in the city of Burgos on Palm Sunday, April 9, 1911.[1] His parents, Rafael Arnaiz and Mercedes Barón, were of upper-class Spanish families with sufficient means to employ a number of household servants. In fact, the young Rafael's maternal uncle, Leopoldo (known in the family by his nickname, "Uncle Polín"), married the future duchess of Maqueda. Rafael's birth was followed in succeeding years by the births of his three siblings, Luis Fernando in 1913, Leopoldo in 1914, and Mercedes in 1917. The senior Rafael was a forestry engineer and owned estates that brought in a comfortable

---

1. Rafael's full name is Rafael Arnaiz Barón. Traditionally Spaniards have two last names: the first one is the father's and the second the mother's—women don't change their maiden name when they marry. Mistakenly, an accent mark was added to *Arnaiz* when Rafael's writings were first published and made available to the public. This mistake has perdured until the most recent edition of his writings.

Currently the only English-language biography of Rafael is Gonzalo María Fernández, *God Alone: A Spiritual Biography of Blessed Rafael Arnáiz Barón*, trans. Hugh McCaffery, ed. Kathleen O'Neill, MW 14 (Kalamazoo, MI: Cistercian Publications, 2008). For more detailed information about Rafael's family and early life, see especially *San Rafael Arnaiz: Obras completas* [OC], ed. Alberico Feliz Carbajal, 7th ed. (Burgos, Spain: Editorial Monte Carmelo, 2017), 27–34, n. 1; 999–1001; and Francisco Cerro Chaves, *Silencio en los labios, cantares en el corazón: vida y espiritualidad del Hermano Rafael* (Madrid: Biblioteca de Autores Cristianos, 2014), 29–64. Others are listed in the bibliography, pp. 265–71 below.

income. An avid reader, he maintained a personal library of some six thousand books. He was later described by his children as loving and available, refined about his dress and dining, but giving no attention to the differences in social classes so prevalent in Spanish society of the time. They described their mother as beautiful, intelligent, and devoted to her husband and children, with a passion for music, literature, and the theater. Active in society life, she also served as a volunteer nurse for the Red Cross. In sum, the young Rafael enjoyed a loving and happy family environment.

The family were fervent and active Catholics, and their life included frequent daily Mass, visits to the Blessed Sacrament, and family rosaries. His mother particularly focused on the religious formation of her children. Over time, in addition to Rafael's vocation, his brother Luis Fernando eventually became a Carthusian, while his sister Mercedes briefly entered the Ursulines, though serious illness prevented her from remaining. The easy shared faith of the family members is apparent in Rafael's later letters to them and in the accounts of his life later written by both his mother and his uncle.

The majority of the young Rafael's elementary and secondary education took place in Jesuit schools, first in Burgos and later in Oviedo when the family moved because of his father's work. Rafael was later remembered by childhood classmates and teachers as a courteous, joyful, and loving child. He was a dedicated student, a lover of nature, one interested in sports as well as in drawing, painting, and music. He was sincerely pious, devoted from his childhood to the Virgin Mary, but he could be humorous, given to innocent pranks, and mischievous in games.

In 1920, at the age of nine, Rafael developed pleurisy, caused by a bacterial infection of his lungs. Gravely ill, he was removed from school for several months. In thanksgiving for his eventual recovery, his father took him to the famous shrine of the Virgen del Pilar in Zaragoza. It is likely that this pilgrimage and the attribution of his cure to the intercession of the Virgin helped to solidify Rafael's lifelong devotion to Mary. The illness is also noteworthy because of Rafael's otherwise apparent good health, until the sudden development of diabetes during his monastic novitiate.

In 1926, at the age of fifteen, Rafael began private art lessons with a well-known artist, Eugenio Tamayo. Drawing and painting became lifelong pastimes for him, though his artistic interests and talents extended less formally to music as well. Without any formal musical instruction, he played and was able to improvise on the guitar, violin, and piano. In hindsight, Tamayo recalled that the young Rafael already manifested a contemplative spirit as he spent contented hours completely absorbed in his art. In fact, Rafael shared with his teacher that he felt an as-yet-undefined attraction to silence.

As a reward for successfully completing his secondary studies, Rafael's parents allowed him to spend the summer with his Aunt María and Uncle Polín (Leopoldo), the duke and duchess of Maqueda. They had a home in the city of Ávila itself as well as a country estate a few miles north of Ávila at Pedrosillo. This was the first of many visits over the next several years, and Rafael formed a deeply affectionate and important spiritual bond with his aunt and uncle. He became very much a member of the family, along with their five children. In the following years he wrote more letters to them than to anyone else; many of the letters reveal his deepening spiritual vision and later served as windows into his spiritual state and maturation as his vocational journey unfolded. (In fact, during a particularly intense and lengthy exchange of letters, after Rafael was forced to leave the monastery for the first time, his brother Leopoldo jokingly asked him if, with all of the letter-writing, he was translating Don Quixote into Greek.)[2]

The duke and duchess came to play an important role in Rafael's vocation and spiritual journey, though their five children, Rafael's cousins, recount that their parents had lived a rather worldly life

2. Saint Rafael Arnaiz, *The Collected Works* [CW], ed. María Gonzalo-García, trans. Catherine Addington, MW 162 (Collegeville, MN: Cistercian Publications, 2022), 282, document 77 (hereafter #). For more detailed information on Rafael's aunt and uncle, see OC 39–44, n. 6.

until they both had a kind of adult conversion. Then becoming deeply devoted as Catholics, the duke with his wife's acquiescence considered entering a Trappist monastery and had made the financial arrangements for his family that might have made it possible, had the abbot not forbidden his entrance until all of his children were independent. It is not surprising, then, that the duke would later introduce Rafael to the Trappist way of life in general and specifically to the abbey of San Isidro de Dueñas, which he himself had hoped to enter. Although the duke was never able to pursue this dream for himself, the duchess, after her husband's death in 1952, entered the Discalced Carmelite Monastery of the Incarnation in Ávila (where Saint Teresa of Ávila had spent the first twenty years of her religious life), dying there in 1980. This was the spiritual ambience in which the young Rafael was formed.

In 1932, Rafael began his studies in the prestigious Escuela Superior de Arquitectura de Madrid. It appeared that his talents for the visual arts would be channeled into a promising career as an architect. With a friend, he found room and board in a Madrid hostel and quickly embraced his life as a student. Although he was appropriately studious, his friends from the time remember him as funny and sociable, apparently not conscious of his family's social status.[3] A long and chatty letter to his brother Luis Fernando from this period—after Rafael jokingly comments on his younger brother's almost illegible handwriting and lack of punctuation— gives funny details of his life in the building, including how he had bought a bird, confessing that even he had found it a little "corny" (*cursi*).[4] In a letter to his parents, he acknowledges their probable concern for his lack of attention to his finances. But even while living much like any ordinary university student, each of his days also included Mass, rosary, and a thirty-minute visit to the Blessed Sacrament in a local church.

3. For personal testimonies about Rafael's personality and character from his siblings and friends, see OC 123–27, n. 103.
4. CW 30, #9.

In January of 1933, Rafael temporarily left his university studies for six months of compulsory military service. For a time assigned to guard duty at the royal palace in Madrid, he got along well with his fellow recruits, from various social and economic backgrounds. They recall him as being funny, especially known for the caricatures he drew of the people around them. At the same time, despite the fact that Spain's government during that period was notably anticlerical and antireligious, he persuaded his companions to pray the rosary with him as they passed the time as sentries. Later he was assigned to a ski regiment before his return to the university in July of that same year.

The First Encounters with "La Trapa"

Sometime around 1929, Rafael's Uncle Polín had given him a copy of a book that the duke had translated from the French, *Del campo de batalla a la Trapa* (*From the Battlefield to the Trappist Monastery*),[5] in order for Rafael to do a drawing for the book cover. It was the story of a highly decorated French military officer, Gabriel Mossier (1835–1897), who had left his promising career to become a Trappist lay brother and died with a reputation for holiness. His story was told with a strong Marian and ascetic spirit. It seems likely that this reading sparked Rafael's personal curiosity and interest in knowing more about the Trappist life, with which his uncle had ample and devoted contact. His uncle arranged his first visit to the Abbey of San Isidro de Dueñas near the town of Venta de Baños, about 160 miles north of Madrid, in late September of 1930.[6]

---

5. Rafael, following a custom of the time, often referred to a Trappist monastery or the Trappist life by the term "La Trapa." To this day, if you want to take a taxi to visit his monastery of San Isidro de Dueñas from a nearby city, you ask the driver to take you to "la Trapa."

6. The Abbey of San Isidro de Dueñas had a history dating back to the Middle Ages, coming to prominence in the early tenth century. In the High Middle

Rafael was enchanted from the start. One biographer summarizes his reaction: "His artistic soul was dazzled by the beauty
of the chant and of the liturgy and by the austere and silent air of
spirituality."[7] In a letter to his uncle of October 11,[8] commenting
on the visit, Rafael reported,

> From this moment I began to see clearly and became inti-
> mately ashamed of myself: when upon entering the church
> to greet the Lord, I saw the monks chanting in the choir,
> and that altar with that Virgin; I saw the respect that the
> monks have in church and, most of all, I heard a Salve that
> . . . dear Uncle Polín, only God knows what I felt . . . I did
> not know how to pray before.[9]

During the visit, as Rafael reported to his uncle, he was given
two books to read. The first was *La vida cisterciense*, which consists
of six chapters in one hundred nineteen pages, explaining the
Cistercian life (including its particular devotion to the Virgin
Mary) as a path to holiness, the process of being admitted, the
vows, and the daily life of the Trappist monk.[10] The second was
La vida del Padre María Efrén Ferrer,[11] the story of a French Trappist who had left behind a wealthy family and a promising future,
dying in 1839 with a reputation for holiness. It would not be

---

Ages, it was a Benedictine monastery of the extensive Cluniac reform. In 1835,
its Benedictine community was expelled during an extended period of anti-
clericalism called in Spain the "*desamortización*" (which included expropriation
of monastery properties). After sitting abandoned with its buildings decaying
for over fifty years, it was "re-founded" by a French community of Trappist monks
who purchased the property in 1890. In 1931, the community numbered almost
120. For more information about and pictures of the monastery and of Saint
Rafael, visit the monastery website: http://www.abadiasanisidro.es/.

7. Fernández, *God Alone*, 9.

8. CW 11–16, #5.

9. CW 12, #5.

10. *La vida cisterciense en el monasterio de San Isidro de Dueñas* (Burgos, Spain:
Monte Carmelo, 1928).

11. For more information on the book, see OC 61, n. 32.

surprising if—as with the earlier book that his uncle had given him to read—Rafael recognized parallels to his own life, perhaps laying the seeds of his later vocation. In any case, it appears that Rafael left that first visit deeply impressed, apparently pondering the possibility of a vocation, but laying it aside for the present. In the letter to his uncle, he said:

> And don't think that upon seeing and admiring them I felt envy, no, for you have taught me something very important that I have heard you say many times: that one may go toward God on many paths and in very different ways. Some fly, others walk, and others, most people, stumble. And since God wants it that way, then so do I.[12]

Rafael returned to the university, but references in his letters suggest that he made another brief visit to the monastery during the next year. During this period he began to write down a more extensive reflection on his visits, which he completed in September 1931, a year after his first visit, now titled *Impresiones de la Trapa*.[13] It is clear that even a year after his first visit, Rafael remained enchanted by his experience of the monastery: the varied sounds of the bells of different sizes, the rough habits of the monks, the beauty of the monastic silence, and the stark contrast between the spirit and priorities of the monks and the people living a purely worldly existence. In contrasting life in the world with that of the monastery, he says, "For setting aside the few little shining lights in this world, one could say that it is ruled by darkness, whereas

---

12. CW 13, #5. Father Teófilo Sandoval, Rafael's Trappist spiritual director, who later played a critical role in preserving Rafael's works and making them known, believes that his Trappist vocation was virtually decided at that first visit. But this is not evident in Rafael's own writings. To the contrary, in writing to his grandmother in December 1933 to explain his decision to enter the monastery, Rafael reports that he had been pondering his vocation for many years, during which God had been calling him "sweetly and gently" (CW 56, #18).
13. CW 20–25, #7.

here in La Trapa, it is never night and it is always day."[14] At times, he speaks in romantic hyperbole of the monastic life as he reports, for example that no one prays to the Virgin like the Trappists, and when he says that when the monks pray, they cease for those moments to be mere mortals but become truly angels. He sees that the monk's purpose is to live totally in and for God: "The Trappist lives in God and for God, who is his only reason to exist in the world."[15] Interestingly, he refers to Saint Bernard as "our father Saint Bernard," as if he were already a son of the monastic patriarch.[16] In the end, he concludes that while the artist or those with heightened sensitivity can be impressed by the externals that they encounter in the monastery, for those with faith, there is a certain "something" ("*algo*" or "*no sé qué*") that works a subtle but real change in the visitor.[17]

In the following year, Rafael returned to San Isidro for a retreat of over a week (June 17–26, 1932), and, in a notebook of that time, he writes rather cryptically, "I have become convinced of many things" ("*Me he convencido de muchas cosas*"[18]). It would not seem unreasonable to assume that he is referring to his own vocation, though he did not move immediately to enter the monastery. In this delay of three years from the first visit to his entrance, for all of his early romanticism about the monastic life, Rafael reveals himself as ultimately a realist. When he finally revealed to his uncle that he intended to seek admission to the monastery, Rafael reported that he had been pondering the idea for at least two years.[19]

---

14. CW 24, #7.

15. CW 23, #7.

16. CW 22, #7.

17. CW 25, #7.

18. OC 88, ¶49. The brief comment—without further explanation—appears in a very brief list or calendar of events and activities that Rafael kept for January through June 1932. The comment appears for the date June 19 with the notation of the place: "Trapa." The text is not translated for the *Collected Works*.

19. His uncle reports on this conversation in Duque de Maqueda, *Un secreto de la Trapa (Beato Hermano Rafael)*, 6th ed. (Burgos, Spain: Editorial Monte Carmelo, 1998), 29–35 (excerpted in OC 131–34, n. 106).

Although his announcement at that time was unexpected, his uncle was not completely surprised. He did worry that Rafael was being romantic and naïve about the monastic life, but he was reassured by the recollection of the words of Saint Paul: "I can do all things through him [Christ] who strengthens me" (Phil 4:13). In fact, it appears that Rafael had already consulted widely: the archbishop of Burgos, the Discalced Carmelite nuns of Oviedo, and some Dominican acquaintances—though they had all apparently advised him to become a diocesan priest.[20] Given the social status of his family, the comfort in which he had been raised, and his own sociability and artistic nature, this advice might not be surprising, given the austerity of the Trappist life, especially in the 1930s.

In a brief but beautiful letter of November 19, 1933, Rafael wrote to the abbot of San Isidro de Dueñas, Félix Alonso García, seeking admission to the monastery. He assured the abbot that he was not acting out of any dissatisfaction or disillusionment with the world: "I am not motivated to change my life in this way because of sadness or suffering or disappointment or disillusionment with the world . . . I have all that it can give me. God, in His infinite goodness, has given me such gifts in this life, many more than I deserve." In fact, he felt blessed by what he had been given in life, but he offered himself humbly, with "a heart filled with joy and much love for God."[21] The monastery's novice master, Fr. Marcelo, responded affirmatively only two days later, cautioning Rafael about the challenges of the Trappist life—undoubtedly aware of Rafael's family background and knowing his uncle, the Duke of Maqueda—but without trying to dissuade him.[22] The door to the monastery now stood open to Rafael.

Having already made arrangements to leave his university studies, Rafael originally planned to seek admission and to inform his parents once he was already in the monastery, because of his fear

---

20. Paulino Beltrame Quattrocchi, *Fascinado por el Absoluto: Hermano Rafael* (Madrid: Ediciones Paulinas, 1991), 60.

21. CW 43, #12.

22. For the novice master's response, see OC 129–30, n. 106.

of the pain that his decision and his departure would cause them and himself when he broke the news to them. His uncle tried to dissuade him from this plan and arranged for him to meet the papal nuncio to Spain, who happened to be in Ávila at the time for an extended visit, an arrangement that indicates the family's social status. The nuncio affirmed Rafael's decision to enter the monastery but, like his uncle, urged him not to leave without softening the blow to his parents with a face-to-face conversation and seeking his parents' blessing.

Rafael finally saw the wisdom of this path. He decided to go ahead with a previously planned Christmas holiday visit with his family and to inform them after the new year. In the end, he found his parents pained by the thought of his leaving (which was bound to be particularly painful for them because of the strict separation required by Trappist life of the time) but supportive, in keeping with their own deep faith and desire to follow God's will for them.[23] It does not appear that Rafael himself had any particular concern about the austerities of the Trappist life that he had decided to embrace or about his own ability to live it.[24]

THE FIRST ENTRANCE

On January 15, 1934, the twenty-two-year-old Rafael arrived at the Abbey of San Isidro de Dueñas. On February 18, he formally received the white habit of a novice and began his novitiate, though he was only to stay for about four months. The life could hardly have been more different from the one that he had just left

---

23. The details of this Christmas visit and the conversation between Rafael and his parents are touchingly recounted by his mother in her biography of Rafael: Mercedes Barón, *Vida y Escritos del Beato Fray María Rafael Arnaiz Barón, monje trapense*, 12th ed. (Madrid: PS Editorial, 2000), 116–19 (excerpted in OC 165–67, n. 154, with a letter from his mother to her own mother, expressing both her sadness and her resignation to God's will for her son).

24. Beltrame, *Fascinado*, 63.

behind. The monastery belonged to the seventeenth-century Trappist reform of the Cistercians, which emphasized penance and austerity. The daily schedule itself was rigorous, with monks rising at two o'clock in the morning, going to bed at seven in the evening, and enduring a sparse vegetarian diet, manual labor, strict silence, and hours of common liturgical prayer.[25] And yet the young Rafael embraced it with fervor, joy, and a sense of adventure, and also with a sense of humor. He was full of youthful health, strength, and desire for the heroic—leaving behind, without regret, his family, the comforts of the life he had known, and the promising future that had been ahead for him had he continued with the plans for his career as an architect.

In his first letter to his mother shortly after his reception of the habit, Rafael reports, "I am ever more convinced that God made La Trapa for me, and me for La Trapa."[26] In a letter of April 1, he writes to his parents: "your son has found the true way . . . and, as the Gospel [Matt 13:44] says, a treasure, one that he has set about digging up without a moment's hesitation."[27] In the few letters that a Trappist novice was allowed to write to his family, Rafael describes with enthusiasm the details of his life, his eagerness to adapt himself to everything, his fervor for the liturgy, his desire for humility and mortifications,[28] and his struggle with what he calls his three enemies (sleepiness, cold, and hunger)—to which he adds his physical fatigue from his unaccustomed physical work, which he had nonetheless embraced with enthusiasm. And in these letters and journals from the monastery Rafael begins to show his keen

25. For the daily schedule at the Abbey of San Isidro in Rafael's time, see OC 187, n. 172.

26. CW 89, #31.

27. CW 96, #33.

28. The Rule of Saint Benedict (RB 58.7) states that the candidate for the monastic life must truly seek God and show eagerness for the liturgy (the "Work of God"), for obedience, and for trials. (All quotations from the Rule are taken from *The Rule of Saint Benedict in English*, ed. Timothy Fry [Collegeville, MN: Liturgical Press, 1981]).

eye for detail, his power of description, and his ability to reveal his inner life through words. As one commentator says, Rafael the artist paints with words just as he did with a brush.[29]

Rafael, who had first been hooked by the monastic liturgy during his first visit, had a special devotion and singular love for the monastery's celebration of the Eucharist and for the Divine Office. Being in choir, Rafael writes to his mother, is what he loves most— what he likes least is getting up at two o'clock in the morning![30] Later, when his health had seriously declined during his final months at the monastery, his inability to participate in community prayer was one of his greatest trials. His early spiritual director in the monastery, Fr. Teófilo, believed that Rafael's artistic and pious spirit could not but be enchanted by the liturgy and by sacred music—so much so that Teófilo believed that in his first fervor Rafael virtually identified the monastic life with the choral office.[31] In fact, the Trappist usages (*"Usos"*) of the time—the regulations governing all Trappist monasteries[32]—include careful and precise manners in which the smallest actions were to be carried out. Rafael embraced all of this with great devotion—even though his own efforts to carry out all of its details could be a little clumsy.[33]

For all of his romantic zeal for the monastic life with all of its rigors, Rafael retained a playful spirit. He wrote to his mother that

29. Antonio María Martín Fernández-Gallardo, *El deseo de Dios y la ciencia de la Cruz: Aproximación a la experiencia religiosa del Hermano Rafael*, 2nd ed. (Burgos, Spain: Editorial Monte Carmelo, 2002), 29 [hereafter cited as Martín].

30. CW 81, #29.

31. Juan Antonio Martínez Camino, *Mi Rafael: San Rafael Arnaiz según el Padre Teófilo Sandoval, su confesor, intérprete y editor*, 2nd ed. (Bilbao, Spain: Editorial Desclée de Brouwer, 2003), 86.

32. *Regulations of the Order of Cistercians of the Strict Observance Published by the General Chapter of 1926* (Dublin, Ireland: M. H. Gill and Son, 1926) [Usages of 1926].

33. A novitiate classmate of Rafael's describes a particular incident that portrays Rafael's earnestness in carrying out his occasional liturgical duties—though without complete success (OC 219, n. 211).

he had adapted well to the monastic life and that it was not as hard as some might think—the only thing that is really hard, he reports, is his bed![34] He reported in an early letter to his father that he often felt a nearly uncontrollable desire to start whistling, and he found himself imagining little acts of possible mischief-making. As he says, though he clearly sees the sublime and solemn aspect of the monastic life, he also sees its little funny realities:

> I'm a rather dissolute monk . . . unfortunately . . . I'm in a good mood, just as I always am, but since I can't talk or shout or run, I have to swallow it. . . . So maybe I get a terrible urge to whistle when I see my brothers, and myself among them, with our hoods up and eating onions. . . . A thousand ideas for mischief come to mind, because while I always see the sublime side of La Trapa, I see the amusing side of it too. . . . Well, that seems like a contradiction, to say La Trapa is an amusing place, . . . but the thing is, I never get bored, I don't even know what that word means.[35]

In a letter of April 1 to his parents, he reports that he has learned to peel potatoes "with all my typical elegance."[36] One of his novitiate classmates reports that while out weeding in the monastery fields—where the monastic silence was to be maintained—Rafael once made a little whistle from a piece of straw, causing the young oblates (candidates for the monastic life) to do the same, provoking laughter—until their superior came along. Rafael owned up to his instigating the event. Another monk of the time describes Rafael as funny, able to see the humorous side of things, with the ability to imitate the voices and gestures of others (though never mocking), and says that in the few circumstances in which conversation was permitted, Rafael was friendly and clever. All together, these characteristics made him much

34. CW 81, #29.
35. CW 91, #32.
36. CW 99, #33.

appreciated and even loved by his peers.[37] Even in the liturgy, to which he was devoted, he saw the humor—at least of his own sometimes awkward participation in it. In the letter of April 1, he describes a humiliating but funny scene of his bumbling efforts to perform his liturgical tasks:

> Recently I've had to sing some readings from the pulpit at Matins [the early morning prayer today more usually known as Vigils], and I'm telling you I've never been in such a fix. My voice was trembling, singing either way too high or too low, tripping on my cape as I climbed up the stairs, in short, a real disaster. But it can't be helped; when I found myself up at the pulpit at three in the morning, looking out over all the shaved bald heads of the monks, the letters danced around the lectionary and I suddenly forgot how to pronounce Latin. I was striking out.

But Rafael's monastic journey was about to take an unexpected turn.[38] In the middle of May, after four months of good health, Rafael suddenly became increasingly fatigued and found himself urinating frequently, day and night. Out in the fields with the other young monks, he was not able to continue working. When the monastery doctor was called, he diagnosed a serious case of diabetes, in an age in which little was known about the treatment of diabetes. Insulin had been used for the first time as a treatment for diabetes in 1922—only twelve years before it was administered to Rafael. Believing that the monastery was a bad place to pursue the necessary medical care, Abbot Félix wrote to Rafael's father asking him to come for his son so that he could get the medical attention that the monastery was unable to provide. So on May 26, a very sick Rafael—weak, nearly blind, and having lost a significant amount of weight in a short period of time—left his beloved Trapa.

---

37. These recollections by his contemporaries appear in OC 250–51, n. 257.

38. Rafael briefly narrates the unfolding events in a later letter of June 3, 1934, to his uncle (CW 106–8, #35).

Rafael's spiritual director, Fr. Teófilo, described his encounter with the anguished Rafael on the night before his departure. Rafael was clearly heartbroken. He admitted that he was thinking about the reaction of the people of Oviedo who had known about and admired his departure—this young man of wealth, high social status, and a promising future who only four months earlier had left it all to enter the Trappists. But, at the same time, he was already anticipating his eventual embrace of these unwanted events as God's mysterious but loving will for him, recollecting the "*nada*" doctrine of Saint John of the Cross—the need to cling to nothing so that one can come to possess the All.[39]

It is difficult to know what brought on this sudden onset of diabetes. It has been conjectured that Rafael's sudden and dramatic change in diet, with little variation or consideration for nutrition, hard physical labor, and significantly reduced sleep on a very different schedule from before—and especially during Lent, which was particularly strictly observed in the monastery—may have caused a latent problem to flare up.[40] There has been some thought, in fact, that Rafael must have known of his diabetes before his entrance, but the facts do not support that hypothesis. His family, friends, and college roommate all attested to his good health before entering the monastery, his medical exam for his compulsory military service shortly before his entrance had given him a clean bill of health, and his good health was clear in his first four months in the monastery as he energetically embraced the lifestyle and work of the monks. But more basically, it would have been highly uncharacteristic of Rafael to enter the monastery through any deception.[41]

39. Father Teófilo's recollection is quoted in Martínez Camino, *Mi Rafael*, 92–93. For an article that appeared in the daily newspaper of the city of Oviedo announcing Rafael's entrance into the monastery, see OC 181–82, n. 165.

40. Martín, *Deseo de Dios*, 189.

41. Fernández, *God Alone*, 18–21; Francisco Cerro Chaves, *Silencio en los labios, cantares en el corazón: vida y espiritualidad del Hermano Rafael* (Madrid: Biblioteca de Autores Cristianos, 2000), 82–85.

BACK IN THE WORLD AGAIN

Rafael returned to his family home, a very sick young man. But, under the care of his family physician and mother, and with the introduction of regular insulin injections and a carefully controlled diet, he began to recover his strength within a relatively short time. And so began what would become almost a year and a half outside the monastery, as he adjusted his insulin dosage and diet and worked to regain his health, but otherwise taking up a relatively normal pattern of life. His confusion and desolation over the sudden turn of events passed quickly as he began to see the mysterious but benevolent hand of God through it all. As he embraced what clearly seemed to him to be the wise and loving plan of God for him, he found greater peace. Meanwhile, although his inner struggle and longing for the monastery were not lost on his family, his external demeanor was that of the jovial and loving person that he had always been. Still, it was clear to everyone that he intended, as soon as his health and God's will permitted, to return to his beloved Trapa. As one commentator has put it, his departure from the monastery became a desert in the biblical sense, as a place for listening anew and more profoundly to the Word of God.[42]

On June 3, 1934, about a week after his departure from the monastery, Rafael wrote to his uncle, explaining what had happened and his unfolding reflection on it.[43] He had already begun to see that the events were a reflection of God's great love for him. In a phrase that later raised the eyebrows of the theological consultant reviewing his writings as part of his beatification process,[44] Rafael concluded that Jesus is "very selfish" (*egoísta*) when it comes to his children's love. He had been too happy in the monastery, he wrote. Although he had thought that he had detached himself from the things of this world and given up life's normal ambitions,

42. Martínez Camino, *Mi Rafael*, 96.
43. CW 106–8, #35.
44. OC 235, n. 239.

God wanted him completely and thus decided to detach him from every lesser love, even his love for his monastery. And although this trial was difficult, he refused to give himself over to worry or to distrust of God. How sweet it is, he writes, to abandon oneself into the hands of so good a God:

> What's happening to me is very simple; in short, God loves me very much . . . I was happy in La Trapa. I considered myself the most fortunate of mortals, having managed to detach myself from earthly creatures, aspiring to nothing more than God. . . . But I still had one thing left: love for La Trapa. So Jesus, who is very selfish when it comes to His children's love, wanted me to detach myself from my beloved monastery too, even if just temporarily. This trial that I am enduring is difficult, very difficult, but I am not shaken, nor afraid, nor have I ceased to trust in God. More and more, I see His hand in everything that happens to me, and truly, it is so sweet to abandon yourself to such a good Father.[45]

In his first letter to his novice master after his departure (June 11, 1934), Rafael expresses his recognition and acceptance of the fact that on entering the monastery, he had given everything to God, body and soul.[46] And so, now, how could he complain that God was dealing with him as God saw fit? He would not complain nor rebel, he said. God in infinite divine wisdom knows what is best for the salvation of each person and simply invites us to trust. As Rafael now saw it, he had been "too happy in the monastery," too focused on his joy in the place and in the life but too little focused on surrendering to God's will. But though the trial was hard, he had put his hand to the plow and would not look back. Rafael repeats the same sentiment a week later (June 17, 1934) in a second letter to his uncle, though he confesses that he thinks constantly of his beloved monastery and his eventual return there:

45. CW 106, #35.
46. CW 110, #36.

I trust deeply in God. Surely He will carry me back to the monastery; I think of nothing else all day . . . The choir . . . the fields . . . the silence, the joyful peace of the cemetery . . . my brothers, my habit, my cell . . . my Tabernacle of La Trapa . . . everything I won with sacrifices and tears collapsed over something so insignificant as a bit of sugar in the blood . . . How great God is, Uncle Polín, who uses the smallest, most insignificant things to show us our own smallness and wretchedness, and to make us understand that we are nothing without Him.[47]

A few months later, in a letter to his grandmother (September 30, 1934), Rafael repeats his now familiar interpretation of events: "It was necessary for me to leave the monastery . . . I was too happy."[48] He had believed that he had entered the monastery seeking God, but he had discovered that he had also been seeking himself—that is, his own ideas and dreams for how his life should unfold.[49] In a letter to his novice master on August 11, 1934, he recalled Job's sentiment that as we willingly receive good from God's hand, we should receive the bad as well. He concluded that he was learning an important lesson, now seeing that he remained attached to creatures, and now God wanted to detach him so that he could truly give himself completely to God. Thus the trial, though hard to endure, was necessary for his own purification: "As I find myself once more in the world, sick, separated from the monastery, in this situation . . . I can see that I needed it, that the lesson I'm learning is very useful. My heart is still so tethered to creatures, and God wants me to free it so that I can give it to Him alone. . . . since God wants me to be better and more perfect, it is clear that this trial He has sent me, however difficult, is necessary."[50]

47. CW 113, #37.
48. CW 188, #53.
49. Letter to his Aunt María Osario, July 23, 1934 (CW 130, #40).
50. CW 135, #42.

It appears that Rafael's interpretation of the recent events in his life was especially influenced by his reading during this time of Saint John of the Cross. He saw in his own disappointments the challenge of Saint John's insistence on leaving aside all attachments to anything less than God. Rafael says in a July 23 letter to his Aunt María that he has learned that "one cannot approach God without having first relinquished *everything* and being left with *nothing*, as Saint John of the Cross says."[51] It is not surprising that the fervent spirit of Saint John's challenge to his readers would appeal to the earnest desire of the young Rafael, a desire undampened by the crisis of his health.

In all of this Rafael had a simple and clear belief that the divine hand was present in all things. His diabetes, though one might find a natural explanation for its sudden appearance, was God's plan for him. God's will for him was being realized in it, whatever other elements might be involved. But the critical thing is the simple and yet mature response of faith in this twenty-three-year-old. He overcame his initial shock and disappointment, reflected on how God might be at work in his illness and its consequences, and responded with a mature faith in the face of his trial. He had no anger, no resentment, no rebellion. He was reminded in his difficulties that it was God whom he sought, not his own satisfaction or will. The faith of this generous young man was being purified and honed to truly seek God alone—the foundational monastic search, which would become one of the principal themes of his life: God alone! (*Sólo Dios!*).

Within a relatively short period of time, it seemed that Rafael's recovery from the sudden and life-threatening appearance of diabetes would be quick and complete. Already on July 22, 1934, Rafael wrote to his novice master that he believed he would be able to return to the monastery within two or three months, to resume his novitiate and his path toward profession

51. CW 124, #40.

and ordination.[52] In a letter of September 15, 1934, to Fr. Francisco Díez Martínez, a young priest of the monastery, Rafael wrote that his doctor had told him that he was actually cured of his diabetes; he had been able to discontinue his insulin, and his task was now to take on the normal diet of the monastery while still at home and determine if and what adjustments might be necessary for his continued health.[53] He reported these details in a letter to his novice master, Fr. Marcelo León, about two weeks later.[54]

With his physical health seemingly restored and his inner equilibrium regained, Rafael settled into a quiet normal life with his family. Although he sometimes found the involvements with family distracting from the time he desired for prayer or quiet, they found him returned to his old self—jovial, generous, and affectionate. He again took up smoking, playing the violin, and painting. In this spirit of optimism and good health he wrote the journal that Father Teófilo would later title *The Trappist's Apologia* (*Apología del trapense*)[55] as a kind of defense of the Trappist life and of his own sense of vocation. Having begun it on September 19, 1934, he appears to have written it over a couple of weeks, probably until October 5, when the beginning of the Spanish Civil War brought a dramatic change for him and his family.

Early in the *Apología*, Rafael describes an encounter with a high school classmate that seems to be at least part of what prompted his writing:

> The other day I came across an old schoolmate of mine, a good kid and a good Christian. Naturally, we started talking about La Trapa, and I told him that when I was entirely recovered I'd be going back there, returning to my monastery . . . Well, without trying to offend me, far be it from him

52. CW 119, #39.
53. CW 156, #48.
54. CW 192–93, #54.
55. CW 167–81, #51.

to do such a thing, he did call me selfish and half suicidal, and on top of all that, dirty.[56] It didn't offend me, because I understand that he is in the world . . . and that's how the world is, it sees only what is external, what is counter to its own ways: an indulgent, comfortable life, eating well, talking and singing and listening to music, washing and bathing.[57]

Rafael's classmate was simply offering the common-sense view of those living in the world, for whom the monastic life made no sense. In fact, as Rafael saw it, living the Christian life in the world, with all of its distractions and temptations, is the harder form of the Christian life. To respond to a call to monastic life was simply choosing to step aside from those obstacles, not as an act of cowardice before the challenge but as a response to a call, the same call as that Jesus offered to the rich young man who had come to him asking how he might attain eternal life (Matt 19:19-22; Mark 10:17-22; Luke 18:18-23). Rafael writes that he knows that struggle from personal experience, but having already experienced the challenge and its difficulty, he is eager to do so again.

Throughout the *Apología*, Rafael contrasts life and attitudes within the monastery and those outside. In doing so, he insists that not everything in the world is evil. He repeatedly explains that the world contains so much good and beauty, so much joy in authentic loves and relationships, as he knew from experience. As he had told the abbot in his letter requesting his initial entrance to the monastery, he was not motivated by any dissatisfaction or disappointment in the world or in his life itself; in fact, he had felt blessed and even spoiled. But he felt the call to give himself simply and completely to God in the freedom of monastic life.

But Rafael did not write the *Apología* in abstraction from the life around him. He comments as well on the reality of social injustice

56. *Dirty* here probably refers to the infrequency of bathing in Trappist monasteries of the time.

57. CW 168, #51.

and unrest that was apparent to him in walking around the city of Oviedo. This unrest was about to engulf his family, overturning his hope for a speedy and complete recovery from his diabetes and his return to the normal monastic path that he had been forced to leave behind. Unsurprisingly, when war broke out on October 5, 1934, it spelled the end to his reflective writing of his *Apología*.

Throughout the 1930s Spain was racked by political instability and social conflict, the forces that would lead to the Spanish Civil War of 1936–1939. On the night of October 5, 1934, in northern Spain a revolution broke out, soon engulfing Rafael's family home.[58] Over the next nine days, loyalists and rebels occupied the house, trashed it, and riddled it with bullets, and Rafael's family had to take refuge from cannon fire in their basement. Meanwhile churches in the city were being attacked and religious killed. They were nerve-racking days for all, especially as they had little food on hand, but Rafael remained calm and a constant support for the family. His mother credited the actions and prayers of her "Trappist angel" in assuring their safety in passing through the crisis. But the trauma of those sleepless, hungry, and stressful days overturned much of Rafael's recovery. He quickly suffered a relapse in his diabetes.

After the crisis had passed, Rafael's parents sent him to Burgos for a time of rest and quiet in the home of one of her mother's brothers. Returning on November 21 to Oviedo, Rafael stopped at La Trapa to report on the events in Oviedo, and on his relapse. The abbot and novice master told him that in light of the situation, it would be better to plan to stay out longer than he had expected, until he had regained his health. Upset by this turn of events, Rafael was able to find his confessor and spiritual director, Fr. Teófilo, and to report the details of his conversation with his superiors.[59] Teófilo first suggested that he might try to enter the Benedictines instead, where the life was not so austere and where greater accommoda-

58. The events of these days are recounted by Rafael's mother in a letter to her family on October 22, 1934 (OC 364–68, n. 386).

59. Fr. Teófilo recounts the details of this conversation in a number of different brief publications compiled in Martínez Camino, *Mi Rafael*, 99–103.

tion could be made to his dietary needs. But Rafael was uninterested, replying that even then his life would require mitigations, in which case he preferred to return to his Trapa. Then Fr. Teófilo first introduced the idea of returning as a claustral oblate—that is, a layperson, without monastic vows, but essentially living the monastic life.[60] As Rafael found this possibility more hopeful, he raised the idea with the monastic superiors, who expressed openness to the possibility but instructed him to continue his recovery for the time being.

It is likely that the idea of Rafael's possible return to the monastery as an oblate had not occurred to either the superiors or immediately to Fr. Teófilo, because it would involve a certain amount of humiliation for a man of Rafael's social standing, whose natural trajectory would have been profession as a choir monk and ordination as a priest. The more typical oblate was a person who because of age or lack of physical or intellectual capacity could not hope to be canonically professed as a monk. Admitting a person with a debilitating illness as an oblate would be unusual.

---

60. The Trappist regulations (Usages of 1926, #26) in use at the time says the following about oblates: "Oblates do not canonically form part of the Order, they are simply aggregated to it; they follow all the regular exercises in the measure appointed by the Superior, but without being bound by vows. The Superior, assisted by the Father-Master, gives them the habit in his room, without any ceremony. They follow for two years the same exercises as the novices. After that time, they are with the professed, if the Superior thinks fit, and fulfil in the community whatever duties are assigned to them. In the choir and everywhere else, they are always placed after the novices. The oblates are buried in their habit, and the same prayers are offered for them and the same ceremonies observed as for a novice. On their part, they ought to say the prescribed prayers for the deceased of the Order" (*Regulations*, #26, p. 11). An addendum made by the General Chapter of the Order in 1935 added, "Oblates can be admitted to profession '*in articulo mortis*,' whatever may be their rank, if the Superior judges it proper, taking care to give them previously the novice's habit, if they have not already received it." The regulations later stipulate: "The habit of the choir oblates is like that of the novices, but instead of the cloak, they have a short mantle which descends to the knees, and their scapular has no hood. For work time they are given a little hooded cape, which ends in a point behind, and is rounded in the front" (*Regulations*, #398, p. 187).

The fact that it eventually happened demonstrates the abbot's belief in Rafael's monastic call. Rafael's own acceptance of this mutation of his own original vision became yet another instrument of his surrender and self-offering to God—but not without a period of struggle.

As all of these circumstances weighed heavily on Rafael's spirit, he entered a period of doubt and spiritual desolation. On February 5, 1935, the novice master wrote to Rafael, worried at his failure to write or respond to letters from the other young monks.[61] Rafael responded on February 21 with a candid admission of his depression and sadness, in a letter demonstrating his ability to express his emotional state honestly and vividly. Even while deeply missing the monastery and his peers there, he had begun to think that he had aimed too high by thinking that he could be a monk: "Sometimes I think that, truly, I don't deserve to be a son of the Cistercian Order; that I've been dreaming too loftily for such a lowly person; that God has chastened and punished me . . . Perhaps I committed the sin of pride, and I assure you, Father, I'm certainly being purified of it . . . Perhaps less than I deserve."[62] Maybe, he thought, his illness and the necessity of his departure from the monastery was a kind of divine punishment for his pride and presumption in thinking that he could aspire to holiness in such a life. At times, he confessed that he felt abandoned and alone, even while surrounded by the affection of his family and the solicitude of the abbot, novice master, and other novices. But in the end, he was sustained by those who cared for him and especially by his faith, maturing and deepening through the crisis.

But events soon called Rafael outside himself. In the early summer of 1935, his sister Mercedes, always of frail health, had become seriously ill with peritonitis.[63] Physicians deemed it incurable,

61. For a copy of the novice master's letter, see OC 375–76, n. 398.

62. CW 203, #61.

63. Rafael's mother narrates these events in her biography of Rafael, excerpted in OC 378–81, n. 401.

and she suffered great pain, not fully alleviated by large doses of morphine. Mother, daughter, and Rafael temporarily found housing closer to Madrid in the hope of finding further medical care. Meanwhile, Rafael devoted himself to supporting and caring for both women, focused especially on trying to amuse and distract his sister from her pain and distress with stories and by drawing caricatures. His mother recounts that as Mercedes's death seemed to be approaching, Rafael went to a local church to petition the Virgin Mary for her help, and Mercedes's recovery began immediately. Their mother credited Rafael's prayers for what she believed to be a miracle. While crediting the cure to the Virgin, Rafael dismissed the idea that he had played any significant role in the healing. Briefly recounting Mercedes's unexpected recovery in a letter to his aunt, Rafael recalls keeping vigil with his sister as her life seemed to be ebbing away:

> In those moments, I saw that she was dying, that she was slipping away . . . And she looked at me in such a way . . . if you could have seen her . . . it was as if she was saying, "But Rafael, what are you doing? Aren't you going to pray to the Virgin for me?" . . . So then I ran like crazy to the Tabernacle, and offered *my sister's prayer* to the Virgin, since my own was worthless.[64]

In his own view, Rafael had simply been a messenger of his sister's prayer.

Requesting Readmission as an Oblate

On October 9, 1935, after almost a year and a half out of the monastery, Rafael wrote to the abbot requesting admission as an

---

64. CW 252, #73 (italics in the original).

oblate.[65] The letter is a jewel in its expression of his earnest and mature faith and sense of vocation, and in its candid expression of the state of his soul and its journey. The letter vividly reveals Rafael's character and depth of faith. Writing to the abbot, Rafael says that he can now thank God for his trial, seeing it in hindsight as a divine instrument for his deeper surrender to God. Although at his first entrance, he says, his self-giving had been sincere, now he sees that it was not the total abandonment that God truly wanted of him. Christians, he goes on, often say that they are willing to embrace the cross, but when it is actually given, they recoil from it or weep at its presence. For himself, however, Rafael believed that he had learned to kiss the cross as God had given it to him and so had united himself more closely with Christ crucified.

As the letter continues, Rafael recalls his earlier visit to the monastery, when Fr. Téofilo had first raised the idea of his being admitted as an oblate. He had waited almost a year since that meeting and was now physically and spiritually ready. He acknowledged that the status of an oblate might seem like a humiliation to some, but not to him. In order to be humiliated, he says, one would have to have been first exalted. He goes on to explain this idea: did not our God choose to be humiliated for us? What then, in that light, could possibly humiliate us creatures? What would monastic profession or the priesthood give him that the simple love of God could not? Their absence would not impede him from consecrating his life to God in silence, humility, and simplicity. Saint Benedict, he says, had permitted the admission of monastic oblates, and many of them had become saints. Why not him, with the help of Jesus and the Blessed Virgin?

It had been almost two years since Rafael had first entered the novitiate. In the eyes of others, he tells the abbot, for a time he

---

65. CW 214–20, #64. A full copy of the letter appears in the Appendix. Rafael was not aware that his novice master, Fr. Marcelo, had died on October 1, 1935. A successor had been appointed a few months earlier when Fr. Marcelo had become seriously ill.

had ceased to be a Trappist, but for himself, not for a moment had he been anything but Brother Rafael, Cistercian novice. Even if he had to spend the rest of his life living in the world, in spirit he would continue to be a Trappist. He carried it deep within his heart, and he knew himself always accompanied by the Virgin of la Trapa.

Rafael tells the abbot that his only fear about returning as an oblate is that the mitigations in the Rule and customs of the monastery that his health would require would make him a bad example to others. But, he says, God has invited him to let go of that fear (though in fact it would haunt him after he returned to the monastery). While it was true, he reasoned, that the full rigors of the monastic life involved sacrifices that he could no longer make, perhaps his own inability fully to embrace those practices would be a form of his own sacrifice.

As to more practical matters, Rafael writes that his father would be willing to provide a regular donation to cover any additional cost to the monastery that Rafael's ongoing medical care and dietary needs might require,[66] though it seems that, in fact, this contribution was never deemed necessary.[67] Such an offer may itself have been humiliating for Rafael. As to his health, Rafael reports that he had recently consulted a renowned doctor in Madrid who assured him that his diabetes was relatively mild and that he should be fine as long as he managed his diet in the monastery. Sadly, the abbot's positive response to Rafael's letter has been lost. But given the abbot's paternal attitude and solicitude for Rafael during his novitiate and his absence, and throughout the events leading up to his death, his response was probably not only positive but welcoming.

In early November 1935, having received an affirmative response from the abbot, Rafael returned to his parents' home in

66. This possibility was reaffirmed in a subsequent letter to the abbot of November 7, 1935 (CW 226, #69).

67. Fernández, *God Alone*, 51, n. 7.

Oviedo after a month in Ávila with his aunt and uncle. He remained there until he returned to the monastery in January of 1936. During this period, his letter writing increased dramatically after the months of struggle, during which he wrote very little. Particularly notable are the series of letters he wrote to his Uncle Polín and especially to his Aunt María (two letters to his uncle and nineteen to his aunt, whom he addressed as "brother" and "sister"). The letters reveal the deep spiritual friendship that had been forged between them. In the letters Rafael reveals both a deep traditional spiritual wisdom and an ability to discern both what his aunt was experiencing and what was apparently the best counsel to offer her. Although the two agreed to destroy their letters once read, Rafael did so with his aunt's letters, but she did not. Taken together, their correspondence creates almost a treatise on the spiritual life, in which Rafael draws together his reading as well as especially his own maturing spiritual experience.

Rafael's biographer, Gonzalo María Fernández, highlights some of the themes of these letters.[68] A first theme is desire and love for God, in which Fernández sees the inner transformation and deepening that occurs in Rafael after the crisis through which he had just passed. In fact, he says that Rafael had attained a "state of unitive love."[69] Such love is not restricted narrowly to God, though, but embraces other persons more strongly, especially those living in a type of spiritual poverty, caught up in purely worldly interests. Rafael's love is one that yearns for God and yet knows how to wait on God's will and plan.

Another frequent theme of the letters is the need for detachment, which Rafael had himself learned to embrace more deeply. Several times he quotes a line from the third stanza of John of the Cross's *Spiritual Canticle*, in which the bride—the soul—in anxious pursuit of the Bridegroom sighs, "I will not gather flowers

---

68. Fernández, *God Alone*, 55–63.
69. Fernández, *God Alone*, 57.

nor fear wild beasts."[70] With his constant devotion to the Virgin Mary, Rafael writes of her often, urging his aunt to turn to Mary for help, as he himself has always done. And he opens up his heart about his reasons for returning to the monastery without his diabetes having been cured, in his new status as an oblate.

In the course of this extraordinary series of letters, Rafael recounts two challenges to his decision to return made by a Jesuit priest who had at one time been his confessor. Ultimately, both merely strengthened his resolve, a notable fact in light of the fact that only a few months earlier he had been plagued by doubts as he passed through his crisis. This priest told Rafael that his decision to return to the monastery was simply absurd, but these words did not disturb or dissuade Rafael.[71] However, not long afterward, as he entered a local church to make one of his frequent visits to the Blessed Sacrament, the same priest was in the middle of a homily during a Mass. This time, the priest's words disturbed Rafael, making him wonder if he was motivated by selfishness:

> Yesterday, when I arrived at church, the sermon wasn't over yet. It was a Jesuit priest, whom I know very well, and he said a few things that left me a bit . . . I don't know exactly . . . He was talking about the active life, and the consolation of being an apostle, and being able to someday present oneself before the Lord alongside all the souls one had helped. He said something about selfish souls who only care about their own holiness, and who hide themselves away from others' sight in order not to be bothered . . . He said a lot of things, and it made me think . . . I don't like what he said. I don't know why, but I was a bit perturbed. . . . Am I doing something wrong? . . . According to this priest, yes. According to him, only those who keep busy like Martha give glory to God. Am I wrong? Am I being selfish? Lord,

---

70. *The Collected Works of St. John of the Cross*, trans. Kieran Kavanaugh and Otilio Rodriguez, 3rd ed. (Washington, DC: ICS Publications, 2017), 78.

71. CW 245, #72.

Lord . . . enlighten me; this conflict is pressuring me from all sides . . . The men of the world call me crazy, and the man of God does too . . . just in a different way.[72]

To be called misguided by people whose only perspective was this world was bad enough, but to be called so by a man of God was unsettling. But Rafael remained in the church to spend time in prayer, as he had originally planned, and he felt that in doing so he received a confirmation of his call to love God and neighbor in the monastic life.[73]

Rafael's time of crisis had passed, leaving his faith stronger and more mature, his prayer deepened, his identification with Christ crucified more focused, his sense of a monastic vocation in its new form reaffirmed, his desire and love for God heightened, and his love for neighbor broadened. But he still deeply felt the pain of leaving his beloved family once again and his sorrow at the pain his departure would bring them. Although he was sure of his vocation, the renunciation of family was deeply painful—even a "battle."[74] But in the end, he concludes, it must be "God alone."[75] In a letter to his maternal grandmother only a couple of weeks before his return to the monastery, he assures her that he now counts it a great favor that God has given him in bringing about his departure from the monastery, maturing his Cistercian vocation and making it all the more precious to him.[76]

THE SECOND ENTRANCE

Rafael, now almost twenty-five years old, re-entered the Abbey of San Isidro de Dueñas on January 11, 1936. He would remain

72. CW 268, #75.
73. CW 268, #75.
74. CW 283, #77.
75. CW 372, #97.
76. CW 333, #88.

only about nine months, though, when together with other young monks he was called up for military service by the outbreak of the Spanish Civil War in July. Things had changed in a number of ways, within himself, in his status as an oblate in the monastery, and in his relationship with the other monks.

Before his return Rafael had pondered the reality of his new life as an oblate, without the possibility of profession of vows. In his letter to the abbot requesting admission, he had acknowledged but ultimately minimized the humiliation of his new status. But living the reality was different from imagining it. The real challenge for Rafael, though, was not so much the reality of being a mere oblate but his inability to live the monastic life to the fullest. His health during this second entrance was not a severe problem, but it did demand certain mitigations: he had a special diet that did not allow for fasting, he could not fully participate in all of the common liturgical life of the monastery, which was especially dear to him,[77] and he could not join the other young monks in the heavier labors in the fields—and Rafael loved the outdoors and working side by side with the others, even in silence. During his first time in the monastery, despite the fact that such outdoor work had been foreign to him, he had embraced it with gusto. Now, however, he was often instead restricted to solitary indoor work, such as cleaning the infirmary, peeling vegetables in the kitchen, or packing the monastery's chocolate candies for sale. All of this made him feel at times isolated and virtually useless—again, a theme that would become spiritually important to him.

While the abbot continued to show a special solicitude and paternal care for Rafael, not all of the monks were so well disposed to his return, feeling that the mitigations meant that he was not

---

77. When Rafael had been singing in choir with great gusto, at times the cantor had to ask him to sing with a little less zeal. Unfortunately, it became evident to the superiors that it was difficult for Rafael to stand throughout the long hours in the monastic choir. At that point, they required him to sit outside the choir, leaving him to recognize his separation (OC 592, n. 617).

suited to the Trappist life and was even a burden on the community. As one Cistercian commentator noted, monks are often
not very tolerant of "exceptional" monks in their midst,[78] and,
apparently, some of them were not reluctant to show or even express that fact. Rafael, always sensitive and feeling himself useless
at times, found their attitude painful and humiliating, though he
soon recognized this challenge as part of his own call to humility
and surrender to God's plan.

Among those who seemed to doubt the appropriateness of
Rafael's return was his new novice master, Fr. José, and Rafael
found no real personal support in him, as he had in his predecessor.
Most vocal of all in expressing doubts about Rafael's monastic
vocation was the older mentally unstable monk who also occupied
the infirmary. This Fr. Pío regularly taunted Rafael and his special
diet and other mitigations, telling him that he had no monastic
vocation and that he was a burden on the resources of the monastery.[79] At times, these attitudes tempted Rafael to think that his
vocation might be just an illusion and that he was a scandal to the
monks because of his lack of full observance of the life.[80] But he
did not complain.

Breaking with the usual practice for claustral oblates, the abbot
still intended for Rafael to be ordained a priest, but this goal required him to take up the study of Latin with the boy oblates who
were candidates for the monastic life. For a twenty-five-year-old,
apparently without a special gift for languages, to sit in class with
twelve- and thirteen-year-old boys was a challenge of another
kind.[81] Moreover, the abbot had changed the regular confessor for

78. Francisco Rafael de Pascual, "Son tus santos, nuestros amigos," *Cistercium*
254 (Jan.–June 2010): 19.

79. For details on the life and situation of this unstable monk, Padre Pío, see
OC 840–43, n. 1022.

80. Martín, *Deseo de Dios*, 221–22.

81. One of those young oblates later recounted that the boys could sometimes
not suppress their laughter at Rafael's errors in elementary Latin, but his response

the novices, leaving Rafael without his former confessor and spiritual director, Fr. Teófilo, who had been such a help to him in his first stay, departure, and return. In addition to the silence that restricted conversation among the monks, the monastic practice of "separation" made it almost impossible for Rafael to seek out Fr. Teófilo rather than the regular, appointed confessor. After the new confessor counseled Rafael that his health could be taken as a good sign that he lacked a Cistercian vocation, confession for Rafael became restricted strictly to the matter of confessing his sins without further report of his deeper spiritual state or concerns.

While Rafael felt the weight of these realities, he nonetheless felt himself guided and supported by God's fidelity and tenderness. He embraced his new reality as God's mysterious plan for him. In a letter of February 23, 1936, to his aunt—a month after his return—he says that he had come to the monastery seeking one thing, but God, in his infinite goodness and mercy, has given him something else. We want the cross, he continues, but we only want the one of our own choosing. And in this we are self-deceived. Rafael had come to see divine mercy at work precisely in placing him in a situation in which he felt useless, burdened with his illness, and unable to live fully the demands of the Rule. In doing so, God reveals to him his own self-love, opening his eyes to see that he must give up his own desires—even to be the Trappist of his previous dreams—and thus abandon himself more completely into the divine hands. He is being invited to love God more completely and to see that God alone can fill his soul. Again, he concludes that his illness is necessary in the divine plan to reveal his own attachments. How great the mercy of God, he exclaims. Echoing the thought of Saint Paul (2 Cor 12:5), he says that he can now say, "I rejoice in my uselessness." His trials became a situation of grace and even of spiritual joy. In his letter to his aunt, he continues,

------

was always a smile (OC 591, n. 617). In a journal entry of March 9, 1938, Rafael prays for patience and humility after a particularly trying experience in Latin class (CW 653, #191).

Look, I can just say that for me, I came to La Trapa looking
for one thing, and the Lord in His infinite goodness and
mercy gave me something else . . . When we want a certain
cross, it's not the right one, because it's ours. We should love
God's cross, the cross God gives us. Am I making sense? We
deceive ourselves so often on this front. . . . Truly, my dear
sister, it is a great thing, a tremendous mercy from God, to
realize that you are useless and to be humiliated because you
are of no use whatsoever, because you can't follow the Rule,
because you're sick. If only you knew how grateful I am to
the Lord on that account. He has shown me my own self-
love with such gentleness, and helped me see my many imperfections. It was necessary for the Lord to put me in this
situation in order for my eyes to be properly opened, and for
my desires to be uprooted, even my desire to be a Trappist;
for me to abandon myself in His hands, and love Him more
and more every day, as I realize that He alone can satisfy my
soul . . . I needed my illness to show me that I was still
attached to the world, to creatures, to my aches and pains
and weaknesses. Living off alms and charity, holding God's
hand tight . . . What a great mercy, Lord! I was so blind![82]

On July 12, 1936 (continuing until August 8), Rafael began to
write his journal *Meditaciones de un trapense*, which consists of
about two dozen reflections and fifteen drawings.[83] During these
months, his health was largely stable, and he was well cared for
by the monastery's infirmarian, Br. Tescelino, who was attentive
to maintaining Rafael's diet and health.[84] Six months into his new

---

82. CW 400–401, #105.

83. CW 412–62, #108–30. Rafael left this journal as well as the one that he
wrote during his third stay at the abbey with his mother when he entered the
monastery for the fourth and last time.

84. Like Rafael and the other young monks, Tescelino was called to military
service and remained outside the monastery during Rafael's subsequent stays in
the monastery, leaving Rafael in the care of less solicitous and understanding
infirmarians. Tescelino remained a consoling friend to Rafael, and they main-

life as an oblate, a spirit of peace and acceptance pervades his journal. In an entry of July 26, for example, Rafael writes of the quiet joy of having two hours of peace and silence to spend alone with God—made possible by his private cell in the infirmary and his lightened schedule. With his characteristic humor, he notes that—on this late July day—he has his (screenless) window open but the hood of his habit pulled up over his head because of wearisome flies, concluding, "I have, then, reasons (except for the flies) to be happy."[85]

In a journal entry of July 19, Rafael (speaking in the third person) reflects on his first months at the monastery as an idealistic young man whose artistic sensibilities had been drawn by the externals of the monastic life—the long line of the monks in their habits, the silence, the sounds of the bells calling the monks to prayer, the sun shining in the cloister, the singing of the birds, and the quiet beauty of the monastery's wheat fields. He had been sincere in his faith and in his sense of vocation, but now he had come to see more deeply the true meaning of his vocation: "Now that Trappist, who was once that young, restless dreamer . . . doesn't care so much about the bells or birds, or even the sun. Now, with Mary's help, he has come to see that the most important thing in a monastery is God."[86]

But shortly after that journal entry the monks learned that the Spanish Civil War had erupted on July 18. The monks in general received little information about its progress. The monastery itself was at times threatened by sporadic encroachments of violence in the area, knowing that priests and religious were often special targets of the leftist side. The war was a frequent topic in Rafael's journal and letters—as well as a subject of his prayers. His brother, Luis Fernando, had joined the army, to the constant worry of his

---

tained a correspondence in which they provided mutual support—Tescelino on the military front and Rafael facing his own struggles.

85. CW 434, #117.
86. CW 417, #110.

family. But the war was soon to touch Rafael more directly and personally: on September 29, 1936, responding to a military call up by the rightist Nationalist government, Rafael and about thirty of the other young monks left the monastery for possible military service. Rafael, to his humiliation, was soon deemed medically unfit to serve because of his diabetes. As the final medical determination took some time, he remained outside the monastery until December, living with his family once again, for about two months.

The Third Entrance

On December 6, 1936, Rafael returned to San Isidro. This time, he stayed only about three months. Shortly after Epiphany, the worsening of his health restricted him almost entirely to the infirmary. This restriction caused in him a deep sense of loneliness but also an opportunity to embrace a deeper silence with God and a deepening identification with Christ crucified. One commentator characterized this period as one of personal ambiguity: "His periods of prayer were prolonged, his suffering greater, his solitude in his infirmary cell more profound. Christ was on the cross, with Rafael, ever-faithful with Mary, at the foot of Calvary."[87] But constrained within the four walls of his monastery and of his cell, Rafael writes that he is finding true freedom. His suffering, he says, is a sign of God's immense mercy toward him:

> Illness . . . separation. Long hours sitting in an armchair, hearing the bells, and directing my intention toward all the community's activities. As for my illness, why bother talking about it? . . . It's just one of many . . . It just makes me tired . . . and hungry, and very thirsty, and totally lacking in energy . . . Otherwise I am fine. I am very pleased to have such an attractive illness that makes me suffer sometimes. I

---

87. Almudena Vilariño Pariáñez, "El Hermano Rafael, modelo de fidelidad y constancia," *Cistercium* 254 (Jan.–June 2010): 41.

was also healthy, once . . . but that was then. Now, thanks be to God, I am sick. When the Lord thinks it necessary, He reminds me of this fact by having me sit in an armchair in the infirmary for a few days and keeping me away from the choir . . . Blessed be God. He is the one who ordains all things, and He does well in leading me into solitude. Showing me the great void that is nothingness, which is everything outside of Him, He invites me to reflect and obliges me, in my uselessness, to seek His aid. He separates me from everything else in order to unite me more closely to Himself. Blessed be God, and blessed be my illness, which is the means He is using to accomplish His designs in me, insignificant as I am. How great God is! . . . How vast is his mercy![88]

Only two days after returning to San Isidro, Rafael began his journal *Mi Cuaderno* (*My Notebook*), dedicated to his brother Leopoldo. Much of it follows and reflects on the liturgy and the liturgical seasons, but always with an eye to the mystery of the cross.[89] Rafael records times of peace and prayer but also of darkness and near desolation. He made his last entry in the journal on the day before his third departure.

The monastery to which Rafael returned had been significantly changed by the circumstances of the war. The abbot had cautioned Rafael about returning because many of these changes would make it even more difficult for him to manage his health. The young monks had been called to military service, leaving Rafael without men of his own age. Resources to care for the sick were reduced. In a time in which monasteries rarely had any professional medical and infirmary staff, the sick and elderly were cared for by monks chosen by the abbot for their perceived ability to carry out that care with diligence and compassion, though most often they lacked any formal training. Br. Tescelino, who as infirmarian had been so

88. CW 523–24, #150.
89. Beltrame Quattrocchi, *Fascinado*, 138–40.

conscientious about Rafael's care, was now a soldier. He had en-sured that Rafael followed medical instructions, ate as appropriate to his condition, and, at least to some degree, fended off the bad-gering of the difficult Fr. Pío. Br. Tescelino's successor, however, lacked the knowledge or focus to keep Rafael on his proper diet as well as the will to confront Fr. Pío, who taunted Rafael, telling him that he should go back to his comfortable home and eat the delica-cies available to him there. Rafael would later blame only himself for his deteriorating health, admitting that he had continued to feel the humiliation of needing more and different food than the other monks, rather than embracing it fully as the path given to him by God. He did not insist when the infirmarian served him only the normal portion available to other monks. Reflecting later on the deterioration of his health that led to his third departure, Rafael wrote to Tescelino, blaming himself, "My relapse was God's will, of course, but it was also my own fault, and no one else's . . . my self-love, my desire to do what I cannot and should not do, my refusal to humble myself in the face of my own illness, my capri-ciousness and disobedience, my inability to see that this is what the Lord wants for me."[90]

During this period at the monastery Rafael's health declined so rapidly that on February 6, 1937, his superiors once again in-formed him that he would have to go home to his family. The last entry of his journal of the period, *Mi Cuaderno*, reflects on the history of his entrances and departures:

> I've left my home and my family three times. Three times now, I've believed that I was leaving everything behind, but I wasn't. If God grants me the grace and health to do so, I will leave it all behind again, not three or four times . . . but a thousand times over, if necessary. This is the third time that

90. CW 596, #168. One of his biographers characterizes this full acceptance of all blame for his decline in health as "*mentiras de los santos*" [little lies told by saints] (Beltrame Quattrocchi, *Fascinado*, 160).

I am taking off my monastic habit and putting on secular clothing . . . The first time, I was so upset I thought I would die . . . I thought that God was abandoning me. The second time, I left for the sake of the war . . . I was happy when I left . . . as if I were *going on vacation* . . . The novelty of war, the curiosity of it, a few days of rest from penance, it all sounded good to me . . . I knew that going back to the monastery would be hard for me . . . I could tell that God was testing me. This is the third time . . . and I see God's hand in it so clearly that it's all the same to me. Suffering is the only treasure that will retain its worth on the last day . . . and wherever you go, you will find the cross, as Thomas à Kempis says.[91]

Rafael sees clearly in this third departure that God is not abandoning him, or even testing him; rather, he is simply experiencing the unfolding of God's love for him. He wants to accept simply and fully what God is asking of him, though not without the sorrow that reveals to him that his renunciation is not yet complete. Rafael concludes the journal entry with praise of God who shuffles him about from place to place—all of it, manifesting the goodness and love of God. It is Rafael's task to let God do what God deems best, trying himself to learn to let it be:

How good God is! He picks me up, carries me, and tosses me about from one place to the next. Sometimes He makes me cry, sometimes He makes me suffer, sometimes He makes me rejoice and laugh . . . One right after the other. How good God is! He only wants what is best for me . . . He knows what He is doing . . . Now that I'm getting used to His way of going about things, I don't even ask Him about it anymore . . . I just let Him lead me, and do whatever He

91. CW 546–47, #158. Rafael here cites Thomas à Kempis, *The Imitation of Christ*, trans. Ronald Knox and Michael Oakley (South Bend, IN: Greenlawn Press, 1990), 2.12.

wants, and that's the best thing to do . . . Woe is me. When will I ever learn?[92]

The final word written in this journal echoes that of the Virgin Mary at the Annunciation: "*Fiat!*" "So be it!"—words of surrender to God's will and mysterious plan. Rafael would be away from the monastery this last time for almost a year.

A FINAL INTERLUDE

When Rafael left the monastery this time he joined his family in their wartime refuge on an estate in Villasandino, outside the city of Burgos. It was a quiet ten months, virtually a time of recollection. Once again he engaged in the normal life of the family and conversed with those around him, with his usual good humor. But he often felt these conversations and activities to be a distraction. He prayed, read Scripture, drew, and painted. As his diet improved, and his health with it, he took long walks alone in the countryside. He spent hours in the local parish church, praying and painting.

He wrote very little in this time—five letters to his aunt and uncle and two to Br. Tescelino on the war front. In two lengthy letters to his uncle in late September, twenty-two times he uses some form of the phrase "God alone,"[93] reflecting the fact that his detachment and embrace of the cross has left him increasingly focused on the "one thing necessary." Now, having deeply embraced the cross in his own life, Rafael was practicing the art of waiting on God—one of his other principal themes in his writing ("*saber esperar*").

On October 19, Rafael was called back to Burgos for another medical review of his fitness for military service but was again judged to be unfit. This conclusion—made already when Rafael had first been called up from the monastery for possible military

92. CW 547–48, #158.

93. Fernández, *God Alone*, 85–86.

service—did not now disturb him. It couldn't have surprised him. He had already grappled with the sense of being "useless" in the monastery, being unable to share in the labors of the other monks. He had already accepted his "unfitness" and "uselessness" in serving in the military for what he had believed was a just cause—Spain and Catholicism.[94] It had become for him another aspect of his surrender to God's plan and to God's action in his life. His task was to wait, to trust, and to obey. At the same time, the very fact that this medical exam had revealed that his blood sugar was running very high—despite his mother's meticulous attention to his diet—suggests the steady advance of his disease.

Two Letters to Br. Tescelino

On November 1, 1937, Rafael wrote to Br. Tescelino, repeating over and over his motto "God alone . . . God alone." He reports that he has written to the abbot, requesting readmission. The novice master has responded that he is welcome to return when he wishes, but he cautions that Rafael should consider carefully the situation in the monastery, which had not changed since his last departure. They still had no real infirmarian and lacked the resources to care for him adequately. It would be a shame, he said, if what had forced Rafael to leave the monastery before should happen again.[95]

---

94. Rafael himself was not a supporter of the Fascist views of the Nationalist side in the Spanish Civil War, nor was his viewpoint particularly political. His letters and journal entries show little interest in political forces at work in 1930s Spain. His concern was not the maintenance of the established social order—in which his own family was well positioned. Rather his vision was fundamentally religious and ecclesial: the Republican side was anticlerical, and, for him, its victory would mean continued violence against priests, religious, and Church institutions and a threat to the faith that was central to his own fundamental view of reality.

95. CW 589–93, #166. A copy of this letter appears in its entirety in the Appendix.

Rafael concedes that the novice master's caution makes perfect sense, humanly speaking. It is a prudent response. But in an imagined scene, he expresses his humanly imprudent response. Imagine, he tells Tescelino, that you are sick in your house, practically useless to those around you, but well cared for and attended. And just then, Jesus passes by under your window and invites you to follow him. Looking into those eyes that radiate such tender love, how could you respond with excuses about one's illness or the need for prudent care? Wouldn't you rather jump up and follow after him—without concern for your sickness, weakness, or any concerns raised by a purely human prudence? Rafael tells Tescelino that he truly feels deep within his soul that sweet gaze of Jesus, and he hears Jesus nearly echoing the words of the novice master: "You can come when you want."[96] The world can call him crazy. People can give him their prudent warnings. But what does that matter when compared to that sweet gaze of Jesus and the invitation to join in his company?

On November 29, 1937, Rafael wrote letters to both the novice master and his assistant, telling them that he hoped to return to the monastery sometime after the feast of the Immaculate Conception. He felt that leaving his family before Christmas would be an act of solidarity with the many soldiers who would be experiencing the same privation. His own brother, Luis Fernando, had been with family for a brief leave before returning to the battlefield, and it was now time for Rafael to return to his own struggle. He also says that this next stay in the monastery will be "of a short duration."[97]

In a second letter to Tescelino, written on December 1, 1937, Rafael confesses that he recognizes the familiar challenges that lie ahead for him with his return to the monastery: his bitter companion in the infirmary, the isolation, the separation from common prayer and work, the absence of human consolations,

96. CW 591, #166.
97. See Fernández, *God Alone*, 89–90.

and the lack of comprehension by others about his decision to return. But Rafael sees in all of this the opportunity to depend solely on God, resting in the divine hand, without anything other than God for help or consolation. He writes of his longing for the silence of the monastery: "All I desire is to love God; all I want is to serve Him. I see La Trapa, I see a cross, and there I go. That's it." And yet, Rafael confesses that he is still human: he feels the pain of separation once again from his beloved family and the loss again of the freedom of life outside the cloister, he sees the privations ahead, and sometimes he feels dread. But even in those moments, when he ponders the goodness and love of God, when he looks to Jesus, who reveals his love in the wounds of the cross, he finds his soul inundated with peace and light. There is struggle, but Jesus triumphs in him.[98]

Rafael was ready to return to the monastery, again to take up an oblate's habit. But he had come to see that the only true habit is the cross of Christ. Even without the formal vow of obedience, he returned with a deeper obedience to God's will for him. Even though he could not follow the full rigors of the Holy Rule, he had come to believe that surrender to the divine will was surely the authentic Rule for all. He was ready to return to the house of God and to embrace its silence.

On December 15, 1937, Rafael left his family home for the last time.[99] His mother later described how, aside from the clothes he was wearing, he took with him nothing more than a breviary, his rosary, and a crucifix. He even left behind his recent paintings and his supplies, though in the past he had found comfort in painting

---

98. CW 596–601, #168.

99. The information about Rafael's final departure from home and return to the monastery—including a touching excerpt from his mother's recollection of the day—appears in a lengthy explanatory footnote in OC 856–58, n. 1033. Fr. Teófilo recounts that he encountered Rafael on the day of his return. The two embraced, and Rafael said, "I return and will not leave again. I come here to die" ("*Vengo para no salir más; vengo a morir aquí*").

during his long hours alone in his infirmary cell. In his farewell to the family, it was clear that he foresaw both the trials that awaited him and his death. His companion for the drive to the monastery was his brother Leopoldo, who later recounted that, within sight of the monastery, Rafael stopped the car and asked for a cigarette. Noticing that Rafael was crying, he asked why. In a mysterious and disturbing response, as Rafael looked toward the monastery, he said, "Look, there is an outpost of hell" (*"Mira, éso, es una sucursal del infierno"*). As he regained his earlier calm, Leopoldo drove the short remaining distance to the monastery. There Rafael said simply, again crying, "I enter the place where I will die." The story highlights Rafael's struggle to embrace the cross to which he felt called and which he was fully embracing—not, we might note, unlike Jesus sweating blood in the Garden of Gethsemane.[100]

The Fourth and Final Entrance

The twenty-six-year-old Rafael arrived at the monastery for the last time on December 15, 1937. How different he was from the young man who had first arrived only a few years earlier. Through his struggles and trials, he had arrived at a deep spiritual maturity. His writings of the brief period that remained until his death reveal a profound embrace and understanding of the mystery of the cross. His physical health was declining, and he had no further illusions about the place, about himself, or about what God was inviting him to. Rafael felt both the dread of it and yet a deep sense of conviction about taking the path before him, feeling more deeply that he was drawing near and conforming himself to the cross of Jesus. The final renunciations lay before him. By living through and accepting such trials as his intense physical hunger and thirst (the result of his worsening diabetes), his feeling of isolation, and the verbal abuse of his infirmary companion as well as the misunderstanding of others, Rafael was entering into the

---

100. Beltrame, *Fascinado*, 175–76.

cross of Christ and into the heart of the Crucified. His "God alone" was now focused and identified with the "God alone" of Jesus on the cross.

The day after his return to the monastery, Rafael began to write his final journal, *God and My Soul: Notes of Conscience* (*Dios y mi alma. Notas de conciencia*). He would continue writing until April 17, just a little over a week before his death. This was the most intimate of his journals, begun at the recommendation of Fr. Teófilo as a way to externalize his reflections in the absence of a spiritual director. It became his only outlet. It was Teófilo's hope that the two would be able to find an opportunity to share its contents. Unlike his earlier writings, Rafael never expected it to be read by anyone other than Fr. Teófilo. But the journal reveals a deeper intimacy for other reasons: the entries are often heartfelt and candid prayers directed to God from the depths of Rafael's soul. They also reflect his profound spiritual maturity, engaged in an ongoing encounter with the cross. The journal reveals a soul in dialogue with God, in prayer, in struggle, in darkness and light, in desolation and in consolation, aridity and sweetness—a rich window into a soul surrendering itself more and more completely to God, being purified to arrive at true purity of heart. *God and My Soul* is a spiritual treasure. How fortunate that Teófilo was able to save it from being disposed of after Rafael's death! The journal is the only source of our knowledge from this period, because Rafael wrote only four letters in these final months of his life.

In the first entry of the journal, Rafael records three reasons for returning to the monastery and three aspirations. He has come to better fulfill his vocation to love God in the cross and in sacrifice, to aid his brothers engaged in the war effort, and to take advantage of the time that God gives him to learn quickly to love the cross. He aspires only to unite himself absolutely and entirely with the will of Jesus, to live for nothing more than to love and to suffer, and to be the least and the last in order to obey. [101]

---

101. CW 607, #170.

The infirmarian did not understand the care that a diabetic required, especially the need for food portions beyond the meager and largely unvarying diet of the monastery. In previous times in the infirmary, Rafael had accepted the situation because he wanted to avoid the humiliation of needing more than the regular portion of food or to blunt the taunting of his infirmary companion. But, now, though he was by no means suicidal, Rafael consciously and freely accepted the slow and virtually inevitable deterioration of his health, simply embracing the reality of his life in the infirmary, which he had fully anticipated. Staying in his family home could have slowed and eased this deterioration, but cure was not a possibility. The result, then, was that Rafael experienced a nearly constant hunger and intense thirst. And yet, at the same time, he found himself at peace and even happy, feeling himself to be at the foot of the cross of Jesus.[102] "What are you complaining about, Brother Rafael?" he felt Jesus say to him. "Love Me, suffer with Me, I am Jesus."[103] At one point, after describing an experience of feeling buried with Christ in the tomb—buried alive in his physical suffering and isolation—Rafael concludes, "All I can say is that I have found true happiness in loving the cross of Christ. I am happy, completely happy, more than anyone could ever imagine, when I embrace the bloodstained cross and realize that Jesus loves me despite my misery, my negligence, and my sins, as does Mary. But I am of no importance . . . God alone."[104]

On January 1, reflecting on the arrival of a new year, Rafael records that he has in prayer vowed to love Jesus always. He sees that he is neither a professed religious nor a lay person. In fact, he is nothing except a soul in love with Christ, who desires Rafael's love in return, freed of attachments to anything or anyone else: "To love Jesus in everything, because of everything, always . . . Only love. A humble, generous, detached, mortified love, in si-

102. CW 635, #184.
103. CW 638, #185.
104. CW 642, #186.

lence. . . . A life of love, that is my Rule . . . my vow . . . That is my only reason for living."[105] And, then, on February 27, he writes that he has offered to the Lord the only thing that remains to him: his life.[106] In coming to the monastery this time, he had consciously and freely left behind the care that his health required, embracing this life in which such care was plainly impossible. But now he offered to the Lord any further concerns about his health, about this or that treatment, about this or that manifestation of his illness. His life and his health are now the Lord's. He will care for it as he can, but, belonging no longer to himself, he chooses to let God act while he lets go of any preoccupation over it. Having left behind all else in coming this last time to the monastery, this offering of life and health is all that remains to be given.

Periods of darkness passed into peaceful light. One commentator, reflecting on Rafael's narration of his spiritual state during this period, sees in those words the desolations and consolations, the anguish and sensible yearnings for God, of Teresa of Ávila's description of the passage from the sixth dwellings of the interior castle to the seventh, in which the person enters into the transforming union with God.[107] In fact, witnesses attest that in these last months, Rafael spent hours before the Blessed Sacrament, appearing by external demeanor to be in the deepest prayer and totally abandoned to God.[108]

Reading Rafael's journal from this period—even more than his previous writings—feels like being privileged to observe his prayer from within. The journal entry of March 13, 1938, offers one of many examples of Rafael's simple ardor and his mature spiritual depth as he expresses his longing for union with God while wait-

105. CW 613, #175.

106. CW 643, #187.

107. Baldomero Jiménez Duque, "La experiencia del Hermano Rafael a la luz de las enseñanzas de San Juan de la Cruz," in *Espiritualidad del Hermano Rafael* (Venta de Baños, Spain: Abadía de San Isidro de Dueñas, 1984), 83.

108. OC 908–9, n. 1082

ing in silence at the foot of the cross. There he wonders at the "miracle" of the transformation that God has been working within him, freeing him from his attachments to everything that is less than God—even from his focus on his trials, his joys, and his dreams. Nothing matters—not his life, not his health, not his illness. All that matters is God's will for him as he waits at the foot of the cross.[109]

In a special way, this change in Rafael is manifest in a new love for those around him. He finds that he no longer judges them and their faults or the little offenses they sometimes seem to give him. He sees now that his former response to them was the result of his own self-love and his pride. But now he feels nothing but a great desire to love the people around him, to show them tenderness, and to serve them. He concludes that it is only such love that can bring true happiness, meekness, and peace, and that only that can allow one to live in community with a spirit of tranquility and peace. In the monastic tradition, it is the freedom that comes with purity of heart that that finally allows one to truly love. Saint Teresa of Ávila wrote that in that arrival at the inmost dwelling place of the interior castle of the soul, entering into union with God, the soul discovers that the task that remains is love of those around us.

RECEIVING THE SCAPULAR AND COWL

The abbot had already shown a distinct regard for Rafael by setting him on the path to priestly ordination through the study of Latin and theology. This was a highly unusual path for an oblate. Perhaps the abbot thought that Rafael would eventually recover, or perhaps he perceived special gifts in Rafael, or perhaps he thought of ordination as a way to alleviate the humiliation of Rafael's status in the monastery, though in his journal Rafael expressed his indifference to ordination. In fact, he did not think that he would live

109. CW 655–58, #193.

to receive it.[110] But even more extraordinary was the abbot's decision to give Rafael the black scapular, to be worn over the white tunic, and the cowl of a professed monk. None of the monks could remember seeing or hearing of doing so for an oblate before or afterward.[111] In his journal entry of March 8, Rafael recalls that his first reaction was joy and gratitude, but he quickly came to see his reaction as a vanity. What does the external matter when one loves God from within? He addresses God: "And so, Lord, I see that all is vanity. You are not in a habit or a crown. Where, then? You, Lord, are in the heart that is detached from everything."[112] He concludes with a popular saying whose English equivalent is "You can't make a silk purse from a sow's ear."[113] Nonetheless, on Easter Sunday (April 17, 1938), he received the black scapular and cowl. And, even while recognizing it as just an external thing, Rafael admitted that he took joy in it.[114]

FINAL DAYS AND DEATH

Just a few days later, on April 21 (Easter Thursday), Rafael's father came to the monastery for a visit. He found Rafael looking healthy and happy, wearing his new cowl and professing that he didn't know what to do in his long sleeves and with so much cloth. But the next day, after his father's departure, Rafael was suffering from a fever and remained in bed. At the time, it didn't seem like a serious cause for concern, but his condition deteriorated rapidly. His blood sugar was now out of control, his fever rising, and his thirst seemingly insatiable, but he did not complain. Then he became delirious. On April 25, he received the Anointing of the Sick but

---

110. OC 962, n. 1165.

111. OC 910, n. 1086.

112. CW 652, #190.

113. In Spanish: "*Aunque la mona se vista de seda . . . mona se queda*" ("Although the monkey dresses in silk, it remains a monkey").

114. CW 693, #206.

was unable to receive Viaticum. On the morning of April 26, 1938, he briefly recovered consciousness, but then died peacefully. He had turned twenty-seven only a few days earlier.[115]

Rafael's brother, Luis Fernando, on a brief leave from his military service, had visited Rafael on March 25, 1938. Like their father, he had found his brother looking well. But in the course of their conversation, Rafael had confessed a terrible suffering—not the privations, the trials associated with his health, or his isolation in the infirmary, but rather his simple awareness in faith of God's infinite love for him. Rafael felt intensely his powerlessness to respond to such unmerited divine love as he longed to do. Luis Fernando asked his brother why he had not chosen the Carthusians, which would have given him more solitude. Rafael had responded that he still "needed to see faces," but he noted that Luis Fernando himself possessed a temperament for the Carthusian life—a path that in fact Luis Fernando took after the war.[116]

Rafael Arnaiz Barón was beatified by Pope John Paul II on September 27, 1992, and canonized by Pope Benedict XVI on October 11, 2009. Fr. Teófilo later noted that during Rafael's lifetime, the vast majority of the monks—though they might have noted his piety and fervor—knew nothing of his interior life. It was revealed to them only later in his letters and journals. Especially in an age of strict silence and separation in Trappist monasteries, many of his brother monks probably did not even know anything of his family status, his earlier studies, or the range of his artistic talents.[117] Such was the nature of life in the monastery . . . and such was the humility of Saint Rafael Arnaiz.

115. Various accounts and brief commentaries by monks and family can be found in OC 971–77, n. 1185.

116. OC 926, n. 1112.

117. Martínez Camino, *Mi Rafael*, 49, n. 17.

CHAPTER 2

Rafael: Writer and Writings

In October 1920, the nine-year-old Rafael was admitted to a Jesuit school in Oviedo, where his family had recently moved. Many years later, one of the Jesuit administrators of the school from that time remembered Rafael fondly. He recalled that the young boy had shown a particular aptitude for mathematics but not so much for writing—ironic, the priest himself notes, in light of the spiritual beauty and depth of his later writing.[1] And beautiful in their simplicity and surprising in their depths provides an accurate description of the writings of Rafael Arnaiz. It would be difficult to read his journals and letters without feeling the draw of his character, his utter simplicity, his sincere piety, his profound faith, and his humble desire to simply love God. These writings reflect what his family and friends said of him—that he was a young man of intelligence and good humor, with a charming and attractive personality and a deep and heartfelt faith.

Except for a few of his earliest extant letters, virtually all of Rafael's writings could be called "spiritual" writing. They are a living expression of a faith vision of his own life and of the world around him.[2] In his journals and even in his letters, he is often

1. Mercedes Barón, *Vida y escritos del Beato Fray María Rafael Arnáiz Barón, monje trapense*, 12th ed. (Madrid: Editorial Perpetuo Socorro, 2000), 63–64.

2. Gonzalo María Fernández, *God Alone: A Spiritual Autobiography of Blessed Rafael Arnáiz Barón*, trans. Hugh McCaffrey, MW 14 (Kalamazoo, MI: Cistercian Publications, 2008), xiii.

offering his reader a glimpse into his own conversations with God. What Rafael writes are not thoughts or concepts *about* God but rather an effort to put into writing his own encounter with God—recognizing that his words could often not adequately express that experience.[3] He is not offering theory or an explanation of a path to God; instead, he is revealing the journey in faith of his own soul, with its ups and downs, his very real struggles, but also his steady—if sometimes hesitant—maturation and progression.[4] Rafael writes without an academic theological sophistication, but his doctrine is nonetheless profound and rich. As we will see, for example, his reflections on the cross in his own life show a deep grasp of Gospel truths—although he was only in his mid-twenties when he wrote and lacked any formal theological training. And yet what he unfolds in his writing is a true theology of the cross, of suffering, of vocation, and of the monastic journey. What Rafael displays may be called a special charism for writing—a special gift and vocation given by the Spirit.[5]

Rafael did not write books or articles for publication. He wrote letters, meditations, and journals. He did not expect his letters to be preserved—in fact, he and his aunt had made a compact to tear up their letters once they had been read. (Happily for future generations, his aunt did not keep her word on the matter.) His final journal was written only for the eyes of his former spiritual director. All of this gives his writings a sense of raw encounter with this young man so full of earnest longing for God. He explicitly wrote one of his journals (*Mi cuaderno / My Notebook*) to be shared with his brother Leopoldo, hoping that it would provide a window into the unavoidable mix of the life of Rafael's soul:

---

3. Tomás Álvarez, "El Hermano Rafael, escritor espiritual," *Cistercium* 179 (Oct–Dec. 1989): 411.

4. Antonio María Martín Fernández-Gallardo, *El deseo de Dios y la ciencia da la Cruz: Aproximación a la experiencia religiosa del Hermano Rafael*, 2nd ed. (Burgos, Spain: Editorial Monte Carmelo, 2002), 220 (cited hereafter as Martín).

5. Paulino Beltrame Quattrocchi, *Fascinado por el Absoluto: Hermano Rafael*, trans. Tomás Gallego Fernández (Madrid: Ediciones Paulinas, 1991), 11.

You'll find a bit of everything in this notebook: faults and virtues, anguish and joy. Between the lines, you'll read about sunny days and cloudy ones, moments of calm and storms . . . but a soul is all of that and much more. All of it is a necessary part of the rhythm of life, both materially and spiritually speaking; and since material matters don't change much in La Trapa, it's the interior life that develops in this way, moved by unfathomable forces . . . A Trappist who *doesn't waste his time* can't help but very often marvel at the work God is doing in his soul . . . In his interior life, he comes across nooks and crannies that are unfamiliar to him at first glance, but in silence and prayer, light is shed upon them.

You'll read many things here that you already know, which might be annoying. There will be a little bit of everything except literary quality and perfection, but it doesn't matter, so long as there's simplicity and good intentions. And believe me, those you will find. I ask you only one thing, which I already said, and that is to read these pages in the same place your Trappist brother wrote them, namely, invoking the Virgin Mary's aid and sitting at the foot of the cross of Jesus.[6]

Why He Wrote

Writing was clearly important for Rafael. It seemed to fulfill a kind of inner need for self-expression, for externalizing his thoughts and feelings, and for focusing his prayer. He was writing basically for himself rather than for publication.[7] While retaining its character as a personal journal, as we have just noted, Rafael did write *My Notebook* with the hopes that his brother Leopoldo would one day benefit from reading it. And since he lacked real spiritual direction

6. CW 480, #136 (Document 136 in *Rafael Arnáiz, Hermano San Rafael: Collected Works* [CW], ed. María Gonzalo-García, trans. Catherine Addington, MW 162 [Collegeville, MN: Cistercian Publications, 2022]).

7. Once Rafael suggested in a letter to his aunt, almost in passing, that one day he might write a little book with his reflections on the Virgin Mary, which she could take to a publisher with the author listed simply as "a Cistercian, a son of Mary" (CW 296, #81).

after his first departure from the monastery, he wrote his final journal with the thought of sharing it with Fr. Teófilo, who had been such a help to him during his first stay. Notably, Rafael left copies of two of his earlier journals with his mother as he was entering the monastery for the last time. Obviously he could have chosen to destroy them.

At the beginning of his journal *The Trappist's Apologia*, Rafael offers two reasons for his writing as well as implying his sense that the journal might eventually be read by others:

> I am writing for two reasons: first, because I believe that writing and thinking about the things of God greatly profits my soul, and delights my spirit, which rejoices at the mention of God, and second, because I have time at my disposal, and so I ought to use it in such a way that serves the greater glory of God.
>
> If someone should read these lines someday, I ask the reader only for their great charity . . . Do not take them for doctrine or teachings, for I attempt no such thing. I write only what I think, what comes to mind, and in a simple way, with no literary aims . . . In these pages I am studying my own soul and my impressions, with no determined plan or set order . . . As such, I repeat, if some curious person should read them (which I will ensure that no one does), I beg them ask for nothing more than that . . . *charity*; that is, a benevolent spirit and understanding. If at any point these pages bring a smile to the reader's lips, may that reader see here only a person who says what he is feeling, even if he might say foolish things sometimes.[8]

Later, in the same reflection, Rafael says that he is not writing for others to read but rather as a method of dialoguing with God—or perhaps a monologue, written as if he were writing to God. At one and the same time, he says, his writing is a manner of self-

8. CW 167, #51.

reflection as well as prayers to God. We can see that writing helped Rafael to externalize, understand, and process his experience, his feelings, his prayer, and his reflections about God's activity in his life. His journals and even his letters became an important tool for the maturation and deepening of his faith and his sense of what God was calling him to do and to be.

At the beginning of his journal *My Notebook*, Rafael again reflects on his reasons for writing. For himself, sitting at his little desk presided over by his crucifix, he often writes as a kind of consolation in his solitude. But with his brother in mind, he also writes with the hope that God is guiding his pen so that the reader may be drawn closer to God. In that way, the reader will come to a way of knowing God that can only be gained—not by studying or by human discussion or debate—by a simple gazing at the crucifix.[9]

Rafael's writing, then, is a manner of self-expression and self-reflection, as well as a manner of praying: writing of God, says Rafael, is itself a method of prayer.[10] In another place, he writes that his writing is often prayer.[11] And in yet another place, he writes that his writing is a consolation to him in his solitude, writing as if he were writing to Jesus, perhaps serving as a kind of prayer that Jesus will hear: "Since I don't talk to anyone anymore, it brings me consolation to fill up page after page writing as if I were writing to Jesus Himself . . . Perhaps it's a form of prayer, and He is listening to me."[12]

LETTERS AND JOURNALS

Rafael's *Obras completas* appeared in Spanish for the first time in 1988. Subsequent editions have appeared as new writings have been discovered and included. The most recent version is the

9. CW 479, #136.
10. CW 533, #153.
11. CW 657, #193.
12. CW 635, #184.

seventh. Rafael wrote no books, articles for publication, or treatises. His collected writings—over 130 letters and 5 journals—were personal expressions of his experience, reflection, and prayer. Although they contain details of his life—in fact, sometimes keen observation of details of life around him—they are more an expression of his inner life. In addition to the letters and meditations, there are also Rafael's paintings, drawings, and holy cards (often with a phrase or spiritual message inscribed on the front or back), as well as notebooks of rather random prayers, very brief reflections, and texts from other authors that he copied by hand without accompanying reflections. These may give us a wider sense of what Rafael was reading.[13]

LETTERS

Rafael's letters reveal a young man of jovial character, compassion, a desire to bring joy to the people around him, and an ability to see the humorous peculiarities of his own life and of the world around him. At the same time, they reveal a man of real faith, of profound yearning for God, and of single-hearted pursuit of the divine will in his life. These letters can largely be divided between those directed to his aunt and uncle, the duchess and duke of Maqueda, and those directed to everyone else. The journals were mostly written while he was in the monastery, serving as a way to externalize his thoughts and prayers when it seemed particularly important for him because of the required monastic silence and

---

13. OC 1065–1116 (*San Rafael Arnaiz Barón: Obras Completas*, ed. Alberico Feliz Carabajal, 7th ed. [Burgos, Spain: Editorial Fonte, 2017]). For seventy-one photos of some of Rafael's notebooks—both the notebooks themselves and individual pages in Rafael's neat handwriting—as well as a few of his accompanying illustrations, see Juan Antonio Martínez Camino, *Mi Rafael: San Rafael Arnáiz, según el Padre Teófilo Sandoval, su confesor, intérprete y editor*, 2nd ed. (Bilbao, Spain: Editorial Desclée de Bouwer, 2009), s.n. (last, unnumbered section of the book: *Fotografías*).

absence of a spiritual director. The letters, on the other hand, were generally written when he was outside the monastery. The Trappist discipline at the time restricted the sending and receiving of personal letters.

Rafael's letters to his aunt and uncle reveal their deep spiritual friendship as well as the depth of his own maturing spirituality. These letters could be quite long, written over several days and often begun immediately upon receipt of a letter from them. In this correspondence, Rafael is sharing his personal reflections, and he recognizes that his letters must sometimes read more like a spiritual diary to which he is making his aunt privy.[14] Sometimes he begins to speak to her about God but ends up speaking to God.[15] Often his letters are a kind of spiritual direction, especially for his aunt but for others as well. Rafael credits his aunt and uncle with mentoring his growth in faith and in his sense of vocation, but the letters show that their roles became reversed; it was Rafael who became the mentor and support.[16] At a number of points, Rafael refers to the agreement between his aunt and himself that they would destroy their letters to each other once read.[17] This would allow them to write to each other with complete candor. While Rafael was faithful to this agreement, despite his frequent reminder his aunt was not, undoubtedly recognizing the spiritual treasure that they contained.

THE JOURNALS

These five journals contain reflections written over days or weeks, almost in the form of diary entries, not really narratives but rather meditations on his experience. Often we are reading Rafael at

14. CW 361, #94.
15. CW 316, #85.
16. Concerning the reversal of their roles, see the following footnotes: OC 409, n. 450; OC 429, n. 468.
17. See for example CW 231, #70; CS 263, #75; and CW 285, #77.

prayer, expressed in writing. At other times we are reading his simple and yet profound theology—the reflections of his maturing faith on the unfolding of the mysterious will of God in his life.

1. *Impressions of La Trapa* (*Impresiones de la Trapa*).[18] In September of 1931, the twenty-year-old Rafael, still enrolled in the School of Architecture in Madrid, recorded his idealistic impressions of his first two visits to the monastery. His sincerely pious and artistic spirit reflects on the solemn and haunting sounds of the bells, the simple beauty of the divine liturgy, the silent witness of the monks whether in the church or on their way to work in the monastery's fields, the tender devotion of the monks toward the Virgin Mary, and the generally pervading atmosphere of prayer and divine presence. He contrasts this sacred and ordered ambience with the cars speeding by on the nearby highway—even as he contrasts his own life of comfort with the contented and chosen poverty of the monks. He concludes that no person of Christian faith could visit such a place without being changed by the almost tangible presence of God.

2. *The Trappist's Apologia* (*Apología del trapense*).[19] The twenty-three-year-old Rafael wrote this journal between September 19 and October 5, 1934, not long after his first departure from the monastery in May of that year. Still recovering physically and spiritually in his family home, Rafael begins the journal by saying that he writes for two reasons: for the benefit that it provides to his own spirit to write of the things of God, and to use his free time in a manner that will give glory to God. But at its heart the journal is a kind of defense of the Trappist life against a general misunderstanding and lack of appreciation even among some in the Church. It is for this reason that Fr. Teófilo later gave the journal its title. More specifically, this spirit of defense was oc-

18. CW 20–25, #7.
19. CW 167–81, #51. For a summary of its content see Francisco Cerro Chaves, *Silencio en los labios, cantares en el corazón: vida y espiritualidad del Hermano Rafael* (Madrid: Biblioteca de Autores Cristianos, 2014), 127–36.

casioned by Rafael's encounter with an old high-school acquaintance who—sincerely and without ill will—called his desire to return to the monastery selfish and virtually suicidal. It is not surprising that many people could not understand why a young man of Rafael's talents and background—and with his recent serious illness—would choose to return to the monastic life.

3. *Meditations of a Trappist (Meditaciones de un trapense).*[20] Rafael was twenty-five years old when he began this journal on July 12, 1936, during his second stay in the monastery. He wrote the last entry on August 8 of the same year. It was a period in which his diabetes had improved, and he was able to participate in many aspects of the normal monastic life and schedule: attend the common liturgies in the monastic choir, work moderately in the fields with the novices, and attend various other community functions. The journal, with about a dozen entries, reveals a sense of inner peace, a contemplative soul deeply in love with God and with the Virgin Mary. In a particularly self-revealing reflection, Rafael looks back on himself as the naïve young man whose artistic sensibilities and sincere piety had first brought him to the monastery, contrasted with the man—the oblate without the possibility of professing monastic vows—who now sees the challenges of the reality of the monastic life as it is lived by flesh-and-blood people of faith.[21] What truly matters, he concludes, is not the externals of the life; rather, "the most important thing in a monastery is God."[22] But, at the same time, the journal reflects the disturbing first news of the eruption of the Spanish Civil War in mid-July of 1936, which would draw Rafael out of the monastery again on September 29.

---

20. CW 412–63, ##108–30. Rafael's mother later added the titles to the journal entries. For a summary of some of the main themes of the journal, see Cerro Chaves, *Silencio en los labios,* 186–200.

21. CW 416–19, #110.

22. CW 417, #110.

4. *My Notebook (Mi cuaderno)*.[23] Rafael began this series of meditations on December 8, 1936, just after his third entrance to the monastery. He continued it until February 6, 1937, right before his deteriorating health forced him to leave the monastery for the third time. The journal is dedicated to his brother, Leopoldo, who was serving in the military in the civil war. It was Rafael's only writing during this period. These meditations, written from his cell in the infirmary, reflect a quiet and peaceful spirit. He clearly uses his prolonged periods in solitude and silence to ponder, to meditate on, and more deeply to embrace his reality—as he says, at the foot of the cross. In a reflection of January 22, 1937, Rafael reflects on a day spent drawing an image of Christ on the cross.[24] As an artist, it is a joy for him to draw and paint, but it becomes clear that in this action, Rafael is meditating on and identifying himself more deeply with Christ crucified. Throughout the journal, Rafael speaks candidly of his trials, but there remains a more fundamental acceptance of his illness and its accompanying restrictions. Rafael writes without self-pity or complaint against God's will, accepting that God's will—no matter how mysterious—is exactly what is best for him.

5. *God and My Soul: Notes of Conscience (Dios y mi alma, notas de conciencia)*.[25] Rafael began this journal on December 16, 1937, the day after his fourth entrance to the monastery. As he found himself again without a spiritual director—at a critical point in his life and in his spiritual journey—Fr. Teófilo recommended that Rafael write down his reflections with the hope that the two might speak about them at some point. Rafael wrote until April 17, 1938, just nine

---

23. CW 479–548, ##136–58. Rafael left the copy of *Meditaciones de un trapense* and his *Mi cuaderno* with his mother when he entered for the fourth and last time on Dec. 14, 1937. For a summary of the contents of *Mi cuaderno*, see Cerro Chaves, *Silencio en los labios*, 203–22.

24. CW 540–41, #155.

25. CW 606–93, ##170–206. For a summary of the contents of this journal, see Cerro Chaves, *Silencio en los labios*, 284–97.

days before his death. It was only then that Teófilo was able to read them—and to save the journal from destruction. Rafael's meditations reflect a deep life of prayer, a profound identification with Christ crucified, and ultimately a complete surrender to the divine will. Martín Fernández-Gallardo, in his *El deseo de Dios y la ciencia de la Cruz*, sees in the first part of these entries a mixture of joy and anguish, peace and struggle, light and darkness—until Rafael's entry of March 4, 1938 (titled "How Long, O Lord?").[26] Then, beginning with the next entry—of March 7, 1938 (titled "Jesus is Where I Belong" [¡*Mi centro es Jesús!*])[27]—we can see Rafael settling more securely into his unfolding "science of the Cross."[28]

SOURCES/INFLUENCES

Rafael's writings make clear that he liked to read and that he gained important insights for his own prayer and reflection from what he read.[29] Mostly in passing, he quotes or refers to authors whom he has read. We know that time was set aside in the monastic schedule for daily spiritual reading as required by the Order's Constitutions and the Holy Rule. Rafael mentions his practice of spiritual reading among his other devotions in a letter to his aunt.[30] In addition to his journals and letters, he left behind two notebooks of his own drawings and of his handwritten quotations from a wide variety of spiritual authors whom he was reading or had read, both classical and contemporary. Although we cannot know in any systematic and thorough way what he was reading, we can get a sense of these sources through a look at which sources he cites, quotes, or mentions in his writings.

---

26. CW 646–58, #188.

27. CW 649–50, #189.

28. Martín, *Deseo de Dios*, 41.

29. Cerro Chaves (*Silencio en los labios*, 13–25) provides a helpful overview of what seem to be some of Rafael's most important sources.

30. CW 403, #105.

Scriptures

Rafael frequently quotes and makes references to biblical texts, suggesting that the Scriptures had an important place in his spiritual reading and meditation. This fact is noteworthy because reading the Bible directly was not so common among the Catholic faithful in this time before the Second Vatican Council. In fact, the Trappist *Spiritual Directory* recommends the daily reading of a passage from the Bible, aided by the use of a brief commentary.[31] It goes on to suggest reverently reading the passage over several times.

Rafael moreover writes to a friend in September of 1934 recommending that he should read the Bible often:

> Forgive me for resorting to citing sacred texts. On my own I know nothing, but we can always find balm for our wounds in the Sacred Scriptures . . . I read them often, and when we read the divine Word there, it seems as if everything quiets down, and we have greater peace of spirit . . . Don't stop reading them, and very often; don't ever stop. If we had true faith, that would be the only book we'd ever have close at hand.[32]

Three years later, in a letter to his aunt, he reports that he has spent the whole morning alone, dedicated to the reading of the Scriptures, in which he always discovers again the inexhaustible depths of the Word of God.[33] It becomes clear that the Bible played an important role in his coming to understand his personal relationship with and journey to God.

When Rafael came to the monastery the second time, he had been allowed to bring with him three or four books for his personal use to serve his prayer and meditation.[34] We know that he brought

---

31. *A Spiritual Directory for Religious* (Peosta, IA: New Melleray Abbey, 1932), 136–37. This is a translation from the French of *Directoire Spirituel à l'Usage des Cisterciens de la Scricte Observance*.

32. CW 164, #50.

33. CW 557, #160.

34. OC 995, n. 1203.

a Bible, a 612-page study of the Psalms, and *The Imitation of Christ.* It may be that he also brought a thick, scholarly book on the life of Jesus, *Jesucristo*, by the contemporary Jesuit Leónce de Grandmaison.[35] In any case, it is noteworthy that among these few books, the Scriptures and serious studies of the Bible should be featured prominently—again, in an age in which Catholics did not usually read the Bible directly.

TERESA OF ÁVILA AND JOHN OF THE CROSS

Surely it is not surprising that Rafael was a devoted reader of Teresa of Ávila and John of the Cross, two great Spanish mystics whose works were so widely known and so readily available in Spain at the time. The editors of the Spanish Cistercian journal *Cistercium* note the clear influence of these two Spanish Doctors of the Church on Rafael's spirituality, suggesting that no other authors influenced him so strongly.[36] We recall that his aunt and uncle, the duke and duchess of Maqueda, had a house in Ávila and an estate a short distance outside the city. Rafael had spent extended periods there, and he reports that he had a great love for the city of Saint Teresa and experienced a spiritual rejoicing walking through its streets.[37] It is a love for the city and a devotion for those two saints that he shared with and to some degree learned from his aunt and uncle.[38] We recall too that after his uncle's death, his aunt became a nun in the Monastery of the Incarnation, where Saint Teresa had first entered some four hundred years earlier.

---

35. The above note in the *Obras completas* does not mention this last book. See Martínez Camino, *Mi Rafael*, 236.

36. Francisco Rafael de Pascual, "Son tus Santos, nuestros amigos," *Cistercium* 254 (Jan.–June 2010): 13.

37. CW 208, #62.

38. Baldomero Jiménez Duque, "La experiencia del Hermano Rafael a la luz de las enseñanzas de San Juan de la Cruz," in *Espiritualidad del Hermano Rafael* (Venta de Baños, Spain: Abadía de San Isidro de Dueñas, 1984), 75.

Rafael cites the works of Saint Teresa about fourteen times in his journals and letters, referring to several of her major works. It is quite possible that his often-repeated phrase "God alone!" (*Sólo Dios*) is inspired by the famous poem attributed to her that ends with the line "God alone suffices" (*Sólo Dios basta*).[39] Rafael quotes this final line from the poem at least three times[40] in addition to referring to other lines of the same poem. But beyond that particular poem, like his references to John of the Cross, Rafael most often quotes selections from Teresa that reflect her deep yearning for God. Having experienced something of the divine presence, she longed for yet-deeper union with God and, by comparison, found the things of this world profoundly unsatisfying. This was an experience that Rafael came to know intimately. He opens his journal *Meditations of a Trappist* with the first, famous, stanza of her poem, *Vivo sin vivir en mí*, which is full of longing for union with God:

> I live without living in myself,
> And in such a way I hope,
> I die because I do not die.[41]

And, about a month before his death, Rafael seems to refer to another poem in which Saint Teresa expresses this same longing for God and her dissatisfaction with what the world had to offer:

> My God, how sad is
> Life without You!
> Longing to see You,
> Death I desire.[42]

---

39. *The Collected Works of St. Teresa of Ávila*, trans. Kieran Kavanaugh and Otilio Rodriguez (Washington, DC: ICS Publications, 1985), 3:286. The poem is sometimes called "Saint Teresa's bookmark."

40. CW 397, #104; CW 411, #107; CW 617, #176.

41. CW 412, #108. English translation quoted from *Collected Works of St. Teresa of Ávila*, 3:375.

42. CW 662, #195. English translation quoted from *Collected Works of St. Teresa of Ávila*, 3:382.

Teresa of Ávila and John of the Cross are both prime examples of the images and themes of searching and longing love that characterize classic Spanish mysticism. The yearnings of Saint Teresa that seem to have resonated so deeply in the heart of Rafael, he found even more in the works of John of the Cross—especially in his poem of mystical love, *The Spiritual Canticle,* which is itself based on the biblical Song of Songs, so often the focus of meditation by mystical authors.[43] Rafael cites or refers to John of the Cross more than twenty times—arguably, along with Thomas à Kempis, the author he cites most often.[44] Rafael records in his journal *My Notebook* that many times he had found passages from John of the Cross that seemed to have been written precisely for him.[45] Especially after his first period in the monastery, when he found himself without a human spiritual director, John of the Cross became a kind of spiritual guide for Rafael.[46]

Rafael's close reading of the spirituality of John of the Cross is evident in his copy of Crisógono de Jesús Sacramentado's well-known 1935 study, *San Juan de la Cruz: el hombre, el doctor, el poeta.*[47] It is a book of about 230 pages in three parts: John's life, an overview and analysis of his spiritual teaching, and an examination of his prose and poetry. Rafael apparently read the book very shortly after its publication, probably in the period after his first departure from the monastery and his later return as an oblate. At that point, it seems that he gave the book to the Poor Clare nuns in Ávila.[48] During this same period Rafael wrote to his aunt that he had been out for a long drive, taking consolation in reading

43. For the influence of John of the Cross on the thought of Saint Rafael, see especially Cerro Chaves, *Silencio en los labios,* 143–54; and the article by Jiménez Duque, "La experiencia del Hermano Rafael."

44. Cerro Chaves, *Silencio en los labios,* 15–17.

45. CW 499, #141.

46. Cerro Chaves, *Silencio en los labios,* 154.

47. Crisógono de Jesús Sacramentado, *San Juan de la Cruz: el hombre, el doctor, el poeta* (Barcelona, Spain: Editorial Labor, 1935).

48. Martínez Camino discusses Rafael's copy of the Crisógono text at some length (*Mi Rafael,* 219–28).

John of the Cross's poetry. He reported that he always carried a text of John of the Cross in the glove compartment of his car.[49]

Rafael's copy of the Crisógono book is heavily marked up, with texts underlined, suggesting Rafael's immersion in the thought of John of the Cross. He double underlined a passage containing a text in which John of the Cross's focus on purgation and self-denial—his famous "*nada*" doctrine—is most starkly evident: "Endeavor to be inclined always: not to the easiest, but to the most difficult; not to the most delightful, but to the most distasteful; not to the most gratifying, but to the less pleasant . . . ."[50] Texts such as these, as Crisógono and other commentators note, have to be understood as the challenge of the soul that yearns for God and thus seeks to be—and must be—purged of all that is less than God. Rafael went on to underline Crisógono's words: "the negation is always absolute; it never admits of degrees."[51]

Rafael's affinity for John of the Cross is not surprising in light of the yearning for God expressed in John's poetry but also in his challenge that seekers must walk in a kind of blind faith—which John calls "darkness" or "night."[52] For a person's yearning love for God to find its goal, he or she must be prepared to give up everything that is not God and is less than God. In a number of places Rafael cites the third stanza of *The Spiritual Canticle,* in which the bride/soul proclaims that she will not "gather flowers."[53] When seeking one's Beloved, "gathering flowers"—as beautiful as they might be—is nothing more than a waste of time. In the same

---

49. CW 279, #77.

50. Quoted from *The Collected Works of St. John of the* Cross, trans. Kieran Kavanaugh and Otilio Rodriguez, 3rd ed. (Washington, DC: ICS Publications, 2017), 149.

51. Martínez Camino, *Mi Rafael,* 223.

52. For a discussion of this theme of "dark" faith in the works of Rafael, see Manuel Sánchez Monge, *La passion de solo Dios: el Hermano Rafael* (Burgos, Spain: Editorial Monte Carmelo 2000), 195–209, chap. 10: "Sólo Dios en pura fe."

53. English translation quoted from *Collected Works of St. John of the Cross,* 74. See, for example, CW 228, #70; CW 289, #78; CW 374, #98.

spirit, Rafael cites a one-stanza poem of John of the Cross titled "The Sum of Perfection":

> Forgetfulness of created things,
> remembrance of the Creator,
> attention turned toward inward things,
> and loving the Beloved.[54]

When we think of Rafael's own journey—with its unexpected turns and disappointments—and of his deep faith that God was acting according to a mysterious but loving plan, it is not at all surprising that words of John of the Cross resonated with his experience and helped him to come to his own rich faith response. Rafael yearned for "God alone," walking along the mysterious path that God was directing, embracing ever more deeply the cross, which would be the pathway to union with his Beloved. In fact, just two months after his first departure, he writes to his aunt that his own experience has helped him to see the truth of John's "*nada*" doctrine—that in drawing close to God, there is no other way than to become free of "all" in order to remain in the "nothing."[55] (Though perhaps without the dramatic starkness of John of the Cross's radical manner of expression, the ancient monastic wisdom sees the same necessity for purgation in order to arrive at purity of heart.) In this same early letter to his aunt, Rafael quickly noted that he recognized that he was daring to speak of "high" spiritual doctrine—he wanted to fly when in fact he was learning to crawl along that path. But Rafael would ultimately fly by embracing his

54. CW 409, #106. English translation quoted from *Collected Works of St. John of the Cross*, 73.

55. CW 124, #40. Fr. Teófilo, Rafael's spiritual director during his first stay in the monastery, later wrote that he and Rafael had spoken of this "*nada*" doctrine of John of the Cross during those months. In fact, Teófilo reported that in a conversation the night before Rafael's first departure, Rafael had already begun to see this unwanted turn of events in light of that teaching of John of the Cross. See Martínez Camino, *Mi Rafael*, 93.

own journey of self-offering as it unfolded before him. And on that journey, John of the Cross's reflections on walking in dark faith along a path of letting go, as well as his poetry that sings of yearning for union with God, resonated in Rafael's heart and gave him language to understand and express his experience.

In a reflection on solitude written shortly after his third entry, Rafael ponders how God draws the soul into an inner solitude separated from what is less than God. But, he reflects, it is only there that one can most deeply encounter God. Twice in this journal reflection, Rafael quotes stanza thirty-five of *The Spiritual Canticle*, ending with the entire stanza:

> She lived in solitude,
> and now in solitude has built her nest;
> and in solitude he guides her,
> he alone, who also bears
> in solitude the wound of love.[56]

And only a month later, he cites the last line of the famous first stanza from *The Living Flame of Love*:

> O living flame of love
> that tenderly wounds my soul
> in its deepest center! Since
> now you are not oppressive,
> now consummate! if it be your will:
> tear through the veil of this sweet encounter![57]

It was this sentiment of longing love that came to fill the depth of Rafael's soul, even as his disease progressed with its accompanying trials.

---

56. CW 488, #138. English translation from *Collected Works of St. John of the Cross*, 79.

57. CW 525, #150. English translation from *Collected Works of St. John of the Cross*, 52.

Many of the principal elements of Rafael's spirituality—devotion to the humanity of Christ, particularly his passion, the centrality of desire, a strongly affective path to God, and a preference for simplicity—were fed by his reading of the works of John of the Cross and Teresa of Ávila. But they are also essential in Cistercian spirituality and frequent themes in the works of Saint Bernard and Cistercian authors of the twelfth and thirteenth centuries. Those writings subsequently inspired and formed mystical writers that followed in the wider Christian tradition that reached the great Carmelite saints. While it seems unlikely that Rafael had the opportunity to read the writings of the Cistercians of the golden age, the pages that follow show that, embracing the monastic life and the Cistercian way, Rafael developed a kind of monastic instinct for what had moved the hearts and enlightened the minds of the earliest saints of the Cistercian reform. Rafael's desire for "God alone" expresses the same determination that guided that great monastic reform to look for simplicity in everything so that nothing would hinder the encounter with the God whom they so ardently loved.

THE IMITATION OF CHRIST

The Trappist *Spiritual Directory* highly recommended the reading of the medieval classic *The Imitation of Christ* by Thomas à Kempis,[58] and Rafael quotes or makes apparent reference to it over twenty times in his letters and journals. In addition, he copied a number of quotations from the *Imitation*—without accompanying comment—into his *Anotaciones*.[59] This was one of the three or four books that Rafael brought to the monastery with him. It is clear that he both read and meditated on it. The particular texts that caught Rafael's attention cover a range of classical piety and

---

58. *Spiritual Directory*, 138–39.

59. See the index of names, OC 1035. For a review of Rafael's quotations from Thomas à Kempis in his *Anotaciones*, see Martínez Camino, *Mi Rafael*, 241–47.

ascetical thought—for example, his reference to a chapter whose English title is "On Disregarding Creatures to Find the Creator."[60] But most notable is the fact that Rafael cites or refers at least five times[61] to the chapter from the *Imitation* titled "On the Royal Road of the Holy Cross,"[62] in which Kempis urges his readers to embrace the cross as they find it in their lives. Wherever we go, Kempis remarks, we will find the cross, and only by embracing it will we find peace. Martínez Camino concludes that the *Imitation* seems to have played an important role in the unfolding of Rafael's understanding of his own trials in the light of the cross as he found it in his own life.

Monastic Sources

Rafael's reading of classic monastic sources does not seem to have been very wide or deep. This was probably typical of the formation of young Trappists in 1930s Spain and elsewhere. Many of these sources would not have been available in Spanish translation at the time. Rafael cites Saint Benedict seven times and Saint Bernard nine times—in the latter case, mostly in reference to devotion to the Virgin Mary. Still, we can be confident that Rafael was formed by the study of the Rule. As we saw in reviewing Rafael's life, before entering the monastery he had read a short book titled *La vida cisterciense,* which is a sort of summary of Trappist spirituality and practice.[63] In it, the novice is urged to read and to study the Rule of Saint Benedict, understanding it to be a kind of spiritual directory whose wisdom has formed a long line of saints. Further, it addresses the practice in the monastery of a daily common reading of a passage from the Rule in the monastic

60. Thomas à Kempis, *The Imitation of Christ* (South Bend, IN: Greenlawn Press, 1990), 3.31. See CW 406, #106.

61. CW 492, #139; CW 533, #153; CW 538, #154; CW 547, #158.

62. Thomas à Kempis, *Imitation of Christ*, 2.12.

63. *La vida cisterciense en el monasterio de San Isidro de Dueñas* (Burgos, Spain: Monte Carmelo, 1928).

chapter, followed by an explanation offered by the superior. The monks are urged to attend prayerfully to this teaching and to nurture themselves by a frequent personal reading of and mediation on the Rule.

Since Rafael refers frequently to the mandated details of Trappist liturgy and life, we can be certain that he had read the Trappist usages (*Usos*) of that time. We recall too that he had read his uncle's translation from the French of *Del campo de batalla a la Trapa* as well as *La vida del Padre María Efrén Ferrer*, both of which probably played a role in his discovery of his Trappist vocation. In the monastic life, it is assumed that the life is learned by living it—and that Rafael did so whole-heartedly as best he could in the midst of his unusual monastic journey. We know that he read at least some of Saint Gertrude's work.[64] But in general, it does not seem that his reading was much focused on specifically monastic sources.

OTHER AUTHORS

Rafael explicitly refers to Saint Thérèse of Lisieux six times, noting, for example, her commitment to smile through her trials so as not to disturb the peace of those around her.[65] He took that example to heart, as those who knew him have attested. He also may be drawing on the thought of Saint Thérèse[66] when he writes of the need to keep secret or hidden one's deepest encounters with Christ—what they both call keeping "the King's secrets"—since such experiences can seem cheapened or even defiled by trying to describe or explain them.[67] Although his references to Saint Ignatius of Loyola are few, it seems likely that his occasional use

64. CW 526, #150; CW 663, #195.
65. CW 118, #38.
66. Thérèse of Lisieux, *The Story of a Soul: The Autobiography of Saint Thérèse of Lisieux*, 3rd ed., trans. John Clarke (Washington, DC: ICS Publications, 1996), 189.
67. CW 494, #140.

of terms like *consolations*, *desolations*, and *indifference* are a reflection of his early education in Jesuit schools. He refers in a few places to the works of Frederick William Faber, the English convert to Catholicism from Anglicanism, whose works were popular in the early twentieth century. Rafael seems to have identified with some of Faber's piety but rejected Faber's more negative view of the world.[68] In addition to the authors mentioned here, we can add the many more whose words he included without comment in his *Anotaciones*. Of their degree of influence on Rafael, we simply cannot know.

First Writings About Rafael

Although Rafael died in 1938, the first edition of his complete works did not appear until 1988, with each subsequent edition adding previously unpublished works of the young Trappist. They are now available in their seventh Spanish edition. Before 1988, Rafael's writings appeared only in select form. In 1944, his maternal uncle, Leopoldo Barón Torres, Duke of Maqueda, published *Un secreto de la Trapa (El hermano Rafael)*. This was a work of about 250 pages that was part biography, an initial presentation of some of Rafael's major texts (including twenty-four of his letters), and his uncle's personal recollections and reflections. Amplified in later editions, this work is now in its sixth edition.

In 1947, Rafael's mother, Mercedes Barón, using a pseudonym, published *Escritos y datos biográficos de Fray María Rafael Arnáiz Barón, monje trapense*. This text included more biographical detail, drawn from her own memories and those of a few monks who knew Rafael. It also included photographs and more of Rafael's writing. With its fourth, expanded edition, the book was published bearing her own name and under a new title: *Vidas y escritos de Fray María Rafael*. Today it appears in its twelfth edition. Rafael's

68. CW 171–72, #51.

mother never considered it a full biography, but both this book by her and the one by his uncle offer unique and privileged views into Rafael's life and thought. An English translation of some of Rafael's works from his years in the monastery (thus beginning in February 1936) as these appeared in *Vidas y escritos* were translated with brief introductions and published in serial form over several issues of *Cisterician Studies Quarterly* between 1998 and 2003.[69] All of these were compiled and published in a single volume in a special edition of *Cistercian Studies Quarterly* in 2003.[70] Cistercian Publications has recently published a slightly abridged English translation of Rafael's complete works.[71]

The first real biography of Rafael—though with a very hagiographic spirit—was published by Jesús Álvarez, OCSO, in 1952.[72] Since then, a number of biographies have appeared, though none of them approach a detailed and definitive study. In 2008, Cistercian Publications published a translation of a biography by Gonzalo María Fernández, OCSO, with the English title *God Alone: A Spiritual Biography of Blessed Rafael Arnáiz Barón*.[73] In addition to these biographies, many other articles and book-length studies about Rafael's spirituality have been published in Spain.[74]

69. "Introduction to Blessed Rafael Baron, OCSO," trans. Juanita Colon and Charles Longemare, *Cistercian Studies Quarterly* 33 (1998): 61–63, 65–79; 34 (1999): 29–30, 31–52; 35 (2000): 75, 77–91; 36 (2001): 41–84; 37 (2002): 71–82; and 38 (2003): 35–83.

70. *The Life and Writings of Blessed Rafael Arnáiz Barón*, trans. Juanita Colon and Charles Longuemare, *Cistercian Studies Quarterly* reprint, 2003.

71. Saint Rafael Arnaiz, *The Collected Works*, ed. María Gonzalo-García, trans. Catherine Addington, MW 162 (Collegeville, MN: Cistercian Publications, 2022).

72. Jesús Álvarez, *Almas selectas, Rafael* (Burgos, Spain: Hijos de Santiago Rodríguez, 1952).

73. Gonzalo María Fernández, *God Alone: A Spiritual Biography of Blessed Rafael Arnáiz Barón*, trans. Hugh McCaffrey, MW 14 (Kalamazoo, MI: Cistercian Publications, 2008).

74. For a bibliography of texts about Rafael, see Martín, *Deseo de Dios*, 15–21; and Cerro Chavez, *Silencio en los labios*, xxvii–xxxv.

Perhaps no one worked more diligently to make Rafael widely known and read than Fr. Teófilo Sandoval, OCSO, Rafael's spiritual director and confessor during his first period in the monastery and later Vice Postulator of the cause for Rafael's beatification. Fr. Teófilo died in 2000. Over the decades, he published a number of Rafael's texts as well as many brief articles with his recollections of Rafael and reflections about his writings.[75] Along the line of personal recollections, Damián Yáñez Neira, OCSO, who was a novice with Rafael, published a number of recollections and reflections on Rafael's life in the monastery.[76]

75. Martínez Camino has drawn together Fr. Teófilo's recollections and reflections in *Mi Rafael*. For a bibliography of Fr. Teófilo's writings together with a further bibliography of works about Rafael, see Camino, *Mi Rafael*, 311–21.

76. See for example Damián Yáñez Neira, *El Hermano Rafael, con quien conviví: recuerdos íntimos* (Burgos, Spain: Monte Carmelo, 2009).

CHAPTER 3

"God Alone" and Purity of Heart

"God alone" (*Sólo Dios*)—a phrase that Rafael repeated over and over again in his writings. From the very beginning of his monastic search, Rafael manifested a single-hearted search for God. And in his pursuit of this God, he would renounce a promising career, the comfortable life afforded by his family, and the ability to remain physically close to the family that he so obviously loved. But he soon discovered that the search for God required a deeper renunciation—the giving up of his idealistic plans, his naïve dreams and illusions about the monastic life, the exact shape of his vocation, and even about himself. Throughout this journey and its many sacrifices, Rafael remained utterly focused on his "God alone"—even as Christ crucified became increasingly the face of the God whom Rafael had sought throughout his journey.

Rafael never writes explicitly about purity of heart. Probably he knew little about John Cassian, who was its principal teacher in the early Christian West. The study of the history of Christian monasticism and the historical foundations of the Benedictine spirit were probably not topics for the early formation of monks in a Trappist monastery of the 1930s. And yet it is clear that Rafael had a profound intuition and spiritual drive to attain the reality expressed in that phrase. In this chapter, we examine his "God alone" as Rafael's own term for this process and goal, along with other related themes. As an earlier translator of Rafael's works concluded, "His one thought was GOD ALONE, and in this we find his message, which is the very essence of PURITY OF HEART" (*emphasis in the original*).[1] An examination of this important theme provides a kind of lens to understand Rafael's spiritual vision as well as his unusual but authentic monastic vocation.

Purity of Heart in the Monastic Tradition

Christian monasticism was born in the deserts of Syria and Egypt in the late third and early fourth centuries, and the spiritual wisdom of those early desert fathers and mothers came to the West especially through the works of John Cassian (ca. 360–435). Cassian had made a kind of extended pilgrimage through various desert communities of hermits, and he gathered these insights into his *Conferences* and *Institutes*—recommended by Saint Benedict in his Rule to the members of his communities. At the very heart of the teachings that Cassian conveyed was the concept of purity of heart (*puritas cordis*), inspired by the Beatitude *Blessed are the pure in heart, for they shall see God* (Matt 5:8). As the Beatitude suggests, purity of heart is understood as essential for those who want to attain a vision of God—in the life to come and in the contemplative prayer of this life. Columba Stewart has called it Cassian's "premier definition of Christian and monastic perfection."[2]

For Cassian and for the monastic tradition that he is conveying in his writings, the monastic life—like all Christian living—has eternal life as its ultimate goal. But it also has a proximate goal, which is purity of heart as the necessary preparation for this final attainment. A clean or pure heart—a heart free of selfish concerns, self-focus, and disordered attachments—is a necessary condition both for an authentic selfless love of God and neighbor and for

---

1. Juanita Colon, "Introduction to Blessed Rafael Baron," *Cistercian Studies Quarterly* 33, no. 1 (1998): 63.

2. Columba Stewart, introduction to *Purity of Heart in Early Ascetic and Monastic Literature: Essays in Honor of Juana Raasch, O.S.B.*, ed. Harriet A. Luckman and Linda Kulzer (Collegeville, MN: Liturgical Press, 1999), 8.

that "pure prayer" that is the divine gift of contemplation.[3] As such, it is both a goal and a process. Cassian defines it as the goal of monastic striving, empowered by God's grace, and, at the same time, as the process of monastic ascetism:

> Everything we do, our every objective, must be undertaken for the sake of this purity of heart. This is why we take on loneliness, fasting, vigils, work, nakedness. For this we must practice the reading of Scripture, together with all the other virtuous activities, and we do so to trap and to hold our hearts free of the harm of every dangerous passion and in order to rise step by step to the high point of love.[4]

To capture this sense of dynamic growth, Cassian turns to the Letter to the Philippians (3:13-14): *forgetting what lies behind, stretching toward what lies ahead, I pursue the goal, the prize of the heavenly call of the Lord.* This sense of an unfolding process is for Saint Benedict the path of what he calls *conversatio morum*—the continual conversion of the monastic person through the daily living of the demands of the monastic life.[5] Its presence is revealed in simplicity and tranquility of spirit—even in the face of trial and real suffering.

Purity of Heart is to Will One Thing is the title of a book of essays by Danish philosopher Søren Kierkegaard (1813–1855), and it captures something of the meaning of the monastic sense of the term.[6] In Thomistic thought, the human will—the foundation of

---

3. Michael Casey, *The Undivided Heart: The Western Monastic Approach to Contemplation* (Petersham, MA: St. Bede's Publications, 1994), v. Thomas Merton summarizes this point by saying: "The whole monastic doctrine of Cassian is summed up in the equation: *perfecta caritas = puritas cordis = pura oratio*" (Thomas Merton, *The Monastic Journey*, ed. Patrick Hart [Mission, KS: Sheed Andrews and McMeel, 1977], 90).

4. John Cassian, *The Conferences*, trans. Boniface Ramsey, Ancient Writers Series 57 (New York: Paulist Press, 1977), 41 (Conf 1.7).

5. Stewart, introduction to *Purity of Heart,* 10–11.

6. Søren Kierkegaard, *Purity of Heart Is to Will One Thing* (New York: Harper, 1956).

freedom and choice—is ultimately a "rational appetite" for God. The human will is given to us ultimately so that we can choose God in all of our choices. But because of sin, our wills are disordered and weak, our desires sometimes out of control, and our choices misguided. The monastic life and its distinctive asceticism aim at bringing the monastic person to be able truly to "will one thing"—a will that, being conformed to the divine will, aims at nothing less than union with the Triune God. Purity of heart is to will one thing. It is an "undivided heart," a single-minded and single-hearted focus on God that purifies the human heart and makes it truly whole. Joseph Nguyen, a Jesuit author, has concluded that it is synonymous with the important Ignatian goal of "indifference."[7]

In a letter to his parents early in his monastic journey, Rafael refers to another Gospel text that captures some of the same idea: *The kingdom of heaven is like treasure hidden in a field, which someone found and hid; then in his joy he goes and sells all that he has and buys that field* (Matt 13:44). Rafael tells his parents that he feels that he has found the treasure and has begun to unearth it.[8] It must have seemed to him that he himself, like the person in the Gospel story, had "sold all that he had" in order to obtain the treasure— though he was soon to discover that the cost was still greater. As Rafael's life continues to unfold—as revealed in his writings—it gives testimony to his having walked along a single-hearted process of conversion with his eye on the treasure, arriving finally at true purity of heart as the goal of his monastic striving.

---

7. Joseph H. Nguyen, *Apatheia in the Christian Tradition: An Ancient Spirituality and Its Contemporary Relevance* (Eugene, OR: Cascade Books, 2018), 50. Rafael, whose early schooling occurred in Jesuit schools, seems to have been aware of this Ignatian concept. See especially CW no. 201.

8. CW 96, #33, in Saint Rafael Arnaiz, *Collected Works*, ed. María Gonzalo-García, trans. Catherine Addington, MW 61 (Collegeville, MN: Cistercian Publications, 2022).

Cassian writes that the monastic life and the attainment of the clean heart require three renunciations—of which Rafael gives ample evidence: "The first renunciation has to do with the body. We come to despise all the riches and all goods of the world. With the second renunciation we repel our past, our vices, the passions governing spirit and flesh. And in the third renunciation we draw our spirit away from the here and the visible and we do so in order solely to contemplate the things of the future. Our passion is for the unseen."[9] Rafael's life, as revealed in his writings and in the testimonies of his life, manifests the ever-deeper renunciations that led him to an authentic purity of heart—very much within the context of his yearning to live the monastic life in its truest meaning and to its most profound depth. The monastic pursuit of purity of heart as well as Rafael's yearning for "God alone" reflect the stark challenge of Jesus in the Gospel: *Whoever loves father or mother more than me is not worthy of me; and whoever loves son or daughter more than me is not worthy of me; and whoever does not take up the cross and follow me is not worthy of me. Those who find their life will lose it, and those who lose their life for my sake will find it* (Matt 10:37-39).

"God Alone"

If Rafael had had a formal motto it would probably have been "God alone." This phrase appears over and over again in his writings over the years. He writes, for example, "God alone . . . God alone . . . God alone. That is my theme . . . that is my only thought."[10] And "God alone . . . God alone . . . God alone . . . may He be my life."[11] At times, the same thought is reflected in different words: "God first, God always, and God alone."[12]

---

9. Cassian, *The Conferences*, 85 (Conf 3.6).
10. CW 606, #170.
11. CW 628, #181.
12. CW 135, #42.

Rafael's "God alone" is an idea apparently inspired by the final line from Saint Teresa of Ávila's famous bookmark:

> Let nothing trouble you,
> Let nothing scare you,
> All is fleeting,
> God alone is unchanging.
> Patience
> Everything obtains.
> Who possesses God / Nothing wants.
> God alone suffices. ["*Sólo Dios basta*"][13]

While all things in this world change, God does not. Rafael writes to his mother counseling her to repeat the phrase "God alone suffices," both upon rising and when going to bed.[14] In a journal entry later titled by his mother "You Alone" ("*Sólo Tú*"), without using his own typical phrase, Rafael expresses the meaning of "God alone" in this way:

> You alone should occupy my life. You alone should fill my heart . . . You alone should be my only thought. God, the only reason to live, to exist . . . God should reign over even the air we breathe, the light shed upon us. God, who is the beginning, middle, and end of all things, ought to be all the more so for a Trappist monk . . . who dwells in the house of God, who lives only to praise Him, and who remains in His presence day and night.
>
> He is in everything . . . in choir, in the fields, in our work, He is there when we eat and when we sleep . . . It's all the same, because it all reminds us why we came to the monastery, which was to seek Him in austerity, in silence, in chapel, and in the garden, to seek Him inside ourselves as well as

---

13. *The Collected Works of St. Teresa of Ávila*, trans. Kieran Kavanaugh and Otilio Rodriguez (Washington, DC: ICS Publications, 1985), 3:386.
14. CW 617, #176.

outside. We should see the Creator in everything that sur-
rounds us, whether it is beautiful and pleasant or ugly and
repulsive . . . It is all His work.[15]

To his uncle, he writes a long reflection on the meaning of this
unofficial motto as a source of peace in the midst of trials and
disappointments:

> God alone . . . How difficult it is to understand and live
> these words, but once you do, even if just for a moment . . .
> once your soul has realized that it belongs to God, that it is
> His possession . . . that Jesus dwells within it, despite its
> wretchedness and weakness . . . once your eyes are opened
> to the light of faith and hope . . . Once you understand the
> purpose of life, which is to live for God and for Him alone,
> there is nothing in the world that can trouble your soul. And
> those who, possessing nothing, hope for everything, can wait
> serenely instead of anxiously. A great peace fills the hearts
> of those who live for God alone, and only those who desire
> God alone find peace . . . God alone! How sweet it is to
> live like this![16]

It is a remarkable reflection offered by Rafael after the disappointment of his third departure from the monastery.

Rafael continues in this same letter to call this "the foolishness
of the Cross" ("*locura de la Cruz*") and the "foolishness for Christ"
("*locura de Cristo*"). And in this condition, he writes, the person
holds "God alone" in his or her heart like a mantra: "when someone says something to you, you'll answer 'yes, yes, it's true, you're
right,' but within yourself, deep within, you'll be saying . . . 'God
alone, God alone.' And when someone makes you laugh, you'll
laugh, and you'll also say, 'God alone.' And when someone makes

15. CW 461–62, #130.
16. CW 566, #162.

you suffer, you'll suffer, but you'll also say . . . 'Well, all right . . . but God alone.'"[17] This is a truth that Rafael, matured and deepened by his own trials, would want to teach the whole world—this madness of the Cross: "Blessed is that foolishness for Christ, which makes us realize how vain and small our suffering is, turning our bitter tears into the sweetest of songs, the pain and heartache of this life into the gentle fetters that bind us to Jesus."[18] Rafael himself has nothing—not even his health—but he feels that he has everything, because he possesses God deep within, and he wants nothing else: "How joyfully one lives when one has God, and God alone."[19]

As he suffers one disappointment after another, Rafael returns again and again to this fundamental theme, recognizing that it often requires walking in "pure faith."[20] Perhaps here again we see the influence of John of the Cross, who urges his readers to pass through the experiences of darkness and night with a "dark" faith—a faith that does not have to see or understand. This was Rafael's own experience, as he saw God calling him into and out of the monastery again and again, making him physically unable to live the monastic life as he had so desired and frustrating his own plans and ideas for the future. Through it all, Rafael continued to yearn for and cling to God alone in such dark and pure faith. This, he believes, is what God has been trying to teach him: "that I must fix my heart on Him alone, that I must live in Him alone, that I must love, desire, and wait for Him alone . . . in pure faith, without the consolation or help of human creatures."[21]

"God alone" becomes, over time, more focused on the cross of Jesus and in the love awakened and called for by it. On the back

17. CW 567, #162.

18. CW 569, #162.

19. CW 568, #162.

20. See Manuel Sánchez Monge, *La pasión de sólo Dios: el Hermano Rafael* (Burgos, Spain: Editorial Monte Carmelo, 2000), 195–209.

21. CW 639, #185. See also CW 416–19, #110.

of a holy card that he had drawn for his aunt, Rafael writes (with phrases obviously inspired by John of the Cross's *Spiritual Canticle*): "Onward . . . Onward . . . Onward . . . , without turning our gaze, with our eyes on the Cross of Christ, and our hearts aflame with Love. Onward, without turning our gaze . . . Love won't let us stop . . . Don't look at the flowers, or the beasts, or even the path . . . Look at nothing but God's Love awaiting us on the Cross, and behind that Cross, Mary. Onward . . . Onward . . . with no other light or guide than Love . . . Love . . . Love. . . ."[22]

Rafael came to see that the common life of the monastery as well as the events of his life, joyful or sad, had come to focus his gaze on God alone: "In the monastery, the days go by . . . but what does it matter? . . . Just God and me. . . . The whole world is reduced to a tiny little dot . . . and on that dot there is a monastery . . . and in that monastery, there's just God and me."[23] For him, this was the very purpose of the life of the monk: to live for God alone. One entered the monastic life in order to seek God and to be conformed to the divine will. Rafael reports that before his first entrance, people would often ask him what the monks did all day, and he writes that what he would have loved to respond was, "Well, it's pretty simple . . . love God and let ourselves be loved by Him, that's all."[24] It was in this increasingly focused gazing on God that freed him to truly love those around him.

RELATIVITY OF CREATED THINGS AND RENUNCIATION

Rafael loved nature, he loved people, and he was deeply devoted to his family. There are regular references in his letters and journals to his wonder at the beauty of creation. He loved solitary walks in nature, and his paintings (as distinct from his many holy cards)

22. CW 304, #83.
23. CW 517, #147.
24. CW 168, #51.

were most often landscapes. When, as his illness progressed, he was isolated in the monastery infirmary, often unable to leave his cell there, he lamented his inability to walk in or even to see much of the world's beauty.[25] But Rafael saw two things clearly: first, that the greatest wonders of the created order are just that—created and therefore relative in value as well as infinitely less magnificent than the God who created it all, and second, that too many people living in the world lived as if the created world were all that is, all that matters, all that has value—when, in fact, it had no value at all apart from God. For Rafael, this was not a cause for condemnation of the people in the world around him; rather, it filled him with sorrow for their blindness, moved him to pray for their eyes to be opened, and filled him with longing to awaken the whole world to the deeper truth of reality.

God's creation, for Rafael, can lift human hearts and minds to God as it sings to the Creator in a sublime harmony:

> How beautiful is the silence of a Trappist as he works . . . The soul stretches as it loses itself in God's greatness, manifested in the skies under which the monk is working . . . All of creation is subject to human hands . . . everything sings God's praises . . . the wheat, the flowers, the mountains, and the sky . . . Together, they perform a concert with sublime harmony. Nothing is missing, and nothing is superfluous. Everything God makes is well made.[26]

Knowing that the creation is always infinitely less than God, people of Christian faith must allow created things to direct their attention beyond them. They are not God. As Rafael's own spiritual vision matures, he glimpses the transcendent beauty that cannot be contained in anything in the created order—neither in

---

25. See especially his January 13, 1937, journal entry titled "The View from My Window" (CW 528–30, #151).

26. CW 527, #114. See also for example CW 359, #93.

the beauty of nature nor in the externals of the monastic life that had been so important in awakening his monastic vocation.[27] And it is for this reason that the monk, possessing or owning nothing that this world can give, is nonetheless far richer, because he possesses the All.[28]

Rafael's "God alone" is grounded in his insight that only God endures. The things of this world and this life pass—the beautiful and the tragic, the good and the bad, the triumphs and the suffering. The sun sets, the seasons change, the flowers bloom and die together with their bright colors—like smoke that drifts away in the breeze: "Everything passes . . . Man grows old, and at last, dies. Behold the one and only truth: God alone remains."[29] For Rafael, this is not a cause for depression or despair, but rather for the question, Why, then, attach ourselves to the things of this life, or give them more attention than they merit? Rafael came to see that this recognition was true of the monastery itself:

> A monastery full of men . . . is a temporary shelter. Penitent monks . . . are migratory birds, singing as they fly. Flowers and thorns. Tears and crosses. Wind and ice. Hymns of joy. Moments of anguish. Bells, incense . . . Everything that moves, everything that surrounds the soul in this life . . . It's all so short-lived, here one day and gone the next. The soul has no interest in anything but Christ. It is not moved by anything but God.[30]

Rafael had come to see that all that is true and lasting lives in God alone.

In an early letter to his aunt, while living again with his parents after his first departure from the monastery, Rafael tells her of his reflection one evening as he watched a large cruise ship leaving the

27. CW 416–19, #110.
28. CW 433–35, #117.
29. CW 418, #110. See also CW 415, #109, and 514–15, #146.
30. CW 516–17, #147.

harbor. He could see the bright lights onboard and hear a band playing, and he thought of the passengers divided into first and second classes and the rest, thinking that their little temporary paradise was the world in its totality. Those people thought, he reflected, that they had set the direction, that they were in charge, that they were self-sufficient and virtually independent of God. For Rafael, this was an image of so many people living in a superficial world that cannot see its deeper reality, with God at its center.[31] Again, this perception was not a cause for his disdain but, rather, of sadness and a call for prayer. He longed to cry out that if only people could catch just a tiny glimpse of the awesome grandeur of the Creator, they would see beyond the merely reflected beauty of earthly goods and join him in his longing for God alone:

> Nobody out in the world listens patiently to the crazy thoughts of someone who, upon glimpsing a small fraction of God's greatness, is stupefied . . . someone who, leaving behind the nothingness and vanity of worldly things, feels the urge to shout, "Senseless fools . . . what are you looking for? Make haste! . . . God alone, what else is there but Him?"
>
> How could we possibly occupy ourselves with so many things—laughing, crying, talking, arguing—and meanwhile, God gets nothing?[32]

For Rafael, the world and the creation are not evil. They are simply infinitely less than God. Their value is merely relative. To the degree that people can become attached to the things of this world, enslaved by them, or deceived by them, material things become a hindrance to be renounced.[33] And it seemed to Rafael

---

31. CW 126–27, #40.

32. CW 566, #162. See the Appendix for longer extract of the letter from which this passage has been drawn.

33. For a more thorough discussion of Rafael's sense of the relativity of creation and the theme of renunciation, see Antonio María Martín Fernández-Gallardo, *El deseo de Dios y la ciencia de la Cruz: Aproximación a la experiencia del Hermano Rafael*, 2nd ed. (Burgos, Spain: Editorial Monte Carmelo), 149–77

that the best place for him to avoid such entanglement was in the life of a strict Trappist monastery. In the monastic life, he could keep his eyes more clearly focused on the fundamental truth of "God alone"—with everything and everyone else in its proper relationship with God. Rafael, then, becomes a kind of monastic prophet, who in the long tradition of Christian monasticism does not hate or disdain the world or see it as evil in itself—but rather, one who tries to see and to offer a living witness to what is always beyond, the more, the All. And, for Rafael, the motto of this monastic witness was "God alone."

As we have seen, in the monastic tradition, purity of heart is the necessary foundation of authentic, selfless loving. At the same time, the graced work of trying to purify our loving is an essential element of arriving at a clean heart. Rafael was a man with a heart for loving others, and he cherished his family until the end of his life. But he realized that such love must be transformed. In an early letter to his father from the monastery, Rafael assures him that authentic love of God does not exclude the love of other persons. But such love must be purified and even sanctified, he says, and thus becomes a greater and more authentic loving: "Love for God does not exclude love for creatures. It's a matter of purifying that love and making it holy, and believe me, now I love you all more and better than I did before."[34] In a letter to his mother, almost precisely two years later, during his final entry to the monastery, Rafael says that love of those dearest to us is purified and even divinized by being united with love for Christ.[35]

The greatest and most difficult renunciation, says Rafael, is detachment from one's self. Rafael sees this reality as the true obstacle to living as God desires.[36] This is at the central struggle

---

(hereafter cited as Martín). See also Antonio María Martín Fernández-Gallardo, "Beato Rafael Arnáiz: algunas claves de su experiencia espiritual," *Cistercium* 241 (Oct.–Dec. 2005): 1051–53.

34. CW 390, #103.
35. CW 617, #176.
36. CW 554, #160. See Martín, *Deseo de Dios*, 201–15.

for arriving at purity of heart; it is the essential foundation of a truly selfless loving. It was the necessary sacrifice that Rafael himself learned through the painful process of letting go of his own aspirations and dreams—especially the ones that had seemed the holiest. Rafael came to believe that God has a loving plan—often mysterious and even difficult to accept—that can be embraced only by letting go of the projects conceived from merely human horizons. In order ultimately to let go of external attachments, women and men must let go of that part of themselves that attaches them to things. This is a graced, active work of detachment, but it is, more deeply, a fruit of contemplating and becoming lost in the immense love of God in Christ. Then, in the face of joys or sorrows, one's only joy or desire is "God alone, nothing but God. A love for God that fills your life, a life that entails renunciation, sacrifice, prayer, and silence . . . that, I believe, is the love that God asks of us."[37] The influence of John of the Cross is clear as Rafael cites John's admonishment that to possess the All—union with God—one must empty oneself of all that is less than God: "And one cannot approach God without having first relinquished *everything* and being left with *nothing*, as Saint John of the Cross says."[38] For both Rafael and John, there is no place for a self separate from God—that is, a self that, in any ultimate way, desires, wills, or attaches itself to anything that is less than God.

SIMPLICITY

Rafael often speaks of the need for simplicity, beginning with the renunciation of attachment to things. In a journal entry just a couple of weeks before his death, he writes,

---

37. CW 555, #160.

38. See, for example, CW 124, #40, in which Rafael refers to John of the Cross's so-called "*nada* doctrine" in *The Ascent of Mt. Carmel* (1.13, para. 11–13). See *The Collected Works of St. John of the Cross*, 3rd ed., trans. Kieran Kavanaugh and Otilio Rodriguez (Washington, DC: ICS Publications, 2017), 150–51.

With Jesus at my side, nothing seems difficult to me, and the path toward holiness looks simpler and simpler. I think it's a matter of subtracting things, rather than adding them. It's about cutting down toward simplicity, rather than cluttering with new things. And I think the more we detach ourselves from disordered love for creatures and for ourselves, the closer and closer we get to the only love there is, the only wish, the only desire in this life . . . true sanctification, which is God.[39]

The path to sanctity requires simplicity, as the Cistercian tradition teaches us. But the path itself is ultimately simple—not in the sense of ease in walking the path that God chooses (as Rafael would have known from his own life experience), but in the sense of its lack of complexity: "Trust me, you don't have to change in order to become a good Trappist. God merely asks us to be simple on the outside, and loving on the inside . . . See how easy that is? . . . And in reality, how easy and simple are God's true paths when you walk them in a spirit of confidence, with a free heart fixed on Him."[40] And a heart free and given over to God is precisely what is needed in order to see God. For Rafael, the "simplicity of heart" by which the human person can come to know God[41] is virtually synonymous with the monastic path of purity of heart. Only two weeks after writing about simplicity of heart, Rafael was forced by health to leave the monastery for the third time. Citing his earlier reflection, he now writes that his task is to carry out what God is asking of him with simplicity and humility.[42]

Cassian had taught that purity of heart was the essential foundation for authentic and deep prayer. Rafael, on the basis of his own experience and reflection, arrives at the same conclusion,

39. CW 680, #201.
40. CW 410, #106.
41. CW 542, #156.
42. CW 547, #158.

expressed in terms of simplicity. In a journal reflection later titled "Simplicity and Openness," he writes,

> The interior life . . . the spiritual life, a life of prayer. "My God! That must be difficult!" But it's not at all. Get rid of everything in your heart that's in the way, and you'll find God there. That's it. . . . Collect yourself within . . . gaze upon your nothingness, gaze upon the nothingness of the world, place yourself at the foot of the cross, and if you are simple, you will see God. . . . Behold, the life of prayer. We don't need to add something that's already there. Rather, we need to get rid of what is in the way.[43]

The person who is free of self—who has become simple and pure of heart—is ready to gaze at Christ in silent prayer:

> That "*deny yourself*" is the work of a soul who wants only to be hidden away, who wants nothing for himself, who longs only for divine love, and who understands that God does not want us to renounce only the world, but to renounce something much more difficult: ourselves. That self-renunciation is a renunciation of something we carry around inside of us, I don't know how to explain it, something that truly hinders us . . . perhaps you'll understand: when you place yourself at the foot of the tabernacle, and look at Jesus, and contemplate His wounds, and cry at His feet, and you realize that in the face of Christ's immense love, you disappear, *your* tears disappear, your entire soul is overwhelmed and becomes like a tiny speck of sand in the vastness of the sea.[44]

Rafael's reflection brings to mind again the Gospel text that had inspired Cassian's thought: *Blessed are the pure in heart, for they shall see God* (Matt 5:8).

43. CW 543, #156.
44. CW 554, #160.

TRUE FREEDOM

The pure heart is a free heart—a heart that knows true liberty, free from sin, free from disordered attachments, ultimately free from self, and thus free to love God. And freedom is a frequent theme in Rafael's reflections. It is clear from his writings that in his life outside the monastery (even during his unwanted departures), he had enjoyed his "liberty"—the freedom to walk alone in nature, smoke a cigarette, or take a long drive in a family car. Giving up this freedom to come and go as he liked was a sacrifice that he felt with each return to the monastery. In a particularly poignant journal entry during his final stay in the monastery, after two months basically restricted to his infirmary cell because of his health, deemed fit only for the solitary work of wrapping chocolates for the monastery's business, Rafael writes,

> I am getting used to being permanently enclosed within the monastery. It's been two months since I last enjoyed a bit of fresh air and sunshine . . . Oh, Lord, how hard that is for me! . . . In the world, I so enjoyed singing Your wonders and glories in the countryside . . . My greatest pleasure was to open my eyes wide to gaze upon the sea . . . My soul would be captivated by star-studded skies, and would bless You whenever it heard the earth's silence upon a gentle, tranquil sunset.
>
> All that is over for me . . . the sky, the sun, flowers. Lord, the human part of me . . . which is a lot of me . . . weeps for my lost freedom [*libertad perdida*]. But You come and console me . . . Is there anything You would not do for me, blessed Jesus?[45]

Rafael goes on to show that he had come to realize that the loss of his external freedom yields a deeper liberty to live in the moment:

45. CW 623, #180.

"Take heart, Rafael," it seemed like God was saying to me
. . . "Everything passes . . ." and blessed Jesus, the sorrow
went away . . . I no longer cared about the beautiful day, or
anything else earthly . . . I knew that God was helping me,
and that God blessed me. As I clumsily worked to wrap
chocolates, I envied no one on earth or in heaven, because I
was thinking: if the saints in heaven could come down to
earth for just a moment, it would be in order to increase the
glory of God here, even if it were just with a single Ave
Maria on their knees in silence . . . or who knows, wrapping
chocolates.[46]

For freedom Christ has set us free, Saint Paul insists without
equivocation (Gal 5:1). But this freedom that is the saving work
of Christ—the true freedom of the children of God—is not, as
Rafael realized, the liberty to come and go as one pleases. And
yet, he says, it is just such superficial freedom that people "in the
world" so value. People value their ability to buy this or that, go
here or there, choose one thing or another. And the same people
can easily look at the monks enclosed in their monastery who
seem to lack such fundamental freedoms, thinking that the monks
are crazy for what they have given up. But, responds Rafael, it is
precisely the enclosure that allows the monk to embrace a deeper,
truer freedom. The liberty to which the monk aspires is the freedom to love God truly and fully, liberated of disordered attachments to things, people and self. To seek such freedom is precisely
to seek purity of heart. It is the only freedom that can bring us to
"will one thing," and it is only in willing one thing that we are
truly free.

In his lengthiest reflection on freedom, in a journal entry later
titled simply "Freedom," Rafael contrasts true freedom and what
passes for freedom among so many people who live "in the world."[47]
He ponders the trains and cars that constantly pass the monastery

46. CW 624, #180.
47. CW 498–99, #141.

on the nearby railroad track and highway and all the people travel-
ing at great speeds here and there. They can see the monastery as
they pass, but they do so without interest. Rafael imagines himself
addressing the people as they pass by: "You 'free' men who roam
the earth! I do not envy your life in the world. Enclosed in this
monastery at the foot of the crucifix, I have infinite freedom, I have
heaven . . . I have God."[48] The person who is willing to ponder the
true reality of freedom will soon realize that what so many people
call freedom is not really so; rather, true freedom is often enclosed
within the four walls of a monastery. Where, then, is true freedom
to be found, Rafael asks. It is found in the human heart that loves
nothing else but God, that is not attached to anything in the material world or even in the spiritual, but only God. It resides in the
soul that can rise above its own preoccupations, thoughts, and
feelings:

> Where, then, is freedom to be found?
> It is in the heart of the one who loves no one and nothing
> but God. It is in the soul attached to neither spiritual nor
> material things, but only to God.
> It is in the soul that does not subject itself to the selfish
> ego. It is in the soul that soars above its own thoughts, its
> own feelings, its own suffering and rejoicing.
> Freedom is in the soul whose only reason for existence is
> God, whose life is God and nothing but God.[49]

It is for just such freedom that Rafael has been petitioning God—
that true freedom of a heart that allows a person to be authenti-
cally free and focused on God and thus prepared for divine union.
Meanwhile, he laments, people continue to speed by the monastery
in their cars and trains, thinking all the while that they are free,
when in fact they are deceived. Theirs is a freedom limited by the

48. CW 499, #141.
49. CW 497–98, #141.

horizons of this world. The freedom to which Rafael aspires is a liberty unlimited before a limitless horizon.

The monastic tradition emphasizes that the true monastic must strive, with God's help, to arrive at that purity of heart that is the necessary foundation for contemplation and for truly selfless love of God and neighbor. Rafael Arnaiz had a deep and essential intuition of this fundamental truth. And, even more than many of the monastic themes that he addresses, it is this relentless pursuit of a pure heart in the monastic way of life that marks him as a true monk. It is true that he never mentioned the phrase, but many of his central themes—God alone, true freedom, detachment from what is less than God and even from self, and simplicity—all of these themes in his writings are nothing less than synonyms for the pursuit of purity of heart. In and out of the monastery, time and again, Rafael sought—and ultimately arrived at—"willing one thing," which is God alone. It is this lens that can help his readers to understand and appreciate his life, his vocation, his spirituality, and his profoundly monastic heart.

CHAPTER 4

The Gift of Discernment

John Cassian devoted his first Conference to purity of heart as the proximate goal of monastic life. When he wanted to show how to attain this goal, he began to talk about discretion. Even though the meaning of *discretion* has partly changed in contemporary English, Sr. Edith Scholl points out that "*discretio* is the past participle of *discernere* [to discern]; discretion is the result of correct discernment."[1] The tradition that comes from the fathers of the desert sees in the gift of discretion the "source and root of all the virtues,"[2] a way of avoiding both excess and lukewarmness in all the Christian practices.[3]

The Rule of Saint Benedict is an eminent expression of discretion in practice. Under its guidance, not only the abbot but each brother is called to discern and find the right response in the present circumstances according to his role in the community and the needs and possibilities of the moment. Saint Bernard's treatise *On Precept and Dispensation*,[4] in which he discusses the binding

---

1. Edith Scholl, *Words for the Journey: A Monastic Vocabulary*, MW 21 (Collegeville, MN: Cistercian Publications, 2009), 16.

2. John Cassian, *The Conferences*, trans. Boniface Ramsey, Ancient Writers Series 57 (New York: Paulist Press, 1997), 90 (Conf 2.9).

3. Cassian, *Conferences*, 85 (Conf 2.2).

4. Bernard of Clairvaux, *On Precept and Dispensation*, trans. Martinus Cawley, CF 1 (Shannon, Ireland: Irish University Press, 1970).

power of the Holy Rule, is a good example of the enduring importance of discretion through the centuries in Benedictine and Cistercian spirituality.

A monk or any Christian who has not sought the grace of discernment, Cassian writes, is "like a person wandering in the dark night."[5] Discernment includes the capacity to interpret our inner world of thoughts and feelings as a realm through which God manifests himself to us, and so too with the external world, where we want to perceive God's action, to collaborate with it.

We are all faced with the need to constantly discern if we want to make progress along the spiritual path. For example, how and when is the best way for me to pray, and what does this experience in prayer mean? There are also decisions that need to be made: big decisions such as what is my vocation in life? or smaller ones, such as what spiritual book should I choose to read to deepen my faith?

Rafael had to face all of these challenges, particularly the discernment of his vocation in what seemed like unfavorable circumstances. His "God alone" became his compass, helping him to choose always to love and serve the Lord above all things. His heart, purified and made whole in this one love, was gradually more able to see God and conform to his will in the events of his life. Following Rafael along the steps of his discernment process and seeing his fundamental attitudes as he advanced can help any Christian in the discernment of his or her vocation and other decisions that our life and faith will bring our way.

A WHOLE LIFE TO DISCERN

Rafael was a rich young man of the early twentieth century. He not only had an abundance of economic resources, but he was also artistically talented and endowed with a charming personality, and

5. Cassian, *Conferences*, 84 (Conf 2.1).

he had grown up surrounded by the love of family and friends. With a promising future ahead of him, Rafael was rich in so many ways, and he knew it, but he didn't ignore the ultimate source of all of his blessings: God himself. This awareness filled his heart with gratitude and freed it from the clutches of pride and self-centeredness. He could repeat with assurance the words of the first letter of John: "So we have known and believed the love that God has for us" (1 John 4:16). This love was more than an idea; it was a reality he savored each day of his life.

When in November 1933 Rafael wrote to the abbot of San Isidro, Dom Félix Alonso García, requesting to be admitted as a novice, he was offering "a heart filled with joy and much love for God."[6] Because he had everything he could desire, he was beyond the common trap that makes happiness dependent on some kind of goal or achievement that is always in the future: "I'll be happy when I. . . ." At the same time, like the rich young man in the gospels,[7] Rafael could intuit in his heart both a promise and a desire for something of a different order. He wanted to go beyond, past what society could offer, because as Saint Bernard wrote, "It is stupidity and madness to want always that which can neither satisfy nor diminish your desire."[8]

When Rafael visited La Trapa for the first time on September 23, 1930, his aesthetic sensitivity allowed him to recognize in the way of life of the monks a narrow gate that led to this "beyond." Probably he still didn't know if he was called to cross this threshold to embrace and be embraced by a deeper reality that spoke to him of peace, attracted him with a different kind of beauty, and appealed to his religious sense, the faith that had grown within him since childhood.

---

6. CW 43, #12.

7. See Mark 10:17-22.

8. Bernard of Clairvaux, *On Loving God, with an Analytical Commentary by Emero Stiegman*, CF 13B (Kalamazoo, MI: Cistercian Publications, 1995), 21.

The Holy Spirit, with "gentle hand,"[9] touched and directed Rafael all his life within the framework of his duties in family and school and his fidelity to prayer and the practice of the sacraments. "What, dear brothers, is more delightful than this voice of the Lord calling to us?" says Saint Benedict in the Prologue to his Rule.[10] Rafael didn't resist the sweet voice of the Savior. He applied to enter the Abbey of San Isidro, was accepted, and gave himself completely to embody the ideal of becoming a Trappist-Cistercian monk. Everything seemed right: he had generously discerned and followed God's will, selling everything to follow Christ, and, for a time, it seemed as though he was receiving the hundredfold.[11] Is this not how it is supposed to be?

But suddenly, all changed for him with the onset of diabetes and his first departure from the monastery. God's hand seemed to withdraw from him, as a former confessor told him: "The other day I went to see my former confessor. He told me that my plan [to reenter the monastery] was absurd, and that God seemed to have abandoned me." Still, Rafael, now a new Job, continued trusting and blessing God, as his following words show: "What he said didn't rattle me or trouble me in the least . . . I didn't make anything of it . . . God alone is enough for me. I've gotten used to that over the past two years . . . That's what the Lord wanted of me. May His will be done."[12]

Letting Himself be Led

On June 11, 1934, in a letter to his novice master written soon after the sudden onset of his diabetes, Rafael summed up the at-

9. Saint John of the Cross describes the Holy Spirit in the second stanza of the poem *The Living Flame of Love* as a "gentle hand" and "delicate touch." See *The Collected Works of St. John of the Cross*, trans. Kieran Kavanaugh and Otilio Rodriguez, 3rd ed. (Washington, DC: ICS Publications, 2017), 640.

10. RB Prol. 19.

11. See Mark 10:18-30.

12. CW 246, #72.

titude needed to discern God's will in his life: "'Trust Me,' Jesus says, 'And I will lead you.'"[13] As he recovered his physical strength in his parents' home, Rafael tried to make sense of what had happened and considered what God wanted from him. Despite his bewilderment after the rapid change in his personal circumstances, the wisdom in this reflection on discernment is remarkable. It reflects the kind of knowledge offered to those who let themselves be led and who open their minds and hearts to the light of Christ.

Being led through an attitude of surrender marked Rafael's monastic journey from its beginning: "When I went to La Trapa, I surrendered to Him all I had and all I possessed: my soul and my body . . . My surrender was absolute and total. It is utterly just, then, that God should now do with me as He wishes and as He pleases, without a single complaint or rebellious move on my part."[14] Vocational discernment is not about fitting ourselves into a mold or category of our own choosing: marriage, priesthood, or religious life. Nor, even more specifically, is it about seeing if this Order or that is a good fit for us according to our own human judgment. If this mental frame is not helpful for anyone, it was even less so for Rafael, who never fit neatly into any category. The precise shape of his vocation needed time to unfold. However, his absolute surrender to God allowed him to surmount this obstacle, discern well, and follow what at first sight seemed like an unusual vocation.

Four years after his first entrance to La Trapa, on the morning of January 1, 1938, Rafael made a vow "to love Jesus always." It had been a long and difficult path, but by then it was clear to him what God wanted and didn't want from him: "I can see that it is not the will of God for me to make religious vows or follow the Rule of Saint Benedict completely. Am I to want what God does not?"[15] He was also aware of the peculiar character of his vocation: "I am not a religious . . . I am not a layman . . . I am nothing."

13. CW 110, #36.
14. CW 110, #36.
15. CW 613, #175.

As he surrendered himself to the manifestations of God's will in his life, he had gradually detached himself from his mental categories and dreams. Abandoning himself in trust, Rafael's mind and heart opened in a way that allowed him to come to the realization of his true self and vocation: "I am nothing but a soul in love with Christ. He wants nothing but my love, and He wants it detached from everything and everyone else. . . . To love Jesus in everything, for everything, always . . . Only love. A humble, generous, detached, mortified, silent love . . . May my life be nothing but an act of love."[16] So while in a certain sense Rafael's vocation was an unusual one, in the singleness and simplicity of what God asked of him, Rafael radically embodied the fundamental call to each Christian disciple: to love God above all things. Moreover, his unqualified response expressed the fire that ignites and sustains each Benedictine-Cistercian vocation: "To prefer nothing to the love of Christ" (RB 4.21). It was this fundamental attitude that allowed him to embrace the distinctive vocation that God had chosen for him.

I Am His Servant

From early on Rafael understood his role in this whole process: that of a servant attentive to the loving will of the divine master. In the letter to his novice master cited above he describes it clearly:

> God is my absolute master, and I am His servant, who keeps quiet and obeys . . . Sometimes I wonder, "What does God want from me?" . . . But as David says, "Who is man to know God's designs?" Therefore, the best thing to do is close your eyes and let Him carry you, for He knows what is good for us.[17]

16. CW 613, #175.
17. CW 110, #36.

A good servant is one who listens in order to be able to obey, as in the words of the prophet Isaiah about the suffering servant: "The Lord God has opened my ear, and I was not rebellious, I did not turn backward" (Isa 50:5). The words of the great commandment and the Rule of Saint Benedict both begin with the word "listen" or "hear": "Hear, O Israel: The Lord is our God, the Lord alone. You shall love the Lord your God with all your heart, and with all your soul, and with all your might" (Deut 6:4-5). If we want to love God with all our being, we first need to listen and then acknowledge the Lord as God alone; we do this by refusing to make other things the guiding principle of our lives. God doesn't impose this choice on us. We can accept or refuse.

TRUSTING IN DIVINE PROVIDENCE

Rafael had a strong sense of divine Providence, which made it possible for him to allow God's plan for him to unfold. Instead of trying to make sense on his own of the apparent chaos of his ever-changing circumstances and those of Spanish society as a whole, he looked deeper, searching for the hand of God always at work. Careful not to hinder the action of divine grace in himself or others, he was able to recognize the invisible threads that held together the events of his life and human history. In this way, what for others appeared to be purposeless events, the result of mere human causes, he recognized as a salvation story that encompassed his own, the experience of a child cared for and taught by his father. This is the blessing for those who trust in divine Providence: a confidence and joy that Rafael expressed in these words: "Happy are those who see God's hand in everything that happens to them . . . Happy, a thousand times over, are those who love everything the Lord sends them affectionately."[18]

18. CW 524–25, #150.

When his diabetes seemed to put an abrupt end to what he thought were the Lord's promises, he waited for the Master to show the path to him once again, instead of giving up or making too quick a move. Full of hope and assurance he wrote to his grandmother,

> I suffered so much the day I had to leave, but when I go back, the monastery won't be big enough to contain all my joy . . . and I know *without a doubt* that I am to die in La Trapa.
>
> My vocation is ever stronger, you could almost say it has grown . . . and as God is giving it to me, He will also give me the means to fulfill it, have no doubt.[19]

How could Rafael himself have no doubts when there were so many obstacles in his path? Rafael had a period of confusion and sadness after his first departure from the monastery, when what was happening in his life went directly against his expectations and desires. Then he could not but ask the Lord, "Why are you doing this?" But he learned quickly that this was not the best approach. His trust in divine Providence helped him to develop a new kind of certainty and increased detachment from his own desires. God was for him a father, whose ways and thoughts were higher than his own[20] but who acted in his life always for his good:

> We human beings can do nothing more than trust in His divine providence, knowing that what He does is well done, even if *at first glance* it might go against our desires. But I believe that true perfection is to have no desire other than "may His will be done in us."
>
> God, in His infinite wisdom, does not ask us what we desire in order to give it to us immediately, because generally

19. CW 188, #53.
20. See Isa 55:8-9.

we don't know what we need for our salvation. Rather, working far above our reason and the designs of His creatures,
He carries us, brings us along, and tests us in a thousand
ways . . . and we say, "Lord, why are you doing this?" . . .
and it seems that God responds, "Trust Me. You are like
children, and in order to reach the kingdom of My Father,
you cannot go it alone, nor do you know the way; I will take
you there . . . Follow me, even if it goes against your
desires."[21]

Some of Rafael's expressions in these lines resemble the attitudes we find in the wisdom literature in the Scriptures and in
later works like the Rule of Saint Benedict. These verses from the
book of the prophet Jeremiah are a good example: "Cursed is the
man who trusts in human beings, who makes flesh his strength,
whose heart turns away from the Lord. He is like a barren bush
in the wasteland." On the contrary, "Blessed are those who trust
in the Lord; the Lord will be their trust. They are like a tree planted
beside the waters" (Jer 17:5-8).

Discernment requires not only knowledge but wisdom. As
Rafael's example demonstrates, wisdom is a gift that we can receive
from God when, trusting in his love for us, we accept becoming,
in a real way, followers and not leaders in our own life story. This
attitude does not devalue our reason and will. On the contrary, it
opens up an authentic path of freedom and fulfillment according
to the divine will and plan, which is always better than our own
because, as Saint Paul says, "What no eye has seen, nor ear heard,
nor the human heart conceived, God has prepared for those who
love him" (1 Cor 2:9).

Rafael's "God alone" worked for him as a principle for discernment, purifying and expanding his mind and heart beyond his
own reasons and desires, and allowing him to recognize God's
presence in the now and to embrace the unfolding divine will.

21. CW 110, #36.

This vision guided his actions in a practical way because it helped him to penetrate more deeply into the truth of things.

"I am the light of the world. Whoever follows me will never walk in darkness but will have the light of life" (John 8:12). Trust in God's Providence allowed Rafael to see the hand of God leading him, precisely in his disappointments. The unexpected turns in his life became a kind of light along Rafael's path. He experienced times of darkness; his trust did not spare him from experiencing fear, confusion, discouragement, and even inner resistance. But because his life was not about himself but about his Master, each day and experience, with all its uncertainties and disappointments, became a source of light for him. What initially appeared as darkness and failure was an invitation to go beyond in faith and love, a call to enter a space in which darkness becomes light.

His life and vocation were not a problem to solve, because he knew they were not only a human project, but rather the craft of divine and human action working together. As he advanced in the assurance of faith and trust, light increased more and more in his life even as he submerged himself in the darkness of the cross. Rafael's attitude of total surrender and trust turned his trials into the blessing of an unquenchable light and a joy that nothing and no one could take from him.[22]

Perseverance

The way of discernment is the way of discipleship. If we want to know the will of God we need to know God, to grow in our relationship with him by following in the footsteps of Christ with perseverance. This is the path on which Rafael advanced with determination. It was his love for Christ that urged him on, not the need to make a decision about what to do with his life. While surrender to following his Master and trust in divine Providence

22. See John 16:22.

kept him open and receptive to a logic and plan beyond what he could foresee or understand, perseverance kept him moving forward, advancing on the path of discipleship through concrete steps and decisions. At every intersection, as soon as the direction to take became clear enough, Rafael didn't linger.

The Lord had told the seventy-two as he sent them out, "Carry no purse, no bag, no sandals, and greet no one on the road" (Luke 10:4). The same kind of determination guided Rafael in his decision to follow Christ. "I will not gather flowers, nor fear wild beasts."[23] This verse from the third stanza of Saint John of the Cross's poem *Spiritual Canticle*, which Rafael liked to ponder, reflects his dogged persistence to go to encounter the one his heart desired above anything else. And so, even though obstacles multiplied on his way, he persevered as one who has no time to waste, one who single-mindedly wants to accomplish the mission that has been entrusted to him, despite the obscurity of the means and circumstances in which this task is to be realized. Rafael's "God alone" was the light that guided him. He would not let his gaze be distracted by other objects that, even though they had traces of Christ's beauty and truth, were not Christ himself. In one of his letters to his Aunt María Osorio, Rafael advises her to respond as Jesus was urging him to do:

> The Lord asks me to keep going and not stop. What am I to do? What I always do: look up, up high . . . and keep going and not stop . . . You ought to do the same. The Virgin is gazing upon you, and God is helping you; don't be concerned with crying or laughing, what's the difference? Clay is clay, we can't change what we are. The important thing is that this clay be given back to God, so may He do as He pleases with it, and may *everything* bring us toward Him.
>
> How difficult it is not to gather flowers! But how easy it is, too . . . Once the initial break has been made, God draws

---

23. Saint John of the Cross, *Spiritual Canticle* 3, in *Collected Works of St. John of the Cross*, 471.

us in such a way, with such gentleness, that it's no struggle at all . . . What difference does it make to cry? . . . Cry as much as you can; laugh and rejoice as much as you can, what does it matter! You're the one who is doing the laughing and crying . . . and you're nobody, you're nothing . . . And believe me, dearest sister—you won't mind if I call you that?— believe me, when you realize that . . . when you become detached from everything, including *your own self*, only then will you see: everything that happens to us is completely inconsequential. Neither suffering nor rejoicing will draw our gaze . . . Then we shall be able to see God better . . . Let's not look at ourselves so much . . . and if we do look at ourselves, and scrutinize ourselves, let it be in order to seek out the God hidden within us.[24]

Watchfulness over the heart has been an important discipline in monastic spirituality since its origin. The spiritual athletes of the desert wouldn't allow anything to distract them from their goal, just as lovers reject any distractions that may delay their encounter and union. At the beginning of his discernment, Rafael thought that the main distraction from his "God alone" was his former way of life: this included his family, his possessions, and his personal tastes. He was determined to "jump over"[25] this obstacle.

With time he realized that there were more subtle obstacles or distractions that could hinder the perseverance in his discernment and the spiritual path: those within himself. Because we can't jump over our own hearts, we need to guard our hearts so as not to be stopped either by attachment to comforts or by fear of suffering. In the commentary to his *Spiritual Canticle*, Saint John of the Cross explains that "seeking God demands a heart naked, strong, and free from all evil and goods that are not purely God."[26] The soul in search of her beloved should not gather flowers, that is, cling to any form of delight, either physical or spiritual, as these

24. CW 228–29, #70.

25. CW 169, #51.

26. *Spiritual Canticle* 3.5, in *Collected Works of St. John of the Cross*, 491.

would distract us from the straight path. Neither should she fear wild beasts, by which the mystical poet meant not to be afraid of the prospect of lacking temporal comforts and facing hardships and temptations.

The ultimate goal of any true Christian discernment is not discovering God's will for one's own sake—if I do what God wants, things will go better for me—but to act according to God's will in order to be more united to him in love. When this is our focus, discerning, even in very complex situations, as was the case for Rafael, brings us closer to God. But the key is that the center of our attention is on the Lord, and not so much on us or the outcome of the process. It is in this sense that Rafael says that "everything that happens to us is completely inconsequential."

"Look up, up high . . . and keep going and not stop," Rafael told his aunt. When we are discerning, perseverance means persistence in doing the things that help us "look up" and "keep going" following the Master. For Rafael, as for any Christian, in practice this meant spending time before the Blessed Sacrament in prayer, reading the Scriptures, and seeking silence, but also serving others and bringing joy to those around him, among other things.

A Love that is not Mercenary

Loving Jesus in suffering and in joy alike: this was the path Rafael trod. The importance of this kind of perseverance in love is as paramount as it is unusual. Often our discernment comes to a halt when the kind of feelings we long for—such as happiness, peace, and sense of purpose—are lacking. The process stops not so much for lack of clarity as because we are seeking other outcomes besides God himself. Rafael also had to grow in this respect, as he explained to his abbot in the letter in which he asked to be accepted as an oblate: "I was searching for God, but I was also searching for His creatures, and I was searching for myself."[27]

27. CW 214, #64.

That being said, in the same letter Rafael also affirmed that his love for God was never mercenary—there could be nothing more contrary to his "God alone." Saint Bernard in his *Letter on Charity to the Holy Brethren of the Chartreuse*, which he included as the final part of his treatise *On Loving God*, distinguishes three kinds of love: the slave's, the mercenary's, and the son's. The slave's love is bound by fear. The mercenary's love is compromised by coveting some profit for himself, but, he says, "Charity is found only in the son. It does not seek its own advantage."[28] But the most important point Bernard makes comes next: "Neither fear nor love of self can change the soul. At times they change one's appearance or deeds; they can never alter one's character."[29] Rafael followed on the path of discipleship out of a love that was tainted neither by servile fear nor by profit. It is this attitude that allowed him to be open to God's will for him, even as the landscape constantly shifted around him.

In later works Saint Bernard used the image of the love of the bride for her bridegroom to better describe pure love for God: "Love is the being and the hope of a bride. She is full of it, and the bridegroom is contented with it. He asks nothing else, and she has nothing else to give. That is why he is the bridegroom and she the bride."[30] This was Rafael's love, a love that held nothing back and asked for nothing in return but to keep loving in total self-gift: "I left my home . . . I pulled my heart to pieces . . . I emptied my soul of all worldly desires . . . I embraced your cross. What are You waiting for, Lord? If what You want is my loneliness, my suffering, and my desolation . . . take it all, Lord. I ask for nothing."[31]

28. Bernard of Clairvaux, *On Loving God,* CF 13B:36.
29. Bernard of Clairvaux, *On Loving God,* CF 13B:36.
30. Bernard of Clairvaux, *On the Song of Songs IV,* trans. Irene Edmonds, CF 40 (Kalamazoo, MI: Cistercian Publications, 1980), 185 (S 37.5).
31. CW 610, #172.

Rafael would have wholeheartedly agreed with these other words of Saint Bernard: "Whatever you seem to love because of something else, you do not really love."[32] The more Rafael advanced in his discernment the purer his love for God became, and his will was cleansed from desires other than to do the will of the Lord: "It is a great desire for everything that is God's will . . . It is not wanting anything but Him . . . It is wanting yet not wanting . . . I don't know, I can't explain it . . . only God understands me, but while I may not know the cause, I do know its effects."[33] A "wanting yet not wanting" is the expression of a will totally surrendered in a love that is not mercenary, a will that wants nothing but God alone. This is the perfect attitude in which to listen and follow without distractions the voice of the Good Shepherd, guiding us through our discernment process.

KNOWING OURSELVES TO GO BEYOND OURSELVES

Given Rafael's natural sensitivity and the many difficulties he encountered in response to the Lord's call, he could easily have fallen into the common mistake of confusing emotional states with the motions of the Holy Spirit—what Saint Ignatius of Loyola in his rules for discernment calls *consolations and desolations*.[34] However, even during trying times, such as when he saw his family suffer when he was about to return to La Trapa, Rafael was not hindered by his feelings, because he realized that they were of no importance compared to his love for God. What mattered was to live and renew his love in acts that led him beyond himself into God. This is how he describes it:

---

32. Bernard of Clairvaux, *On Loving God*, CF 13B:20.

33. CW 626, #181.

34. David L. Fleming, *The Spiritual Exercises of Saint Ignatius: A Literal Translation & a Contemporary Reading* (St. Louis, MO: The Institute of Jesuit Sources, 1978), 208.

Some days I'm very happy, I don't know what is going on
with me . . . Well, I do know . . . I know nothing except
that God loves me, that's enough for me . . . Other days,
when I see my parents and brothers and sister, I want to cry
. . . Everything intensifies, and without wanting to, I start
worrying. But neither my joy nor my sadness matters to me.
I absolutely could not care less. I have to go beyond myself
in order to get to God. I make an act of love for Him, and
everything passes . . . It's necessary. How little everything
is. I don't want to look at myself, I don't want to suffer or
rejoice, it's all the same to me, I assure you . . . I want only
to love God. I want only to give myself over to Him, so much
so that even my very breath belongs to Him.[35]

Rafael was aware of our risk of getting stuck in ourselves and
overthinking what is happening to us, so he advised his Aunt
María, "It's best for us to dispense with ourselves, so that we can
climb toward Him."[36] Similarly, Abba Poemen, a fourth-century
desert father, said, "If you take little account of yourself, you will
have peace, wherever you live."[37] This is the peace Rafael discovered in the midst of so many conflicts within and without. His
peace was not the result of having no struggles—which he learned
was the most superficial aspect of peace—but of throwing himself
before the Lord and letting God lead him beyond himself.

This is what we see in many of Rafael's journal entries, where
he displays all that was happening within him, not to analyze it
or to come to terms with it himself, but to surrender himself into
the hands of the Father and the action of the Holy Spirit. It is
precisely through this attitude that he was freed from getting
entangled by the complexity of his interior world and discovered

35. CW 351–52, #92.
36. CW 291, #78.
37. *The Sayings of the Desert Fathers: The Alphabetical Collection*, trans. Benedicta Ward, CS 59 (London and Oxford: Mowbray; Kalamazoo, MI: Cistercian Publications, 1975; revised ed., 1984), 178.

the peace of those who are not overly concerned about themselves because their focus is on God alone: "Suffering and rejoicing are the least of our concerns. Whether we are suffering or rejoicing doesn't matter at all. Ultimately, that's about us. No . . . Lord, You alone are our life. You alone should be our only reason for living . . . You alone . . . not us, not at all."[38]

ACCOMPANIMENT FOR DISCERNMENT

William Harmless says that John Cassian in his first Conference, in the dialogue with Abba Moses, "stresses that monks need to learn the fine art of discernment, to sort through the inner stream of thoughts and discern their origin, whether they arise from God, from the devil, or from themselves."[39] This process is essential so as not to get stuck in oneself, in one's expectations and fear. But throughout the monastic tradition, there is a repeated warning that this task cannot be acomplished without the wise advice of an elder, before whom the disciple displays his or her thoughts in humility and trust.

No monk or nun discerns his or her vocation alone, and neither did Rafael. The guidance of the superior, formators, and a spiritual director are very important tools for discernment within religious life. Rafael had greatly benefited from them during his first stage at La Trapa, but his first novice master, Fr. Marcelo León, passed away before his second return, and his second novice master, Fr. José Olmedo, never got to know Rafael well or to understand his particular call to monastic life. Similarly, Fr. Teófilo Sandoval, Rafael's first confessor at the abbey, who had been so instrumental in inviting him to consider becoming an oblate, was not available to him after the confessors assigned for the novices were changed.

---

38. CW 341, #89.

39. William Harmless, *Desert Christians, An Introduction to the Literature of Early Monasticism* (New York: Oxford University Press, 2004), 390.

Rafael regretted this situation, but once again he entrusted himself to God's providential help, knowing that God would provide what he could not. Still, aware of his own weakness, he was cautious not to end up following his own will instead of God's, and so he prayed, "Do with me as You will, Lord, but listen, my Jesus: do not permit the devil to deceive me. Show me what You want so that I can do it, and give me a humble spirit so that I can see it and do it. My Jesus, do not permit me to refuse Your divine intimations."[40]

It is important to notice that Rafael also learned to use well a form of guidance that was at his disposal: the spiritual treasury of the Catholic Church. Rafael discerned within the context and the tradition of Benedictine-Cistercian monasticism, which flowed from the first Christian desert dwellers and was enriched through the centuries. To this spiritual source he added the wisdom he encountered particularly in the writings of Teresa of Ávila, John of the Cross, and Thomas à Kempis. His complete openness to grace and the tools he found in these spiritual masters made up for his lack of human guidance.

Still, despite the precariousness of his situation, Rafael was not discerning alone.[41] The final confirmation of Rafael's discernment, as of any vocational discernment, came from the Church's representatives. Dom Félix Alonso, abbot of San Isidro de Dueñas, approved each time Rafael returned to La Trapa. It was this confirmation from his legitimate superior that gave the last seal of approval to Rafael's path as God's will for him. Expressing this fact, Rafael wrote, "At present, I believe I am following it [his vocation], obeying the superiors of the Cistercian Abbey of San Isidro de Dueñas without vows and with the status of an oblate."[42]

---

40. CW 687, #203.
41. See the Appendix for Rafael's letter to Dom Félix Alonso García on October 9, 1935, where Rafael asked for his abbot's advice.
42. CW 606, #170.

On April 17, 1938, Rafael received the cowl from the hands of his abbot. This was a totally unusual event, Rafael being the only oblate ever to receive it in the history of San Isidro de Dueñas.[43] It was a private ceremony in the abbot's office because Rafael was not able to make vows—the moment when ordinarily the cowl is received as part of the celebration of a solemn profession and monastic consecration. Beyond the expression of affection and recognition of his abbot toward Rafael, we can notice in this fact one more sign of God's providential care: underneath the surface of what looked like a rather chaotic life marked by constant struggle, a good Father was attentively watching over his beloved son, even to the last detail.

Rafael always trusted that the voice of his superiors was the voice of God for him, and in this confidence, he opened his heart to them at every fundamental step of his discernment. It was also through the hands of his abbot, as Rafael received the black scapular and the monastic cowl, that he received the main external sign that confirmed his discernment. With unsuppressed joy Rafael wrote in his journal pondering over the coming event:

> I was with Reverend Father Abbot the other day. I went to ask Him to permit me some penance during this holy season of Lent, which he refused. Instead, he told me that he would give me the monastic cowl and black scapular on Easter. How joyful I was, my good Jesus! I wanted to hug Rev. Fr. Abbot . . . he is too good to me.
>
> I've dreamed of wearing the cowl for such a long time now . . . What a joyful thought, that in just a short time, I won't be any different from a real monk.[44]

---

43. *San Rafael Arnaiz: Obras Completas* [OC], 7th ed., ed. Alberico Feliz Carbajal (Burgos, Spain: Grupo Editorial Fonte/Editorial Monte Carmelo, 2017), 910, n. 1086.

44. CW 651, #190.

KNOWING THE SHEPHERD

In *The Trappist's Apologia*, Rafael drew a parallel between himself and the rich young man in the gospels,[45] noting that, difficult as it was, he had been willing "to jump over"[46] any obstacle that would have prevented him from following the Master. But there is another decisive difference between these two young men confronted with the Lord's calling: Rafael dared to look deeply into the eyes of Jesus, the eyes that gazed at him with an indescribable love. This is the key to Rafael's discernment and life as a whole. In a letter to Br. Tescelino, his former infirmarian at the monastery, he speaks eloquently about Jesus' gaze, a gaze before which the excuse of the hardships of illness cannot stand:

> If you saw the tenderness in Jesus's eyes, you wouldn't say any of that. Rather, you'd get up from your bed without a care in the world, without thinking about yourself at all, and you'd join Jesus's retinue, even if you were the last one . . . you hear, the *last one* . . . and you'd tell Him, "I'm coming, Lord. I don't care about my illness, or death, or eating, or sleeping . . . If You'll have me, I will go."[47]

We take on the work of discernment because knowing and doing the will of God means following the one we love. Surrender, trust, perseverance, self-knowledge, unconditional love—all of these elements are essential for a good discernment because they allow us to know the shepherd we want to follow, and they prevent us from being deceived by the voice of *a stranger*.[48] Going always deeper into God's designs for him, Rafael got to know his Shepherd and Master and followed him faithfully, even through the dark valley of suffering. He was disposed to press after his Master,

45. See Mark 10:17-22.
46. CW 169, #51.
47. CW 591, #166. See the rest of the letter in the Appendix.
48. See John 10:1-18.

carrying his own cross, because he knew that Jesus, his Shepherd, had searched and found him first. As Gilbert of Hoyland explains, commenting on the words of the bride of the Song of Songs, "'I found him,' she says, 'I found him,' though previously he sought and found me like a stray sheep, like a lost coin, and in his mercy anticipated me. . . . He found me not that I might choose him but that he might choose me. He anticipated me that he might love me before I loved him."[49]

Knowing our Shepherd allows us to say in truth, "We love because he first loved us."[50] This was Rafael's experience. For him loving Jesus also included sharing in the sufferings of the Shepherd who lays down his life for his sheep, but who often receives no love in return. Rafael's Shepherd was still hanging from the cross and calling his own to himself. To Rafael he whispered, "Love Me, suffer with Me, I am Jesus."[51]

While all Christians are called to love Christ and share in his sufferings, there is something distinctive in this "Me" in the words "Love Me, suffer with Me, I am Jesus." The original words in Spanish, "Ámame a Mí, sufre conmigo, soy Jesús," have a particular emphasis that is more difficult to capture in the English translation. In the paragraph that precedes these words, Rafael is explaining how God, who has offered him "a little corner of this earth so that I might pray," speaks to his heart in silence and teaches him to detach himself from creatures. In the invitation "Love Me, suffer with Me, I am Jesus," the Lord was redirecting Rafael's capacity to love toward God himself and asking Rafael to give him his suffering and share in his own—the pain of a shepherd wounded by love.

---

49. Gilbert of Hoyland, *Sermons on the Song of Songs I,* trans. Lawrence C. Braceland, CF 14 (Kalamazoo, MI: Cistercian Publications, 1978), 124–25 (S 8.8).

50. 1 John 4:19.

51. CW 638, #185.

When Rafael repeated to himself "God alone, God alone," he understood that in his case he was being called not only to love God above all things, but to sacrifice anything and everything for this one love. This is an essential part of the monastic form of Christian discipleship, as Thomas Merton wrote: "The specific value that draws a Christian into the 'desert' and 'solitude' (whether or not he remains physically 'in the world') is a deep sense that *God alone suffices.*"[52] The twelfth-century Cistercian abbot John of Forde put it in this way as he spoke to his monks: "now your soul refuses to be comforted by anyone except Jesus and, no less, it refuses to be made desolate by anyone except him either."[53] To share in the love and suffering of Christ, our wounded Shepherd, Rafael returned to La Trapa.

A Distinctive Path Toward Holiness: Foolishness for Christ

The day after his last entrance, Rafael wrote in his journal the reasons that had brought him back to the monastery:

> I have come for the following reasons:
> 1. Because I believe that here in the monastery I can better follow my vocation of loving God on the cross and in sacrifice.
> 2. In order to help my brothers in the fight, because Spain is at war.
> 3. In order to make use of the rest of the time that God has given me in this life, and make haste in learning to love His cross.[54]

---

52. Thomas Merton, *Contemplation in a World of Action* (Notre Dame, IN: University of Notre Dame Press, 1998), 24.

53. John of Ford, *On the Song of Songs II*, trans. Wendy Mary Beckett, CF 39 (Kalamazoo, MI: Cistercian Publications, 1982), 86 (S 20.5).

54. CW 607, #170.

These reasons are very clear; what might not be so clear is why Rafael was so convinced that the monastery was the place where God wanted him. After all, there was an undeniable obstacle on his path: because of his illness, he didn't have the necessary aptitude to live all that was entailed in pursuing a Trappist-Cistercian vocation. This fact wasn't of little consequence given that an essential element to consider during the process of vocational discernment is whether the person has the indispensable abilities to be able to respond to the call he or she is experiencing.[55] God enables those he calls by giving them the gifts and talents that make a response possible; when these are lacking it is usually a sign that the person doesn't have a vocation to that particular way of life.

Even after the onset of his diabetes, Rafael experienced a persistent call of the Lord to return to La Trapa. He initially thought that he would be cured to make his response possible, but when the cure didn't happen, after some time of confusion, Rafael found in the possibility of becoming an oblate the way in which he could continue following his Master within the monastic life. It was not a new call. After his initial discernment to enter the Abbey of San Isidro, Rafael didn't follow the ordinary steps of the formation process. Yet all the stages of his discernment were linked to his Trapa, and it was in the context of Trappist-Cistercian life and through the essential elements that make up this vocation that Rafael was able to follow Christ wherever he led him. Still, it is important to consider why this apparently impossible path, monastic life, was the way to holiness that God had chosen for him.

Rafael firmly believed that each Christian vocation can lead to holiness: "one may go toward God on many paths and in very

---

55. From the *Constitutions of the Cistercian Order of the Strict Observance*. Constitution 46: "They are to be received as brothers only if they manifest the spiritual attitude needed for monastic life and give evidence of adequate maturity and health. When these qualities are present their desire to embrace this life can be recognized as an indication of God's call and of their intention of truly seeking God with all their heart."

different ways."[56] His vision of holiness as of the spiritual life was uncomplicated, but, at the same time, he was very aware of the obstacles that could prevent *anyone* from advancing on this path; the distractions of the life in the world and not knowing how to suffer were essential ones:

> It is a matter of doing something for Him . . . keeping Him in mind . . . Location, place, occupation are irrelevant.
> God can make me just as holy through peeling potatoes as through governing an empire.
> What a shame that the world is so distracted . . . because I have seen that people are not evil . . . and that *everyone* suffers, but they don't know how to suffer.[57]

During his time outside the monastery Rafael came to understand, not without struggle, that love and service to our neighbor are not a distraction from our interior life as long as we keep God within us; he shared this fundamental lesson with his Aunt María, who was going through a similar trial:

> You think that in order to *immerse yourself in God*, you have to *forget* that you are among creatures . . . and that's not so. . . .
> The Lord made me see, though it took some tears . . . He made me see that I was wrong . . . That I could love Him very much and maintain an intense life in God, but at the same time, I could dwell among creatures with true joy . . . I could invite others to participate in what I carried inside me . . . I could hide God away inside me first . . . but then not hide myself away. Am I making sense? Sometimes it requires effort . . . but then, the Virgin makes everything possible.

56. CW 13, #5.
57. CW 492, #139.

Now I'm more loving toward my parents, and I'm more charitable toward my brothers and sister . . . There's no other way about it. This is what God wants, and if He wanted me to continue like this forever, without going back to La Trapa . . . what do I care, so long as I have His love? Don't you agree?

If only you could see how much joy that thought gives me. Nothing matters to me . . . Wherever I go, there He is.[58]

"So long as I have his love": this is what mattered to Rafael. Loving God above all things in constant acts of love was his one and immutable aspiration. It was his way to the holiness he desired: hidden, ordinary, and human.[59] Rafael lived and encouraged others to live in this way. As he told a layman, Marino del Hierro, "We must love Him [God] above all things. And how hard that is! Only the saints achieved that, but then, the saints were human beings like us . . . Why, then, should we not achieve that too?"[60]

Rafael had not joined the monastery to escape the world. On the contrary, he clearly affirmed his appreciation for all that is good, true, and beautiful in the world—"I enjoy flowers and birds and children. *Everything* is a reason to praise God: stars, nighttime, fields covered in light."[61] In his discernment, Rafael was not closed to the possibility of remaining in the world generously loving God and neighbor, as we read in the letter above—"if He wanted me to continue like this forever, without going back to La Trapa . . . what do I care?" After all, since the beginning of monasticism, monks have added no other goals to their vocation, but simply wanted to live to the full the common call shared by all Christians, that is, to love God above all things and spread his love through work and prayer.

58. CW 324, #86.
59. See CW 320–21, #85.
60. CW 151, #46.
61. CW 172, #51.

Still, in Rafael's heart, as in the hearts of all those who had preceded and followed him on the monastic path, there was a dynamism that drove him forward and beyond the family circle to the desert of his Trapa: the battleground where he needed to engage in the spiritual battle that allowed him to enter into the mystery of God and, in grace, to overcome the distractions and fear of suffering that are proper to the ego. As we see in the *Life of Antony*, the first great model for monks, "To respond to the touch of God upon the soul is to be 'called forth,' to transcend the confines of the domestic sphere and enter into an ever widening, ever deepening circle of self-knowledge and knowledge of God."[62] Rafael expressed this interior dynamism in a letter in which he opened his heart to Br. Tescelino:

> I feel Jesus' sweet gaze deep within my soul. I know that nothing in this world can satisfy me, just God alone . . . God alone, God alone . . .
>
> And Jesus is saying to me, "*You can come whenever you want* [The words in a letter from his novice master welcoming him back] . . . Don't worry about having the last place. Would I love you any less for that? Perhaps even more."
>
> Don't be jealous, brother, but God loves me very much.
>
> On the other hand, my flesh is weighing me down; the world calls me crazy, senseless . . . I'm getting all kinds of prudent warnings . . . But what's all that compared to just one look from a God like Jesus of Galilee as He offers you a place in heaven and eternal love? Nothing, brother . . . even if it meant suffering until the end of the world, it would never be worth it to stop following Jesus.[63]

---

62. Harriet A. Luckman and Linda Kulzer, eds., *Purity of Heart in Early Ascetic and Monastic Literature: Essays in Honor of Juana Raasch, OSB* (Collegeville, MN: Liturgical Press, 1999), 51.

63. CW 591–92, #166. See the Appendix for the rest of the letter.

Rafael understood that for him following Jesus meant taking up the cross that awaited him at La Trapa. Becoming an oblate turned out to be much more than just an exterior arrangement for the peculiarities of his personal circumstances, but rather the way God had chosen for Rafael so that he could join in the oblation of Christ for the salvation of the world: "*My vocation is to suffer*, to suffer in silence for the whole world; to immolate myself with Jesus for the sins of my brothers and sisters, for priests, for missionaries, for the needs of the church, for the sins of the world, and for the needs of my family."[64] Rafael needed the monastery as his school of the cross, the school where he learned to suffer well, and even to rejoice in suffering with Christ for his body the church.[65]

The definite proclamation to the world of Rafael's "God alone" is the silence of Christ crucified. "The world calls me crazy, senseless," Rafael wrote; it couldn't be otherwise, as he had joined Saint Paul and many others who had become fools for Christ, carried away by a mad love for their Master: "We are fools for the sake of Christ, but you are wise in Christ. We are weak, but you are strong. You are held in honor, but we in disrepute" (1 Cor 4:10). Rafael's life becomes one more witness that "the lives of the monk and of the fool show us that the Gospel must be preached as a challenge to the world, and that we must do nothing to minimize or eliminate this challenge."[66]

Accepting the challenge of the Gospel implies responding with specific actions. In his Rule, Saint Benedict explains how to respond to a particularly difficult challenge: what to do when one is assigned an impossible task. When a brother is assigned something he cannot do, he should accept it with gentleness and obedience. If the

64. CW 649, #189.

65. See Col 1:24.

66. John Saward, "The Fool for Christ's Sake," in *One Yet Two: Monastic Tradition East and West*, ed. M. Basil Pennington, CS 29 (Kalamazoo, MI: Cistercian Publications, 1976), 50.

task is still too much, a process of discernment begins in which the brother explains the situation to his superior: "If after the explanation the superior is still determined to hold his original order, then the junior must recognize that this is best for him. Trusting in God's help, he must in love obey" (RB 68.4-5).

In this short chapter of his Rule, Benedict displays his characteristic wisdom. He doesn't take for granted that God's will means doing the hardest thing or that superiors always get it right without any need to listen to what a brother has to say about a situation. All are called to discern and search together for the best course of action. In the end, the greatest benefit of accepting what seems like an impossible task is that in those situations we can experience that God's grace is real, that "nothing will be impossible with God" (Luke 1:37). This is even more important than the completion of the task.

If the onset of diabetes had not affected Rafael's monastic path, he probably would have become the "perfect monk" by all standards, but he was called to give witness to the love and power of God in another way. It was God's persistent call that invited Rafael to do the impossible: to persevere in the monastic way of life despite his lack of aptitude for it. In this way Rafael became a fool for Christ, a witness that God's "power is made perfect in weakness" (2 Cor 12:9).

The Gospel challenge to do the impossible has little to do with the grandiose actions that would feed our egos. Rather, as we see in Rafael's life, it implies the total surrender of ourselves in weakness, relinquishing our control or understanding. This is why it feels impossible, like a form of madness. But Rafael welcomed the challenge in humble trust, just as Mary, the mother of Jesus, and Joseph, his foster father, did in welcoming Jesus into their lives. Rafael let himself be carried away by God's power and logic, the power and logic of love, which is madness to the world.

Discerning our vocation, our distinctive way to holiness, requires that we embrace this new logic at the core of the Beatitudes, and that reaches its climax in the foolishness of the cross. Rafael let himself be transformed by this logic and discovered not only his vocation but the lasting joy and peace he desired, hidden in the mystery of love in suffering. For love of Christ, he became holy through the foolishness of the cross: a fool not only in the eyes of the world but also in the eyes of many of his fellow brothers.

He was a monastic fool, the "circus clown,"[67] not through God's capriciousness but so that he could deliver a message and become a prophet to the world and his own brothers. As Saward says, "Monastic fools reveal something to monasticism, so that monasticism may reveal something to the Church—the madness of the Gospel, and the impossibility of an adaptionary, 'business as usual' Christianity. And it is revealed to the Church, so that the Church may proclaim it to the world."[68]

Faithfulness to the Gospel often demands consciously putting ourselves in the most vulnerable position, so that God's power can show forth in our weakness. Rafael's vocation made him appear like a fragile earthen vessel in the sight of all, to make it clear that the treasure and power within him belonged to God alone.[69]

God had made Rafael's heart to love him, as he declared vehemently: "My soul dreams of love, of pure and sincere affection. I am a man made for love, but not to love creatures, but rather You, my God, and to love them in You . . . I only want to love You. You alone do not *disappoint*. In You alone are hopes realized."[70] *Dreams, disappointment,* and *hope*: these words are an integral part of all discernment processes. They are also evocative of the *Suscipe,* Psalm 118:116, which Saint Benedict prescribed in his Rule as part of the ritual of solemn profession: "Receive me, Lord, as you have promised, and I shall live; do not disappoint me in my hope" (RB 58.21).

---

67. CW 425, #113.
68. Saward, "The Fool for Christ's Sake," 79.
69. See 2 Cor 4:7.
70. CW 610, #172.

Rafael never got to sing this verse surrounded by his brothers in his profession ceremony, but his hopes were not disappointed. He had found a love stronger than death, a love no riches can buy, but for which it was worth selling all he had with joy.[71]

71. See Song 8:6-7, and Matt 13:44.

CHAPTER 5

Rafael, the Monk

In our previous chapter we saw why Rafael persevered on the monastic journey despite the many obstacles he encountered in his path. In Rafael's last letter, written on April 17, 1938, as affectionate as usual, he asked his brother Leopoldo, "when you write, give me all the details. I may be a Trappist, but I'm still interested in everything back home." Then, among the questions about family news, he shared a bit of his own: "Today, on Easter, Father Abbot gave me the black scapular and cowl, so other than the crown, I look just like a real monk now." Rafael finally looked like a real monk, but was he one? Rafael was never able to profess vows and didn't actually live long in a monastery. Looking at his life, we will try to answer this question: What does it take to make a monk a monk?

It seems that it would be easy to identify a monk with what he does. In this same letter, Rafael tells his brother how he spends his days at the monastery:

> My life carries on amid studying Latin, holy reading, and singing in choir, praising Jesus and Mary. Some days, my work involves a pencil and paintbrush, when Reverend Father Abbot asks me to use them for an assignment. Other days, a broom, to help the infirmarian . . . I assure you that I live a happy life, and I don't even notice the days flying by.[1]

1. CW 694–95, #207 (document 207 in Saint Rafael Arnaiz, *The Collected Works*, ed. María Gonzalo-García, trans. Catherine Addington, MW 162 [Collegeville, MN: Cistercian Publications, 2022]).

However, without denying the great importance of monastic discipline, there is a risk of reducing monasticism to the letter of a rule and the exterior practices it prescribes, forgetting the true impulse, the desire for God that puts life into these practices. This has been a constant risk with monastic history, as we can see in this story from the *Apophthegmata* of the desert fathers:

> Abba Lot went to see Abba Joseph and said to him, "Abba, as far as I can I say my little office, I fast a little, I pray and meditate, I live in peace and as far as I can, I purify my thoughts. What else can I do?" Then the old man stood up and stretched his hands towards heaven. His fingers became like ten lamps of fire and he said to him, "If you will, you can become all flame."[2]

This fire burned in Rafael's life throughout his whole monastic journey until it consumed him completely. Because of his illness, he could easily have said to himself, "I will do a little bit of this and a little bit of that according as I am able," but no. This would have never done, either to satisfy his desire for God or to satisfy God's desire for him. These words to his Aunt María are an eloquent expression of his fiery desire: "How could we lead *calm* lives, possessing what we possess? . . . It would be impossible . . . We can't let our love for God sit still . . . More, always . . . always more. We must never abandon the fight, even if it's difficult." "More"— that was his measurement. And he continued, "Let us love God more and more, always . . . Let us not settle for less. And if one day we catch fire . . . isn't that what we are looking for?"[3]

Rafael was not the kind of person who cannot accept his own limitations. The origin of this "more" was quite different. Its origin was in the call Rafael experienced to go beyond what had been his

---

2. *The Sayings of the Desert Fathers: The Alphabetical Collection*, trans. Benedicta Ward, rev. ed., CS 59 (London and Oxford: Mowbray; Kalamazoo, MI: Cistercian Publications, 1984), 103.

3. CW 365, #94.

ordinary Christian life with his family and friends, the call to love more, to give himself in return to the God who had always loved him. But later Rafael came to understand that it was not only he who wanted more, but that God wanted more of him. God's desire for him was the deepest foundation of his calling to monastic life.

What did this "more" mean, and how was he to respond to it? Rafael found in Cistercian monastic life the answer to these two questions, even as his understanding developed and matured. It was not a theoretical answer but a personal invitation to a concrete reality: his own reality as a person and the reality of the community of San Isidro de Dueñas. This invitation also meant saying "yes" to a deep process of transformation, the purification of the heart that, as we have seen, leads to contemplation—the goal of monastic life and the fruit of *conversatio morum*, that is, the practice of all the elements comprised in the monastic discipline.

Rafael found words that described the transformative process he was meant to embrace within the monastic way of life in this verse from the prophet Hosea: "Therefore, I will now allure her, and bring her into the wilderness, and speak tenderly to her" (Hos 2:14). In these words we encounter a central aspect of monasticism, what we can call the desert experience: the monk or nun, like Christ, is guided by the Spirit into the wilderness,[4] and, placed in a space of vulnerability and temptation, he or she begins to rely on God alone. There, listening attentively, the monk or nun will learn to distinguish God's voice from that of the evil one.

While the monk finds himself in the midst of this spiritual battle that will gradually make his heart pure, God is the one leading the process. He searches and works on the soul he wants to attract to himself with such zeal that Rafael dares to call him "selfish" to express this determination:

> God is selfish, and He doesn't let His friends seek any consolation outside of Himself . . .

4. See Luke 4:1-12.

At the beginning, He pacifies them with consolation from other human beings, but there comes a time when human beings have nothing more to give, and what little they can offer cannot satisfy the soul . . . Tears may come, or disappointment, or heartbreak . . . but what does that matter? . . .

Little by little, sometimes gently, sometimes all at once, he goes about stripping away the many things that bind the soul to the earth and its creatures . . .

Let Him do it . . . He is the master of everything. And indeed, if God wants us for Himself, we can't stop Him from leading us into solitude, where He shall speak to our hearts, as Hosea says.[5]

William of Saint-Thierry, a twelfth-century Cistercian writer, expresses the same idea of God wanting us exclusively for himself, not in the sense that nothing else can be loved but that all needs to be loved for his sake:

Then to want you [God], to want you vehemently—that is, to love you and to love you exclusively, for you will not tolerate being loved along with any other thing whatever, carnal or spiritual, earthly or heavenly, that is not loved for your sake—to want you thus is to want nothing but what is good; and that is tantamount to having all one wants.[6]

La Trapa became Rafael's desert, the place where God stripped him and spoke to his heart, cleansing it from attachment to other loves that needed to be set in order—as the twelfth-century Cistercian writers liked to repeat following the Vulgate translation: "He set love in order in me" (Song 2:4). The monastic *conversatio* was the narrow road Rafael was meant to traverse to be led into life. Driven by the love of Christ, Rafael chose to live under a rule and

---

5. CW 486, #138.

6. William of St Thierry, *On Contemplating God,* trans. Sister Penelope [Lawson], CF 3 (Spencer, MA: Cistercian Publications, 1971), 56.

an abbot in a monastery to learn to renounce his self-will, just as Saint Benedict explains to those ready to follow the monastic path:

> It is love that impels them to pursue everlasting life; therefore, they are eager to take the narrow road of which the Lord says: *Narrow is the road that leads to life* (Matt 7:14). They no longer live by their own judgment, giving in to their whims and appetites; rather they walk according to another's decisions and directions, choosing to live in monasteries and to have an abbot over them. Men of this resolve unquestionably conform to the saying of the Lord: *I have come not to do my own will, but the will of him who sent me.* (John 6:38).[7]

Despite Rafael's comings and goings in and out of the Abbey of San Isidro, from the time of his first entrance, and even before, the monastery (and all the elements that make up the Trappist-Cistercian way of life) remained the context and main reference for all of Rafael's experiences, as he wrote: "I am a Trappist, and I feel, see, and think like a Trappist."[8] Inside or outside the cloister, he advanced along the narrow road marked out for him, never setting aside the guidance of the Rule and the authority of his abbot; doing so, Rafael lived and died as a monk, just as God had promised him—"I'm so sure that I am to die a Trappist! . . . I don't know why . . . but even though it seems as though everything is against me, humanly speaking, it's really not."[9]

Conversatio Morum and Community

For the Cistercians of the Strict Observance, often known as Trappists, fraternal life in community is an essential part of the monastic *conversatio*, that is, all the elements that fill up the day

---

7. RB 5.10-13.
8. CW 167, #51.
9. CW 546, #157.

of a monk or nun in the Order, such as the Divine Office, manual labor, *lectio divina*, etc. When a monk or nun makes solemn vows, his or her final commitment publicly manifests the desire of living until death according to the monastic vocation as it is described in the Constitutions of the Order and embodied by the particular community. In this way, a bond is created not only with God but with the brothers or sisters who make up the community that receives the new solemnly professed as one of them. This is expressed in what is called the vow of stability, which implies that the monk or nun will remain in the community of his or her profession until death.

The vows of obedience, stability, and *conversatio morum*—translated as fidelity to the monastic way of life, which also includes the vows of poverty and celibacy—reflect the strong cenobitic character that Saint Benedict impressed in his Rule, a Rule that the Cistercians have followed since their foundation in 1098. As cenobites, or members of a community, spiritual warfare is not only a personal but a communal endeavor—in contrast with the hermit, the cenobite monk fights alongside his brothers in his battle against the evil one.[10]

When Rafael joined the Abbey of San Isidro de Dueñas, he not only wanted to take on a tradition, but he also was embracing a new kind of family, even if so different from the bonds that come from blood and common parentage. He expressed in these words the fellowship he felt he had become part of:

> In La Trapa, we have silence. If only you knew how much that silence, which the world assumes is so gloomy, helps us to understand one another . . . Words are always clumsy, while silence can be rather expressive . . . There, we love one another deeply and truly; our love for God unites us in spirit, while our bodies are united by the Rule, by penance, and sometimes by suffering . . . As for the heart, ours is also very

10. RB 1.1-3.

united . . . in silence we tell it . . . If you knew how beautiful it is to be a Trappist!!![11]

Part of Rafael's first attraction to the monastic life included a certain idealization of the monks of San Isidro, as we can note in this letter to his uncle Polín after his first visit to the abbey: "When I arrived at the station, dealing with men after having been among angels—it produced a certain disgust in me, to be frank with you. When I saw the train arriving in all its imposing grandiosity, I wanted to throw away my luggage and return to La Trapa."[12]

Often, those who come to a Cistercian abbey wanting to discern their vocation are struck by the fact that at the monastery they can be always with Jesus, a simple but deep and joyful realization. Rafael's first experience of monastic life was similar; he found in his fellow monks a visible expression of the "God alone" principle: the monastery was a place where God was not only acknowledged but worshiped as the foundation and end of all that is, because the only occupation of the Trappist is to love and be loved by God:

> The Trappist ought not desire anything but what God desires. He must be the Trappist's only occupation, only desire, only love and occupation . . . Trappists must be filled with the Spirit of God, and all their actions in this life must be oriented toward Him alone and His greater glory, and done in His name. . . . One need only "love God above all things," and that is so pleasant, so sweet, that one might say that the Trappist's occupation on earth is the most *pleasant* of all occupations, the most *divine*, the most *useful* if I can employ such a word . . . When people ask me, "Tell me, what do you do in La Trapa?". . . Many times I have wanted to answer, "Well, it's pretty simple . . . love God and let ourselves be loved by Him, that's all."[13]

11. CW 188, #53.
12. CW 13, #5.
13. CW 168, #51.

The monastic schedule is structured in a way that fosters an uninterrupted encounter with God. While Jesus is always available to us no matter where we are, at the monastery all the central activities of the day intentionally promote the mindfulness of his presence, strengthening and assisting the monk or nun to live for God alone. Rafael was aware of how the monastic *conversatio* helped him to live for God alone, as he explained in a letter he wrote to his parents on the first Easter Sunday he spent at La Trapa: "My sole pursuit is loving God. That fills up everything, and every moment of the day."[14] The fact that in the Trappist-Cistercian life he could intentionally devote each moment of his day to loving God was what brought him back to the monastery time and again. God's closeness, either in suffering or in joy: this is what La Trapa meant to him, as he explained to his Uncle Polín in a letter he wrote soon after his first departure:

> I can promise you that while the life there [at La Trapa] is hard, very hard, God is so close by that you don't even notice the austerity of the Rule. I breathed in joy through every pore . . . God was my one and only desire, and I felt Him so close to me that I forgot about everything else.[15]

Rafael was convinced that despite the many challenges and even hardships of monastic life, it is easier to live for God alone in the cloister than in the world. John Cassian, sixteen centuries before, had already pointed out in his nineteenth Conference a similar line of thought: one of the benefits of cenobitic life is that it allows one to fulfill the Gospel command of having "no thought for the next day."[16] In other words, a person doesn't have the constant distraction of having to provide for oneself (as it is the

14. CW 96, #33.

15. CW 113, #33.

16. John Cassian, *The Conferences*, trans. Boniface Ramsey, Ancient Writers Series 57 (New York: Paulist Press, 1977), 675 (Conf 19.8).

case of the hermit and single person) and for one's family (if one is a married man or woman). This is how the monk or nun has greater freedom to make the love of God the only occupation. This is the greatest gift of their vocation, in which Rafael rejoiced, but he also understood that it is their greatest responsibility.

Rafael suffered any time he pondered the fact that God's love was not reciprocated by humankind. Nevertheless, he understood that the many tasks and responsibilities of secular life could hinder people in their awareness and response to the love of their Creator. But the monks had no excuse, because they were in the most favorable circumstances to love God in return. When, after his second return, Rafael began to discover the failings of his religious brothers and the starker side of fraternal life that he had not seen at first, he could not initially find in his heart the mercy that he held for other Christians. How difficult it was for him to come to terms with the fact his brothers were just ordinary men!

In this journal entry during Christmastime, burdened by the loneliness that the season made him feel more intensely, Rafael expressed his sense of disappointment:

> Poor Brother Rafael, his heart is too sensitive to creaturely things . . . You suffer when you don't find love and charity among human beings . . . You suffer when you see nothing but selfishness. What do you expect of things made of misery and clay? Place your hope in God and leave creatures be . . . you won't find what you're looking for in them.
>
> But what if God hides Himself? . . . How cold it would be in La Trapa then. La Trapa without God . . . is nothing but a bunch of men.[17]

Cassian explains that to reach purity of heart, detaching oneself from the exterior is not sufficient. Only love can make the heart whole again: "perfection is not immediately arrived at by being

17. CW 609, #172.

stripped and deprived of all one's wealth or by giving up one's honors, unless there is that love whose elements the Apostle describes, which consists in purity of heart alone."[18] Rafael left behind riches and honors, but he had transferred many of the old dreams and ideals of his childhood and young adulthood into the monastic setting. As he acknowledged to his abbot before his second return to the monastery, his spiritual search had so far not been for God alone: "I was searching for God, but I was also searching for His creatures, and I was searching for myself; and God wants me all to Himself."[19]

Rafael wanted a community of brothers who would perfectly reflect his ideal of living for God alone. This was his desire, his dream, but not God's plan for him. His heart needed a deeper purification than exterior detachment from family and riches to discover God's unfathomable love. The monastic *conversatio*, and particularly the relationship with his brothers in community, would provide this purification for him: the interior detachment from his own hopes and expectations. This conversion of the heart can only happen when the cross of Christ takes root in one's life. In Rafael's life, the cross made its appearance under the shape of his diabetes, but it was through the pains and blessings of fraternal life in community that it bore its most perfect fruit: Christ's compassion.

Another benefit of cenobitic life that Cassian points out is that it helps us to become aware of our imperfections.[20] The monastery is a school of love and humility because in the interactions with the brothers or sisters in community monastics are confronted with their own imperfections; the failings they see in others mirror their own. As Saint Bernard explains, "You will never have real mercy for the failings of another until you know and realize that you have the same failings in your soul."[21] The ego resists this

---

18. Cassian, *Conferences* 45 (Conf 1.6).

19. CW 214, #64.

20. Cassian, *Conferences* 676–77 (Conf 19.10).

21. Bernard of Clairvaux, *The Steps of Humility and Pride*, trans. M. Ambrose Conway, CF 13A (Kalamazoo, MI: Cistercian Publications, 1989), 35.

process, but when one fully embraces it, as Rafael did, it cleanses the soul from its last remnants of pride and self-righteousness. Full of wonder, Rafael described the change that had happened to him in this way:

> One of the great things You have done is a transformation in my soul with respect to love of neighbor. I will explain.
>
> Before, when I looked for a *monk* and instead I found an *ordinary human being* . . . I suffered so much, my good Lord! [. . .]
>
> Something strange happens to me now. Some days, when I leave prayer, even if I feel that I didn't do anything while I was praying, I have such a great desire to love all the members of the community with such great longing . . . as Jesus loves them.
>
> Some days, after receiving the Lord in communion, and realizing that He loves me *despite what I am*, I feel like enthusiastically kissing the ground that the monks walk on. I have such a great desire to humiliate myself before those who I thought had humiliated me. [. . .]
>
> Oh, Lord! I feel great peace in such moments . . . While I used to get upset over a brother's fault or weakness before, and feel almost *repulsed* by him, now I feel great *tenderness* toward him . . . and I want to do whatever I can to make reparation for that fault . . . He is a soul loved by Jesus. He is a soul for whom Jesus is bleeding on the cross . . . Who am I to scorn him?! . . . God forbid . . . Rather, I feel great love for this soul. This isn't just hot air, it's actual fact, and I am positive that I am not the one who has done this, but rather Jesus has done this in my soul . . . And that is the tremendous miracle.[22]

Rafael had learned to love people as they were and not as he wished them to be. In the process he discovered a new form of

---

22. CW 657–58, #193.

peace that he called "serenity."[23] Now he had become a monk, according to the wisdom of the Desert Fathers: one who had found rest fulfilling the Lord's commandment of not judging others:[24] "Abba Poemen said to Abba Joseph, 'Tell me how to become a monk.' He said, 'If you want to find rest here below, and hereafter, in all circumstances say, Who am I? and do not judge anyone.'"[25] Purity of heart consists not only in the heart's being free from evil but in gazing mercifully on everything, as God does. Gradually, through the monastic *conversatio*, Rafael's heart was made whole in the love of God alone, but it was in the new compassion for his brothers and the whole world that the transformative process reached its peak and confirmation.

MONASTIC PRAYER

In the life of the monk, liturgical and contemplative prayer are meant to flow naturally into each other. As Thomas Merton explains, "The personal prayer of the monk is embedded in a life of psalmody, liturgical celebration and the meditation and reading of Scripture (*lectio divina*). All this has a personal and a communal dimension."[26] Rafael assimilated this rhythm of prayer effortlessly from the time he first entered La Trapa because it perfectly expressed his own desire to pray constantly. His writing and the books he used for meditation show his love for the Scriptures, particularly for the psalms, and how they nurtured his prayer life.[27] From his first visit to La Trapa, the celebration of the liturgy in the monastic church and the praise of God in the Divine Office

23. See CW 550, #159.

24. See Matt 7:1-2.

25. Ward, trans., *Sayings of the Desert Fathers*, 102.

26. Thomas Merton, *The Climate of Monastic Prayer*, CS 1 (Kalamazoo, MI: Cistercian Publications, 1981), 40.

27. See Juan Antonio Martínez Camino, *Mi Rafael: San Rafael Arnáiz, según el Padre Teófilo Sandoval, su confesor, intérprete y editor*, 2nd ed. (Bilbao, Spain: Editorial Desclée de Brouwer, 2009), 229–40.

were his delight. In a letter to his Uncle Polín after this initial visit, Rafael expresses the deep impression it had on him:

> From this moment I began to see clearly and became inti-mately ashamed of myself: when upon entering the church to greet the Lord, I saw the monks chanting in the choir, and that altar with that Virgin; I saw the respect that the monks have in church and, most of all, I heard a Salve that . . . dear Uncle Polín, only God knows what I felt . . . I did not know how to pray before.[28]

As a novice, Rafael had to learn the ceremonies or ways of doing things in the monastic church that were regulated by the *Book of Usages.* These details enchanted Rafael, as a way to give God the glory he deserved and a genuine expression of his love for him. In a letter to his parents, he describes his experience:

> I've also been an altar server, or rather, a "candle snuffer," which is a job I like very much. Also, don't get me wrong, it has its importance. Here at La Trapa, any ceremony acquires a great importance; to light or snuff out a candle, one must follow all the rubrics laid out by the Laws of the Order . . . Everything is accounted for: the steps, the minutes, the bowing.
>
> In church we are always ceremonial. We do not speak for any reason or make any signs; we walk slowly, making no noise; we bow deeply to the Lord who is in the tabernacle . . . In short, what divine worship ought to be and demands. This delights me. You know that I've never liked informali-ties anywhere, least of all at church. You could say that Trap-pists are formed exclusively for God. First they form the soul, but then the body and its manners . . . and it's not that I wish to praise my Order above any other, but you could say that when it comes to celebrating worship, the Trappist way is the most elegant.[29]

28. CW 12, #5.
29. CW 94–95, #33.

Besides the externals of the liturgy, which appealed to Rafael's sensitivity for the aesthetically beautiful, he was also moved by the interior reality taking place during the chanting of the psalms. The way he depicts the Divine Office at the hour of Vespers shows his deep awareness of the Lord's presence among those gathered in his name:

> Those moments of great solemnity during the psalmody, with great peace in one's heart, bring such consolation! . . . The hour of Vespers contains so much joy! What a happy thought, that the day is now spent . . . and it was spent before the tabernacle of the Lord . . .
>
> The soul is so moved upon having completed another day in the Lord's service. Our hearts are so grateful for the sublime privilege of having been able to spend the day singing before the Lord . . .
>
> In such moments, the soul longs to fly up to the glorious heights of heaven, in order to keep singing there alongside the angels, the saints, the Virgin . . . The soul wishes the day would never end . . . that Vespers would go on eternally . . . The soul wants to hold back the sun . . . and rise up to heaven with a *Gloria Patri*.
>
> Anyway, the ramblings of a mad monk.[30]

Other forms of prayer during the day were also essential for Rafael. He would sing quietly to himself as he worked in the fields and make a visit to the Lord present in the tabernacle to offer him the fruit of his labor once he returned to the abbey from his workplace. He interceded for priests and missionaries as he walked through the cloisters, as well as for his family and loved ones at other times during the day. When the Spanish Civil War started, his whole life became a constant prayer of intercession, joining his own sacrifices to the supreme sacrifice of Christ. And prayer—an outpouring of a heart in love with God—was also the main

30. CW 430–31, #116.

reason for his writings. In other words, Rafael fulfilled the apostle's invitations to pray unceasingly,[31] and as his heart was purified and expanded, being transformed more and more into the heart of Jesus, his prayer became the channel and response to the bountiful love that flowed into him from Christ crucified.

In accordance with the Cistercian and Carmelite traditions, Rafael's prayer was mainly focused on the humanity of Christ: Jesus of Nazareth as he is described in the Scriptures, particularly at the time of his passion. As was true then, when Rafael looked at the cross, he found Mary, always close at the side of her Son. Rafael explains in a simple way the focus of his prayer: "my heart and even my eyes are fixed on that sweet, calm Jesus of Nazareth, who is looking at me, waiting for me, loving me more than I'll ever know . . . What am I to do? I don't know. Be astonished, get confused, kiss the ground . . . go mad with joy."[32]

Rafael's heart and prayer were purified by what the Cistercian tradition calls the experience of alternation: the way the Lord seems to be so present at some times and totally absent at others.[33] As Thomas Merton explains it, "This alternation of darkness and light can constitute a kind of dialogue between the Christian and God, a dialectic that brings us deeper and deeper into the conviction that God is our all."[34] It was in prayer that Rafael discovered that he was called to live for God alone, and through prayer that he received the strength to do it, not because prayer was always a source of consolation to him, but because he persevered in it even when it was dry and hard:

> How good it is to be at the foot of the Lord's Cross, when
> He is looking at us . . . The hard thing is to stay on the Cross

31. See 1 Thess 5:17.
32. CW 280, #77.
33. See Bernard of Clairvaux, *On the Song of Songs IV*, trans. Irene Edmonds, CF 40 (Kalamazoo, MI: Cistercian Publications, 1980), 91 (S 74.6).
34. Merton, *The Climate of Monastic Prayer*, 50.

when Christ disappears before our eyes and the Cross remains, all dry and black and bloody . . . And neither Saint
John nor the holy women nor Mary is on Calvary . . . We
are all alone in darkness with the Cross. We neither know
how to pray nor do we hear God, *nothing* . . . all we know
is suffering . . . we look for Christ . . . and He is not there.

What does that matter to us? . . . Is that not what the
Lord wants? . . . Well then! . . .

Take heart, my dear sister; Jesus is on the other side of
everything that you can't see.[35]

Rafael also shared in the monastic tradition recommending that
the simplicity that needs to pervade all the aspects of the life of the
monk should also inspire the way he prays, not looking for extraordinary experiences but keeping heart and mind open through the
awareness of a loving silence:

You told me about your prayer, about remaining in silence
before God . . . I understand. Neither desire nor ask for
anything more. If only I could talk to you about this! But
it's so hard in writing, even though I know what you're describing . . . How good it is to pray like that! Isn't it? God
fills the soul with such gentleness . . . Lord, Lord! What
have we done? What will we do with ourselves, sister?

Anyway, let us be quiet, these noisy words are a hindrance.[36]

Rafael doesn't give details about his experiences in prayer, and
on numerous occasions he manifests the difficulty to put into
words what was happening in his soul at the touch of divine grace.
But reading between the lines, in the unembellished account of
what was taking place within him, we can recognize signs of what

35. CW 239–40, #72. See the Appendix for a longer extract of the letter with
this passage.
36. CW 278, #77.

Cassian called "fiery prayer"[37] and what Saint Bernard described as the fourth degree of love.[38] Rafael's union with God was such that as God filled everything, nothing else mattered, and Rafael felt himself disappear:

> How good is Jesus! With a tender gaze, He commands you to draw near, tell Him everything, let Him console you . . . You see His immense love for you . . . *Everything* disappears, the disciples, even your own self . . . He fills it all . . . How good is Jesus! Then there are no more sorrows or joys, and we don't know what to say . . . we can't speak. We stay there, lost in His embrace, and then He speaks to the soul with such great gentleness . . . My dearest little sister, how good is Jesus! And He loves us so . . . I'm telling you, it's enough to make you melt . . . Does this happen to you too?[39]

THOUGHTS/*LOGISMOI*

One of the greatest disciplines we can learn from the Desert Fathers and Mothers is to manage the influence our thoughts[40]

---

37. Fiery prayer according to Cassian is a form of wordless prayer that transcends human understanding: "it gushes forth as from a most abundant fountain and speaks ineffably to God, producing more in that very brief moment than the self-conscious mind is able to articulate easily or reflect upon" (Cassian, *Conferences*, 346 [Conf 9.25]).

38. This is the highest form of love according to Bernard's treatise *On Loving God*. The one who has attained it "no longer even loves himself except for God. . . . Inebriated with divine love, the mind may forget itself and become in its own eyes like a broken dish, hastening toward God and clinging to him, becoming one with him in spirit" (Bernard of Clairvaux, *On Loving God, with Analytical Commentary by Emero Stiegman*, trans. Robert Walton, CF 13B [Kalamazoo, MI: Cistercian Publications, 1995], 29).

39. CW 248, #72.

40. In Greek, *logismon*. "Once the monk is able to leave behind worldly attachments, thoughts are his or her chief distraction. As such, the 'treatment' of thoughts became a great concern in monastic spirituality and pastoral care"

have over us. The main reason for this arduous endeavor can be found in the words of Cassian at the end of his second conference on prayer: "For whoever is in the habit of praying only at the hour when the knees are bent prays very little. But whoever is distracted by any wandering of heart, even on bended knee, never prays."[41] The wisdom of the desert teaches us that this wandering of the heart or the mind is inevitable. What we are trying to control is not the influx of thoughts but their impact on us—all for the purpose of unceasing prayer and union with God.

Anyone who has tried to pray silently for more than five minutes soon becomes aware of the flood of thoughts that try to push their way into our minds and hearts, trying to get our attention and preventing us from focusing on God alone. This kind of distraction was not foreign to Rafael. He, not unlike Saint Antony and other desert dwellers, had to learn "a technique of introspection that enabled him to attend to, without being seduced by, the flood of feelings and memories that might divert him from his single-minded purpose."[42] This was not an easy task, as Rafael's journal entry on December 29, 1937, testifies:

> An hour at prayer without a single thought of God. I hardly noticed time was passing. The clock struck five and I'd already been on my knees for an hour . . . What about prayer? I don't know . . . I didn't do it. I was thinking about myself, about my personal suffering, about my memories of the world. What about Jesus? What about Mary? Nothing . . . All I have is selfishness, a little bit of faith, and a great deal of pride . . . I think I'm so important! I hold myself in such esteem! [. . .]

(Athanasius of Alexandria, *The Life of Antony: The Coptic and the Greek Life*, trans. Tim Vivian and Apostolos N. Athanassakis, CS 202 [Kalamazoo, MI: Cistercian Publications, 2003], 65, n. 37).

41. Cassian, *Conferences*, 386 (Conf 10.14).

42. William Harmless, *Desert Christians: An Introduction to the Literature of Early Monasticism* (New York: Oxford University Press, 2004), 62.

Lord, have mercy on me . . . Yes, I am suffering . . . but I wish my suffering weren't so self-centered. . . . If I could forget myself, it would be better, Lord.[43]

But why is it so difficult to let go of these thoughts and forget ourselves? Another saying of the Desert Fathers shows the connection between the struggle with our thoughts and our self-will:

Abba Ammonas was asked, "What is the 'narrow and hard way?'" (Matt. 7.14) He replied, "The 'narrow and hard way' is this, to control your thoughts, and to strip yourself of your own will, for the sake of God. This is also the meaning of the sentence, 'Lo, we have left everything and followed You'" (Matt. 19.27).[44]

Rafael came to understand that leaving everything to follow Christ ultimately meant confronting his ego and some of its most insidious manifestations: the memories of his past life, as well as his own hopes and expectations.

In the stories of the first Christians who went to the deserts of Egypt and Syria, we see how this discipline of the thoughts is connected to the battle with the evil one, who would tempt the monk with disturbing thoughts and memories, trying to arouse his passions or persuade him to give in to discouragement. Similarly, Rafael describes in detail how, as he peeled turnips on a cold and rainy day, little devils brought him memories of his family and his lost freedom, to steal the joy from his heart and prevent him from praising God as he worked:

Time passes slowly and my knife does too, moving between their skin and flesh, leaving the turnips perfectly peeled.

---

43. CW 611, #173.
44. Ward, trans., *The Sayings of the Desert Fathers*, 28.

The little devils continue to wage war on me. To think that I left my house to come here in this cold and peel these stupid turnips!! It is a truly ridiculous thing, this business of peeling turnips with the seriousness of a magistrate in mourning.

A tiny, shrewd devil infiltrates me, and from deep within it reminds me subtly of my house, my family, and my freedom . . . which I left behind in order to lock myself in here with these lentils, potatoes, collard greens, and turnips.

It's a melancholy day . . . I'm not looking out the window, but I can guess as much. My hands are chapped as red as the little devils; my feet are frozen solid . . . And my soul? Lord, perhaps my soul is suffering a little. But it doesn't matter . . . let us take refuge in silence.

Time kept on going, along with my thoughts, the turnips, and the cold; then suddenly, quick as the wind, a powerful light pierced my soul . . . A divine light, lasting but a moment . . . Someone saying to me, "What are you doing?!" What do you mean, what am I doing? Good Lord!! . . . What a question! Peeling turnips . . . peeling turnips! . . . "But why?" . . . And my heart, leaping, gave a wild answer: I'm peeling turnips for love . . . for love of Jesus Christ.[45]

Rafael learned to overcome the effects of disturbing thoughts by becoming mindful time and again of why he was doing what he was doing. This "why" was not a well-constructed theory or explanation, but the image of Christ crucified, toward whom he reached out in humble faith:

> Whenever I doubt, or am uncertain about something, or feel a temptation pressing upon me, or let myself be carried away by some weakness . . . I try to make an act of humility at the foot of your cross, and kissing Your divine blood as it drips from the wounds in Your feet over the wood, I ask for

---

45. CW 490–91, #139.

Your protection, help, and counsel . . . and whatever You
inspire me to do in that moment, I do it.[46]

Rafael learned that victory over disturbing thoughts or difficult
emotions is not in gaining control over them but in turning himself towards Jesus time and again, asking for his "protection, help,
and counsel." It was the same discipline that Saint Antony of
Egypt implied in his fight against the demons who tormented
him: "I will not run from your blows! Even if you do worse things
to me, nothing 'will separate me from the love of Christ.'"[47]

SILENCE AND MISSION

From the time of his first visits, Rafael became enamored of the
silence he discovered at La Trapa. These were some of his first
impressions, written in September 1931:

> People say that the silence of the monastery is sad, and hard
> to maintain under the Rule . . . Nothing could be more
> wrong than such an opinion . . . The silence of La Trapa is
> the most cheerful celebration imaginable . . . Oh! If God
> let us see into the heart of another, then we would see within
> the soul of a Trappist—who looks miserable on the outside
> and lives in silence—a glorious song of jubilation bursting
> forth constantly and abundantly, full of love and joy, for his
> Creator, his God, his loving Father who cares for him and
> consoles him . . . The silence of the monastery is not sad,
> quite the opposite; one could say that there is nothing more
> joyful than the silence of a Trappist.[48]

The strict silence of the Trappist monasteries at that time was
so prominent that for Rafael it was one of the hallmarks of the

46. CW 627, #181.
47. Athanasius, *The Life of Antony*, CS 202:81.
48. CW 21, #7.

religious order: "The life of a Cistercian monk is . . . love for God, love for Mary, and silence among men."[49] Silence is the environment for the spiritual life of the monk: "It is in silence that the monk finds balm for his wounds, and sometimes for his distress . . . It is in monastic silence that the soul who delights in God hides his joys . . . ,"[50] as Rafael wrote in one of his meditations.

Rafael's love for silence never declined. With time, it took for him the place of the ocean and the montains, which in his youth had powerfully spoken to him about their Creator: "The Trappist loves his silence as a sailor loves the sea," he wrote.[51] Silence contained for him a hidden treasure, revealing God to those who seek him in a way that nothing and no one else can. Silence was also the only space where Rafael's desire for God could express itself without restrictions: without the limitations he found in his own words, which would not allow him to say what he felt,[52] the noise of conversations that forced him to divert his attention from the Beloved, and the curious gazes of those who could not understand the exuberance of a soul madly in love with God. This is why Rafael longed to come back to the monastery each time he was forced to leave it: "My soul is a burning volcano about to erupt. I can't go on like this, Lord, I can't . . . I have this urge to lock myself away in the monastery, so that among men's silence, I can let God hear this clamor I carry around inside me, these cries that *won't stop coming out*."[53]

Silence had on Rafael a double effect: a desire for more silence, and an intense longing to cry out the love that had been revealed to him:

49. CW 441, #120.

50. CW 426, #114. See the Appendix for the rest of the meditation.

51. CW 440, #120.

52. CW 532–33, #153: "Sometimes I put my pen down when it doesn't express what I want it to, because it doesn't know how, and it can't. Then I prostrate myself before the tabernacle, and while there, I write, sing, pray, or cry . . . about whatever God tells me to . . . and nobody will ever read it, ever."

53. CW 263, #75.

What I can say for certain is that a great deal of silence
and continual reflection brings about a state of mind that
is good for two things. The first is prayer . . . a desire to
remain silent and not interrupt the interior peace that leads
us to kneel at Christ's feet or Mary's heels, and tell Them
about our struggles and ambitions . . . to remain silent
among men so as to love God better, and adore Him without distraction.

The second thing that the soul feels is odd, it's the complete opposite . . . A desire to shout out and proclaim to
the whole world that what you are *feeling* is God . . . the
reason you are *suffering* is God . . . what you are *thinking* is
God . . . the reason you are *living* is God . . . The soul wants
to get everyone else to feel, suffer, think, and live in God and
for God too . . . But everything stays inside. Everything is
reduced to remaining silent and feeling, suffering, and living
for God . . . but in silence. I have two paths . . . prayer in
the presence of Jesus, and my notebook.[54]

Rafael was aware that his mission was to love God and God
alone, but he wanted everyone to join him in this mission. With
painful acuity he contemplated the indifference of humanity
toward the God who yearned for his love:

The world doesn't see, it's blind, and God needs love, so
much love. I can't give Him enough, I'm small, I'm going
crazy trying. I wish the world would love Him, but the world
is His enemy.

Lord, what a great torture this is! I see this, but I cannot
fix it . . . I am so small and insignificant. The love I have for
You overwhelms me. I wish my family and friends, all of
them, would love You very much, so that I could rest a little
. . . But the world, which is so busy with its concerns and
affairs and discussions, takes me for a madman.[55]

54. CW 532, #153.
55. CW 243, #72.

Rafael gradually understood that his whole life, the total offering of himself, was meant to be a "silent shouting,"[56] whispers of love for his Master and intercession for the world: "I wish I could fly around the world and shout to every creature that they should love God, and yet that same God has bound me to His tabernacle, so that all the shouts I'd like to let loose in the world might be transformed into loving silence for His ears only."[57] But Jesus didn't want to hide under a bushel basket the light that he himself had lit in Rafael's heart, and Rafael was aware of that fact: "I've realized that, as long as I am in this world, the mission entrusted to me by the Lord is to help others love Him."[58] How was he meant to accomplish his mission? Rafael responds to this question in a letter to his Aunt María. Through the correspondence with her Rafael had realized that his words could bring help and light to others: "I've offered myself to Him so that I might help souls to get to heaven, as best I can . . . I believe that the best way I can do that is by offering . . . a bit of silence. Nevertheless, the Lord has placed in my path a soul, your soul, whom I look at, and He asks me to give her help and advice."[59] Did Rafael realize that through his writings he would help many more souls to get to heaven, enkindling in them the desire to love and live for God alone?

"Those who abide in me and I in them bear much fruit" (John 15:5 NRSV). A good image of monastic life is that of a tree: a tree cannot be moved around if it is to bear fruit. The vow of stability in the community of one's monastic profession helps monks and nuns to abide in Christ and not to run away in times of trial or be distracted by the desire of novelties. Silence is the interior disposition that makes this abiding fruitful, fostering the main mission of any monastic: the search for God. Silence is the privileged space in which to seek God, because it helps to develop the spiritual or interior senses by the restriction of the exterior

56. CW 280, #77.
57. CW 399, #105.
58. CW 281, #77.
59. CW 322, #86.

stimuli; the silent atmosphere in a monastery not only reduces noise but decreases the exposure to images and other forms of distraction. While this search is deeply personal, it is not individualistic. The monk or nun seeks God not only for his or her own sake but also to bring all humanity into closer union with the divine Bridegroom. Monastic communities are meant to be houses of prayer that by their hospitality—an essential characteristic of monastic life through the centuries—invite others to share in the beauty and joy of a life centered in Christ.

Rafael's life became more and more fruitful as he learned in silence how to abide in Christ. In the midst of a chaotic world—Spain ravaged by civil war—Rafael realized that what was greatly needed was souls ready to listen to Christ in silence. In listening to Christ, receiving his love, and loving him in return, Rafael found the way of accomplishing his mission. He gave his heart to Christ so that Christ could love in and through him. But it all began, and was ultimately accomplished, in the silence where Rafael gradually identified himself with the Crucified One:

> Jesus is whispering from the Cross.
> May human beings fall silent, may creatures fall silent . . . May we all be silent, so that in that silence, we might hear those whispers of Love, of the humble, patient, infinite, boundless Love that Jesus is offering us with open arms from the cross.
> This mad world doesn't listen . . . Crazy and foolish, it rushes about, drunk on its own noise . . . it doesn't hear Jesus, who is suffering and loving from the cross.
> *But Jesus needs souls who will listen to Him in silence.*
> Jesus needs hearts who, forgetting themselves and going far away from the world, will adore His heart, injured and ripped apart by so much neglect, and love it madly, with wild abandon. My Jesus, sweet master of my love, take mine.[60]

60. CW 676–77, #200.

Solitude

Very much related to silence is another essential element of monastic life: solitude. Silence provides solitude for Cistercian monks and nuns even when they live in close relationships with their brothers and share common spaces at work and meals. Likewise, solitude and separation from the world (more concretely, from the ways of the world) provide silence for the life of prayer and contemplation.

Saint Bernard encouraged his brothers to embrace solitude with these words: "O holy soul, remain alone, so that you might keep yourself for him alone whom you have chosen for yourself out of all that exist."[61] The goal of the monastic enclosure and the solitude it fosters is none other than to provide a space for the encounter between God and the monk, who have mutually chosen each other.

Loneliness and solitude are two ways in which we experience the reality of being alone, either physically or emotionally. These two aspects are expressed by a single word in Spanish, *soledad*. In Rafael's experience, these two aspects blended together: solitude was his trial and his blessing, as he made clear in this journal entry:

> Solitude . . . that word brings so many things forth in my soul. It's so difficult to express the joy of solitude when it has caused you to shed so many tears in the past.
> Nevertheless, how joyful it is to be alone with God . . . Such great peace prevails when we are alone . . . when God and the soul are alone.[62]

Rafael was well aware that it was God himself who had led him into solitude with a clear purpose: "He separates me from every-

---

61. Bernard of Clairvaux, *On the Song of Songs II*, trans. Kilian Walsh, CF 7 (Kalamazoo, MI: Cistercian Publications, 1976), 202 (SC 40.4).
62. CW 486, #138. The complete text appears in the Appendix.

thing else in order to unite me more closely to Himself."[63] What God wanted was more than just physical separation. God had led Rafael to his desert of La Trapa to speak to his heart, purify it, and make it whole in the love of him:

> It's not the solitude of the body that is pleasing to God . . . That is pleasing to our bodies . . . What draws us closer to Jesus is the solitude of the heart that is detached from the world and its creatures and from its own will . . . That is what it means to deny yourself . . . that is death, that is the cross. But blessed be the cross whose suffering is the source of eternal life.
>
> Loving God in silence and solitude, with a heart detached from the world, and only one will: that of Christ. With these three things . . . one can become perfect, so long as one doesn't forget about Mary.[64]

"[For the one who] wishes to live in solitude in the desert . . . there is only one conflict . . . and that is with the heart."[65] These words of Saint Antony of Egypt could well apply to Rafael. His conflict until the end was with his own heart, in the solitude of his personal desert. There the content of the heart comes to the fore:

> Poor Brother Rafael! Sometimes, in his Trappist silence, he remembers the world . . . but not the world of pleasure and fun, even if it was perfectly licit amusement . . . No, it's good that all of that, all that freedom, is locked away . . . What's harder is the world that cannot be locked away, the world of the flesh, which is in your heart, with all its affections and

63. CW 523, #150.

64. CW 711, #216.

65. Harriet A. Luckman and Linda Kulzer, eds., *Purity of Heart in Early Ascetic and Monastic Literature: Essays in Honor of Juana Raasch, O.S.B* (Collegeville, MN: Liturgical Press, 1999), 45.

pure loves. In enclosure, these things do not die, but are rather purified and divinized through enclosure with Christ, even if they can sometimes cause suffering.[66]

Rafael was not a solitary person by nature. During Rafael's canonization process, his brother Luis Fernando testified about the last time he visited him at the monastery: "I asked him how he could spend all his time surrounded by the same people who were so different from him in their ways, and why didn't he go become a Carthusian so he could live in solitude. He told me, 'Luis Fernando, I cannot bear loneliness. I have to see faces, even if they make me suffer.'"[67] But there was an aspect of solitude that was connatural to him: hiding away from the view of others his passionate love for Jesus, more specifically the suffering and inexpressible joy of being carried away by this love into the foolishness of the cross. This was the "secret of the King," a secret so deep and intimate that is "tarnished when made known."[68] Rafael found consolation, peace, and the balance he needed in the hidden character of Trappist-Cistercian life:

> One of the joys, or rather, consolations of the monastic life is being hidden away from the world's gaze. Those who delight in meditating on the life of Christ will understand this.
>
> In order to devote yourself to a certain art . . . or to grow in wisdom, the spirit requires solitude and isolation, it needs recollection and silence. Now for the soul in love with God, for the soul that no longer has eyes for any art or wisdom but the life of Jesus, for the soul that has uncovered hidden treasure on this earth, silence is not enough, nor is recollection in solitude. For such a soul, it is necessary to hide away from everyone, to hide away with Christ, to seek out a little

66. CW 617, #176.
67. CW 665, #196, n. 1.
68. CW 494, #140.

patch of earth where the world's profane gaze cannot reach it, and to be alone there with its God. . . .

Let us hide ourselves away so that we can be with Jesus on the cross.[69]

A well-known saying from the fathers of the desert is this: "Abba Moses instructs, 'Go, sit in your cell, and your cell will teach you everything.'"[70] Rafael learned to remain in the cell of his heart, waiting for the Beloved. In his struggle with loneliness, and even when forced to be back in the world, he received the blessing of solitude: a heart always available for God alone:

> You, Lord, are in the heart that is detached from every-
> thing.
> You, good Jesus, my divine Beloved, find joy in . . . Oh,
> Lord, what can I say! . . . in the human heart . . . I offer
> You mine.
> Let me make my cell in Yours. Let me make my bed there,
> too. Let me live alongside Your Divine Heart, alone and
> stripped of everything.[71]

MARY

After Jesus, no one brought more comfort and strength to Rafael in his struggles than the Blessed Virgin Mary. He would call out to her in all his needs and in times of suffering, "I am suffering greatly . . . Mary, my Mother, help me."[72] Rafael considered her his champion in his battle against the spirit of the world, and the one who supported him in his vocation: "She is invincible. She will thwart your worldly spirit, and everything you offer me fades away, becoming insignificant when the Blessed Virgin Mary turns

69. CW 494, #140.
70. Ward, trans., *The Sayings of the Desert Fathers*, 139.
71. CW 652, #190.
72. CW 606, #170.

Her gaze toward me . . . and I know that She loves me very much."[73]

Rafael was faithful to the honor and obligation of all of the children of Cîteaux to sing the praises of and spread devotion to Our Lady. He followed to the letter Saint Bernard's advice: "Asking her help, you will never despair. Keeping her in your thoughts, you will never wander away. With your hand in hers, you will never stumble. With her protecting you, you will not be afraid."[74]

Rafael, like all Cistercian monks and nuns, took the name *Mary*, *María* in Spanish, before his baptismal name, when he received the habit. He rejoiced in being consecrated to her and offering her his love and labors from day to night: "How gentle and sweet it is to devote oneself to Mary. It is the one consolation in La Trapa, to know that Mary is protecting us. And last, the *Salve* at dusk, before heading to the dormitory; they are the Trappist's last words at the end of the day."[75]

Rafael's devotion to Mary pervades all his writings. As his devotion to her increased, he proposed that he would not write anything without mentioning her.[76] His love for her took nothing away from his love to Jesus. On the contrary, Mary was for him the fastest way to go to her Son, and as such he recommended her to others, as he wrote to his Aunt María: "I'm a bit mad when it comes to the Virgin; forgive me."[77]

Our Lady was always in Rafael's heart as the only creature to whom he could confide himself completely, the only one who would never disappoint him, while she pointed for him the way towards God alone:

---

73. CW 170, #51.

74. Bernard of Clairvaux, *Homilies in Praise of the Blessed Virgin Mary*, trans. Maria-Bernard Saïd, CF 18A (Kalamazoo, MI: Cistercian Publications, 1993), 30–31 (Homily 2.17).

75. CW 129, #40.

76. See CW 235, #71.

77. CW 277, #77.

God, who is so good to me . . . God, who speaks to my
heart in silence and teaches it, little by little, sometimes
through tears and always through the cross, to detach from
creatures and seek perfection in Him alone . . . who shows
me Mary, and tells me, "Behold, the only perfect creature
. . . you will find in Her the love and charity that you do
not find among human beings."[78]

Rafael's love for Our Lady was faithful, uncomplicated, and
sweet, a perfect expression of his heart, equally as ready to love as
to be loved. But maybe the most distinctive feature of the love of
this monk for his heavenly queen was his absolute confidence in
her; his trust in her was that of a child who lives always under his
mother's loving gaze:

I hope for everything through You . . . for who am I to
dare to ask for anything? But if You intercede for me . . .
then there's nothing I won't dare to ask for.
And how could You not hear my prayer, knowing how
much Your poor Trappist loves You so?
Oh sweet Virgin Mary! Pray for me, and for all sinners
like me. Don't forget, Mother, that I am Your son, though I
am the littlest.[79]

HUMILITY, OBEDIENCE, AND WORK

Saint Benedict clearly states from the first lines of his Rule a
prerequisite for following the spiritual plan he is about to spell
out: "This message of mine is for you, then, if you are ready to give
up your own will, once for all."[80] As André Louf explains, the
word *will*, and even more specifically *self-will*, has a particular
meaning in early monastic writing:

78. CW 638, #185.
79. CW 294, #79.
80. RB Prol. 3.

In these texts, the will is obviously not understood as the spiritual faculty that loves or as the source of freedom and self-gift. No one is being asked to eliminate within himself the deep dynamism of personhood. To the contrary, the cutting off of self-will aims at the enhancement of freedom, but a freedom in harmony with the truth of the human being.[81]

In the Holy Rule, we find a practical way in which our will can be purified and effectively achieve the purpose it was designed for: union with God and our fellow human beings in love. As Saint Bernard explains, "The will, properly so-called, is that by which we assent, and by which our human liberty inclines. This means that the desires and longings that hold us without our consent are not the will, but a corruption of the will."[82] The monastic *conversatio* is the means to cleanse the will of this corruption, which Bernard considers a leprosy of the heart. This process is to be accomplished following the example of Christ, in this way passing from our self-will (*voluntas propria*) to a will that is common to God and the other members of the religious community (*voluntas communis*). This fundamental conversion of the will occurs when monks or nuns focus on searching for the glory of God and the profit of their neighbor instead of being centered in the self in exclusion of others. In the Benedictine-Cistercian tradition the conversion of the will is accomplished through the free embrace of humility and obedience.

Obedience is a practical way of living in humility. It shows outwardly that we recognize the truth of our dependence on God and on those who legitimately represent his authority. It cleanses

81. André Louf, *In the School of Contemplation*, trans. Paul Rowe, MW 48 (Collegeville, MN: Cistercian Publications, 2015), 60.

82. Saint Bernard explains the conversion process of the will to which monastics are called in his third sermon *On the Resurrection of the Lord* (Bernard of Clairvaux, *Sermons for Lent and the Easter Season*, trans. Irene Edmonds, CF 52 [Collegeville, MN: Cistercian Publications, 2013], 170).

us from the second expression of the leprosy of the heart, according to Saint Bernard: self-counsel—"taking counsel with yourself alone"—and preferring one's "own judgment to [that of] the whole community."[83]

Obedience and humility were the form of Christ's existence on earth: "for I have come down from heaven, not to do my own will, but the will of him who sent me" (John 6:38). The emphasis that Benedictine and Cistercian spirituality puts on humility and obedience is meant to foster the transformation into Christ of each monk and nun, not to serve other practical purposes, such as facilitating the practical functioning of the monastery. But neither obedience nor humility comes naturally. Both of them are the lifelong interior task of the monk, the work within any other work, an expression of one's love for God and neighbor, and openness to the truth about oneself and the source of all truth: God.

The daily round of work in a monastery is a basic means and expression of both obedience and humility. Traditionally, a task was assigned to each monk every morning, and the monk's only acceptable response (without a word's being said) was to go ahead and perform it. Rafael participated in this daily ritual with sincere humility and obedience. The fact that he had been brought up as a pampered child didn't prevent him from fully embracing this aspect of the community life at San Isidro and the community's way of supporting itself through humble manual labor. On the contrary, he quickly understood the role of mutual service according to the Rule of Saint Benedict:

> Here we all sweep and help each other with everything
> . . . Last week my esteemed Father Master was serving food
> . . . This morning a respectable priest with white hair helped
> me wrap chocolates, and later I helped him at the conventual
> Mass.

83. Bernard of Clairvaux, *Sermons for Lent,* CF 52:171.

So, life at La Trapa is not well understood, because it is compared with the world, but in truth, life in the world is completely different.

At work, at mealtimes, and at rest, and in the cemetery, we are all equal . . . even though there is a pyramid from Reverend Father Abbot down to the newest novice, on which each of us has his place, his role, and his dignity. That is, in a Cistercian monastery, hierarchy and equality are blended together: it is a perfect society, as much as can be expected among men.[84]

For these reasons, in the same letter quoted above, Rafael explained to his parents the honor of performing any task for the glory of God:

What you shouldn't do is worry about whether my hands are using a paintbrush or a hoe . . . in the eyes of God it's all the same, so long as they are being used for His greater glory . . . and He can be praised through anything . . . With the hoe in the fields, with the pen at home . . . with the thurible in church, so long as you don't put them down . . . so that one day you can present yourself before God and, showing Him your hands covered in calluses and chilblains, say to Him, "Lord, the works I have carried out are poor and insignificant, my hands have labored poorly . . . but, Lord, I did it all in Your name, and every time my body bent down over the ground to earn my daily bread, my heart was lifted up to You so that I might someday gain heaven." It is a great consolation to have calluses for love of God.[85]

Rafael came back to the monastery because he wanted to obey and embrace the humility, and even the humiliation, it implied. This fact may sound strange to our contemporary mentality, which

84. CW 99–100, #33.
85. CW 97, #33.

mistakes freedom for having no limitations to pursue our own desires. Conversely, Rafael was aware that only obedience and humility can purify our wills from superficial desires and lead us to the fulfillment of our deepest desire of union with God. He explains this fact in a letter to his Aunt María Osorio:

> In the world, I did whatever I wanted, I sought out the consolation that my soul demanded, and my actions were for the sake of God's glory, but I was always guided by my own will and my own way of seeing things.
>
> Now it's different, I can't do whatever I want . . . well honestly, I don't want anything, but you know what I mean. My renunciation is not yet as perfect as it ought to be, but my desire is to give myself over to Jesus in all things, and I can clearly see that obedience is the way to do that . . . If only you knew, it's not difficult when you truly see the Lord's will in even the most minor details. Anyway, it is all a great mercy.[86]

Through this process of renunciation and self-gift in the humble work traced by daily mutual obedience in community, the harmony between the divine will and the human will grows. Within the Cistercian tradition, this harmony of wills is the best expression of union with God in love, love understood not so much as a feeling but what Elizabeth Connor describes as "a deep intentional concurrence of human will with the divine will,"[87] an inclination of the heart or ability to love what God loves, which is shown through actions. This is the framework of monastic conversion that Rafael embraced wholeheartedly, as we see in these words:

> There's something better than cilices and disciplines, and that is conforming *entirely* to the will of God and asking nothing

---

86. CW 398–99, #105.

87. Elizabeth Connor, *Charles Dumont, Monk-Poet: A Spiritual Biography*, MW 10 (Kalamazoo, MI: Cistercian Publications, 2007), 122–23.

of Him, and desiring nothing. Often, in thinking about those words *ask and it will be given you,* and how needy we are, even as I would ask things of God . . . I'd say to myself, "Lord, I ask *nothing* of you . . . but enclosed in that dry 'nothing' is everything that You can give me, which I cannot quite understand, for you give me so much that my imagination cannot encompass it . . . May my will be Your will; my desires, Your desires; my interests, those of Jesus; my loves, those of Jesus. I want nothing that You do not want."[88]

As Rafael kept surrendering control of his life to God, accepting his illness and the humiliations that followed, he was stripped of more and more layers of his self-will, until only the desire "to be the last in everything, except *obedience*" and to love remained.[89] In his own eyes he was like a circus clown[90] when, because of his fragile health, his work was reduced to wrapping chocolates in the factory of the abbey, peeling vegetables, or sweeping the infirmary. The feelings of embarrassment and humiliation for his personal situation weighed on him, as well as the lack of fresh air and of the contemplation of nature, in which he had formerly delighted. But still he pressed on, and found a new form of freedom and joy, born of humility and obedience. He had become a living example of the internal dispositions that Saint Benedict depicts in his steps of humility (RB 7), as he shows in his words after accepting the distress of being sent once more to work in the darkness of the abbey factory: "I will not ask You for rest on this earth, Lord. I want to obey Your will until the very end . . . Teach me, just as You have been doing up to now . . . in solitude and distress, in pure faith . . . in the abyss of my nothingness . . . in the arms of the cross. What do I need in order to be happy? Nothing, for I desire nothing."[91]

88. CW 131–32, #40.
89. CW 607, #170.
90. CW 425, #113.
91. CW 624, #180.

It is significant that this process brought Rafael, probably without his knowledge, to the core of Saint Bernard's understanding of the word *labora*. In Bernard's works, Charles Dumont points out, the word *labora* "means *dolor* or affliction and toil of the monastic ascesis, and only rarely denotes manual labor."[92] In Rafael's humble obedience to God and his legitimate superiors as mediations of his will, he embraced to perfection the main work of the monk: that of searching for God and becoming one with him.

HOLINESS AND ASCESIS

The experience of God's profound love for him awakened Rafael's desire to respond in kind by becoming holy, a hidden, ordinary holiness that simply meant to love God without reserve, "*God alone.*" Becoming a Trappist, one of those "whose only occupation is to become saints,"[93] seemed the best path to follow, giving himself to love God without reserve in the silence and solitude of the cloister. Rafael found in his life in La Trapa a way to suffer with the Christ who suffers, a way to love the God who loves and is not loved. Embracing the ascetical aspect of the monastic way of life, accentuated by his own illness, Rafael was able to respond to the God who longed for his love.

The Cistercian tradition, and even more the Trappist reform, has always emphasized the connection between the ascetic and the contemplative dimensions—there is no real prayer without the cultivation of virtue. This teaching was very much in force when Rafael joined the Abbey of San Isidro: the penitential part inherent in monastic practices was the purification voluntarily embraced to free heart and will for the contemplation of God. As in Gilbert of Hoyland's beautiful image of the bride of the Song

---

92. Connor, *Charles Dumont, Monk-Poet*, 107.
93. CW 161, #49.

of Songs,[94] the hands of the one who earnestly awaits the arrival
of Christ need to be scented with myrrh—a symbol of the passion—to be able to open the door to the Beloved as soon as he
comes: "Good indeed are hands scented with myrrh, which practice mortification of the flesh, which check its laxity, constrain its
wantonness, that the entrance may be wider for the enjoyment of
the Word. Do you not regard as drops of myrrh these works of
regular observance, which following one upon another anoint the
mind and constrain the flesh?"[95] Vigils, a simple diet, manual
work: all these are ways to open wide the door to the Word, but
when Christ enters, he enters not only into us but also into the
world to bring his salvation, just as he did through Mary's *fiat*.

This dynamic has been the program for spiritual progress since
the times of early monasticism, when as Harmless writes, "the
regimen was intensely physical, both its initial renunciations (of
homeland, wealth, pleasures, and marriage) and its daily disciplines
(fasting, vigils, and manual labor). Every human art has its tools,
and these renunciations and disciplines were part of the monastic
"art," the "tools of perfection."[96] Rafael, himself an artist, understood this well, and to his initial renunciations when he joined the
monastery, he added those that God granted him through his
illness: hunger and thirst, the loneliness caused by the separation
from and misunderstanding by the community, and the humiliation of not being able to follow the Rule in its entirety.

Saint Benedict, at the end of his Prologue, clearly states that
the path toward God "is bound to be narrow at the outset."[97] In
Rafael's case, the path narrows, and narrows at a quick pace, stripping his heart from everything but God alone. But as the patriarch

94. "I arose to open to my beloved, and my hands dripped with myrrh" (Song
5:5).

95. Gilbert of Hoyland, *Sermons on the Song of Songs, III*, trans. Lawrence
Braceland, CF 26 (Kalamazoo, MI: Cistercian Publications, 1979), 523 (S 43.8).

96. Harmless, *Desert Christians*, 390.

97. RB Prol. 48.

of monks recommends, Rafael didn't "run away from the road that leads to salvation."[98] On the contrary, he made of the cross his mirror, the example to guide him along his path toward God alone, just as Aelred of Rievaulx recommended to his brothers:

> In Christ's cross there is nothing tender, nothing soft, nothing delicate, nothing pleasant for the flesh and blood. So let this cross be henceforth like a mirror for the Christian. Let him look at himself in the cross of Christ to see if his own life and his way of living is in agreement with this cross. To the extent that he participates in the cross of Christ, he can hope to share in Christ's glory [see 2 Tim 2:1-12]. . . . You, my brothers, see how you should rejoice, you are crucified with Christ himself.[99]

Rafael found his place in the church and the world by embracing monastic life, and through it by joining in the oblation of Christ. On this path he also discovered lasting joy and peace as his heart, transformed into Christ's, expanded with new love not only for God but for all human beings:

> You've already given me *light* so that I might see and understand, Lord; now give me a very, very big heart so that I can *love* human beings, who are Your children, and my brothers and sisters. My great pride saw flaws in them, while I was blind to my own. [. . .]
> I'm so happy. I have it all! . . .
> When you love Jesus, when you love Christ, you also *necessarily* love what He loves. Did Jesus not die of love for human beings? As our hearts are transformed into the heart of Christ, then we too feel this and note its effects . . . and

98. RB Prol. 48.

99. Aelred of Rievaulx, *The Liturgical Sermons: The First Clairvaux Collection*, trans. Theodore Berkeley and Basil Pennington, CF 58 (Kalamazoo, MI: Cistercian Publications, 2001), 180 (S 10.29–30).

the greatest of them all is *love*. [. . .] In short, who can comprehend the heart of Christ? No one. But there are those who have tiny pieces of it . . . very hidden away . . . very much in silence, without letting the world notice.[100]

God gave Rafael the "very big heart" he prayed for. This is precisely the kind of heart that Saint Benedict had described at the end of his Prologue, the outcome of persevering on the narrow road that leads to salvation: a heart expanded and "overflowing with the inexpressible delight of love."[101] On his last Holy Thursday, twelve days before his death, Rafael recorded in his journal what his heart, stretched by his sufferings in and for Christ, experienced. Now the whole world had found a place within him. Joining himself to the oblation of Christ, his vocation and mission were fulfilled. In his prayer, he had told Jesus, "Lord, *take me and give Yourself to the world*. Take what You have given me and give it to them . . . Let me distribute the treasure I have to the needy of the world . . . there are so many! Let me be poor at Your side . . . I want nothing more than Your love, Your friendship . . . Your companionship . . . Take me, Lord, as I am."[102]

Transformed into another Christ, Rafael had become the kind of saint he had desired to be: his life cast like the seed into the darkness of the earth to die and bear abundant fruit.[103] He had become a true monk: one who is unified in the love of God alone. With a heart purified, made whole, and overflowing, now he could see God even in the obscurity of the cross, and with him become fire.[104]

100. CW 683–84, #202.
101. RB Prol. 49.
102. CW 689, #204.
103. See John 12:24.
104. "For indeed our God is a consuming fire" (Heb 12:29).

CHAPTER 6

A Spirituality of Desire

"Is there anyone here who yearns for life and desires to see good days?" This is the question that Saint Benedict asks in the Prologue of the Rule, quoting Psalm 34:12. The Rule addresses those who yearn or long for more. "The voice of the Lord is calling to us," it continues. And, in response, the Rule offers the way to those who are filled with longing: they must "run on the path of God's commandments, our hearts overflowing with the inexpressible delight of love." Saint Benedict devotes his penultimate chapter to the "good zeal of monks" (RB 72). Zeal is a characteristic of the true monk, he teaches. *Yearning, desire, running, a heart overflowing with love, a passionate zeal*—all these words describe both the monastic vision of Saint Benedict and the monastic journey of Rafael Arnaiz. Virtually every page of Rafael's writings reveals his passion for God. And it is his yearning love for God that impelled him to keep returning to the monastery despite whatever obstacle might arise.

Saint Benedict teaches that newcomers to the monastery are not to be granted an easy entrance (RB 58). They must "keep knocking," showing themselves patient in bearing with this apparent slowness to receive them, and they must be persistent in the face of the difficulty of entrance. When discerning the candidate's vocation, Benedict advises, "the concern must be whether the novice truly seeks God and whether he shows eagerness for trials. The novice should be clearly told all the hardships and

165

difficulties that will lead him to God" (RB 58.7-8). In writing his Rule, Saint Benedict cannot have conceived of a distinctive monastic vocation like that of Rafael, but there can be no doubt that Rafael showed himself ready to keep knocking and even eager for whatever trials might come—all because of his passionate seeking of God.

CARMELITE . . . AND CISTERCIAN

The spirituality of the great sixteenth-century Spanish mystics John of the Cross and Teresa of Ávila was characterized by a strong element of affectivity. On the surface was the language of desire and yearning, but beneath the level of simple, natural feelings and emotions was a profound existential need and hunger for God. Speaking in poetic terms, John of the Cross spoke of the deep caverns of the soul that, activated by God's grace, are an infinite capacity to receive the inflow of God. And since the soul's capacity is infinite, it experiences an infinite thirst and hunger for the infinite God, and its "languishing and suffering are infinite death."[1]

As we have noted—and will examine more closely below—Rafael's spirituality shows the influence of the strong affectivity of the great Spanish mystics. What appears less explicitly but is nonetheless true is that his spirituality also resonates with themes central to the works of early Cistercian writers, such as a focus on the humanity of Christ—particularly his passion—on the centrality of desire, on simplicity, and on the mutual love of God and human persons. For example, Saint Bernard presents Jesus as "A dear friend, a wise counselor, a strong helper."[2] The humanity of Christ, and particularly his sweetness (of which the Cistercian writers repeatedly speak), have a function in the salvation of humankind:

1. John of the Cross, *The Living Flame of Love*, stanza 3, paragraph 22 in *The Collected Works of St. John of the Cross*, trans. Kieran Kavanaugh and Otilio Rodriguez, 3rd ed. (Washington, DC: ICS Publications, 2017), 681.

2. Bernard of Clairvaux, *On the Song of Songs I*, trans. Kilian Walsh, CF 4 (Spencer, MA: Cistercian Publications, 1971), 149 (S 20.3).

"to capture the affections of carnal men who were unable to love [Christ] in any other way, by first drawing them to the salutary love of his own humanity, and then gradually to raise them to a spiritual love."[3] In Rafael's life we recognize the same process that Bernard describes in the lives of the apostles: moving from a fleshly love to a spiritual love, that is, from an unwise form of love ("following your human feeling in opposition to the divine plan"[4]) to a love that has been purified and strengthened by entering into the Paschal mystery and the grace of the Holy Spirit.

Even though Rafael rarely uses spousal imagery, the way in which he lived his relationship with Christ is indebted to these forms of theology and spirituality that present love as the way to God *par excellence.* The Cistercian writers of the twelfth and thirteenth centuries interpreted the mutual search of God and the soul in the light of the Song of Songs, animated by ardent spiritual desire. Bernard passionately asks, "When will our frailty be able to sense this about God: that he loves us with the same deep affection that a bridegroom has for his bride?"[5] This is the golden thread that runs through the mysticism of the Cistercian and Carmelite writers, a love characterized by mutuality and desire. Thinking about it, Rafael felt deeply moved, as he wrote to his Aunt María: "As I walk, I do nothing but ask the valleys and mountains, and the creatures I encounter on the way, and humans and animals, and the earth and the sky, if they have seen my Beloved,[6] 'him I love most.' This thought gives me wings; I am always so moved inside."[7]

---

3. Bernard of Clairvaux, *On the Song of Songs I,* 152 (S 20.6).

4. Bernard of Clairvaux, *On the Song of Songs I,* 151 (S 20.5).

5. Bernard of Clairvaux, "On Changing Water into Wine," in *Sermons for Advent and the Christmas Season,* trans. Irene Edmonds, Wendy Mary Beckett, and Conrad Greenia, CF 51 (Kalamazoo, MI: Cistercian Publications, 2007), 187.

6. *Have you seen him whom my soul loves?* (Song 3:3).

7. CW 279, #77 (Document 77 in Saint Rafael Arnaiz, *The Collected Works* [CW], ed. María Gonzalo-García, trans. Catherine Addington, MW 162 [Collegeville, MN: Cistercian Publications, 2022]).

Mutuality in love is a distinctive feature of Cistercian mysticism. Bernard speaks about it in these terms: "Love is the only one of the motions of the soul, of its senses and affections, in which the creature can respond to its Creator, even if not as an equal, and repay his favor in some similar way."[8] Later he adds, "Although the creature loves less, being a lesser being, yet if it loves with its whole heart nothing is lacking, for it has given all."[9] Rafael found an application of this principle in Saint John of the Cross's poetry. John wrote along the same lines in his explanation of the twenty-eighth stanza of his *Spiritual Canticle*: "For the property of love is to make the lover equal to the object loved. Since the soul in this state possesses perfect love, she is called the bride of the Son of God, which signifies equality with him."[10]

The security of being loved and being able to love supported Rafael's search for God even during its most trying moments. Rafael knew and trusted that his desire for God was founded in God's desire for him. Bernard expresses this same confidence: "Since I love, I cannot doubt that I am loved, any more than I can doubt that I love. . . . In what have I known it? In this—not only has he sought me as I am, but he has shown me tenderness, and caused me to seek him with confidence."[11] Similarly, John of the Cross affirms, "In the first place it should be known that if anyone is seeking God, the Beloved is seeking that person much more."[12]

These few examples show that even though Rafael probably did not have the opportunity to study the writings of the Cistercians of the golden age, his monastic instinct allowed him to find in the spiritual sources that were accessible to him the essential

---

8. Bernard of Clairvaux, *On the Song of Songs IV*, trans. Irene Edmonds, CF 40 (Kalamazoo, MI: Cistercian Publications, 1980), 184 (S 83.4).

9. Bernard of Clairvaux, *On the Song of Songs IV*, 186 (S 83.6).

10. *Spiritual Canticle* (28.1) in *Collected Works of St. John of the Cross*, 584.

11. Bernard of Clairvaux, *On the Song of Songs IV*, 192–93 (S 84.6).

12. "The Living Flame of Love," in *Collected Works of St. John of the Cross*, 684 (LF 3.28).

elements of an authentic Cistercian spirituality. He was, after all, called to the same life that these men and women had lived, and he freely embraced that call. Rafael's desire for God alone expresses the same determination that had guided the Cistercian reform to look for simplicity in everything, so that nothing would hinder their encounter with the God they ardently loved.

TEARS AND COMPUNCTION

At a purely natural level, Rafael was a man of deep emotion and heartfelt affection for family and friends. This is obvious in his letters as he writes to family and in his journals, describing, for example, the pain of telling his parents about his decision to join the monastery and the difficulty of leaving them with each return to the monastery. The word *tears* appears frequently in his writings.[13] He was not a man afraid to express his feelings in tears or to speak of them, whether tears of sorrow or tears of joy.

But Rafael himself describes two different types or experiences of tears.[14] One type is very human and sometimes a sign of weakness in bearing the trials of life, leading to bitterness: "weeping sorrowful tears that embitter the heart and do not bring consolation."[15] He was no stranger to these very human tears—whether in departing from home and family or in experiencing the trials of monastic life, community interaction, and his repeated personal setbacks. The other type of tears, he says, is of fundamental spiritual value and

13. See the many citations of his tears ("*lágrimas*") in Alberico Feliz Carbajal, ed., *Hermano Rafael: escritos por temas*, 2nd ed. (Burgos, Spain: Editorial Monte Carmelo, 2000), 453–56.

14. Antonio María Martín Fernández-Gallardo, *El deseo de Dios y la ciencia de la Cruz: aproximación a la experiencia del Hermano Rafael* (Burgos, Spain: Editorial Monte Carmelo, 2002), 248–56 (hereafter cited as Martín). See also Francisco Cerro Chaves, *Silencio en los labios, cantares en el corazón: vida y espiritualidad el Hermano Rafael* (Madrid: Biblioteca de autores cristianos, 2000), 142–43.

15. CW 486, #138.

even a divine gift—what the monastic tradition calls tears of compunction.[16] These tears flow as a recognition of the sins that separate one from God and prevent one from realizing the goal of one's deepest yearning. Tears of compunction promote humility and surrender to God, and they serve as a further impetus to overcome obstacles to attaining communion with God. These tears, writes Rafael, are an expression of love; they are precious, and they intensify one's yearning for God:

> There was a poor brother at La Trapa who often wept before the cross. The world was saying to him, "You're an idiot, weeping by choice is foolish, you're uselessly wasting your life with all that silence and penance. Why love the cross when life is so beautiful? Freedom is bright, not gloomy!" But that Trappist kept on weeping and weeping, and his tears were sweet sighs in his heart, placed lovingly at the Virgin's feet. He wouldn't have traded a single one of his tears for all the gold in the world . . . That Trappist wept, but he wept for joy . . . What does the world know of love? Blessed is foolishness for Christ, which turns tears into pearls and makes us love the cross.[17]

Rafael believed that Christ values such tears, viewing them as an offering to God: "If only you realized that each tear shed for My love while doing penance in the cloister is a gift that makes all the angels of heaven sing for joy."[18] And, he says, in the offering of one's tears, there is comfort and renewed strength even in the midst of trials: "Tears shed at Your cross's side are a balm in this life of continual renunciation and sacrifice, and those sacrifices

---

16. John Cassian, whose works so influenced the Rule of Saint Benedict, writes of the relationship between compunction and tears. See Columba Stewart, *Cassian the Monk*, Oxford Studies in Historical Theology (New York: Oxford University Press, 1998), 122–29. See also RB 20.3; 49.4.

17. CW 570, #162. See also CW 597, #168.

18. CW 623–24, #180.

and renunciations are made pleasant and easy when the soul is alive with love, faith, and hope."[19] They also bring one into communion with Jesus in his sufferings: "What great intimacy Jesus has with those who mourn! Blessed are our tears, sorrows, and illnesses, which are our treasures, all that we possess. They make us draw near to Jesus, since the love we have for Him is so little, so feeble, so weak that it is not enough on its own . . . !"[20]

At the level of personality and character, Rafael describes himself as prone to being overly sensitive to the perceived rudeness or criticisms of others:

> There is one thing that causes me alarm, and makes me suffer greatly . . . and that is my excessive sensitivity. Anything can bring me joy, but any mishap can make me cry; this demonstrates how far behind I am when it comes to virtue. One time, a brother struck a very personal nerve with me, without meaning to, and I cried bitterly. At first, I thought my tears were because I was humiliated; later, upon reconsideration, I realized that they were also imbued with some pride. I am like a very finely tuned guitar, whose strings vibrate at the slightest twitch in the air or the slightest graze . . . I should make myself stronger; souls that have truly been entrusted to God do not cry when somebody offends them . . . Did they not scourge Christ?[21]

This affective bent of Rafael's personality and proneness to tears may help to explain, to some degree, his attraction to the language

---

19. CW 684, #202.

20. CW 569, #162.

21. CW 180, #51. See also the several examples of Rafael commenting on his sensitivity listed in *San Rafael Arnaiz: Obras completas* [OC], 7th ed. (Burgos, Spain: Editorial Monte Carmelo, 2017), 860–61, n. 1036. In fact, the editor notes that one of the official censors who reviewed Rafael's work as part of the beatification process commented on this characteristic as perhaps weighing against the authenticity of Rafael's heroic virtues. The editor strongly refutes this idea, and it did not obstruct Rafael's beatification process.

of affective spirituality. But the explanation is more fundamentally his deep-seated and awakened desire for God. One Spanish Cistercian commentator has concluded that Rafael's desire for God was perhaps the foundational element of his entire spirituality.[22] That desire runs through all of his writings, gaining in intensity as he passes through each trial. Rafael's constant mantra "God alone" (*Sólo Dios*) is a kind of shorthand expression of his longing.

A Longing for Holiness

Early in his writings, Rafael often expresses his desire for God as a longing—for holiness, to be a saint. He describes "a mad desire to be holy."[23] In a letter to his novice master, written shortly before his first entrance to the monastery, Rafael writes that he is seeking to be a saint in the hidden and ordinary life of the monastery. In expressing the shape of the sanctity that he is pursuing, he already demonstrates a maturity in his desire as well as a sense of authentic monastic holiness:

> The monastery will be two things for me: first, a corner of the world where I can praise God night and day without obstacles, and second, a purgatory on earth where I can become purified, become perfect, and become holy . . . Saying it like that, so casually . . . "become holy" . . . it seems like an aspiration that's a bit . . . I don't know how to put it, but that's the truth. I want to be holy in the eyes of God, not in those of men; a holiness that develops in the choir, in the fields, and above all, a holiness that develops in silence, and that only God knows about, that not even I should discover, for then it would not be true holiness.[24]

22. Martín, "El deseo de Dios," in *Deseo de Dios*, 115–47, chap. 4.
23. CW 281, #77.
24. CW 66, #21.

After the disappointment of his first departure, Rafael sees that his desire for holiness, though real, had been too narrow and even naïve. True holiness, he realizes, requires embracing reality as we find it—not as we dream it to be—and, fundamentally, surrendering completely to God's will just as it is.[25] As his faith matures, Rafael writes less explicitly about holiness and being a saint, and his focus turns to living a life surrendered to the will of God, embracing the cross as he finds it before him. He no longer idealizes holiness but rather simply tries to pursue it and live it out in the circumstances of his life, even as he experiences within a deeper longing to love Christ even more madly, with greater excess.[26] His desire and pursuit of holiness becomes increasingly expressed in terms like *ofrecerse* (to offer oneself), *abandonarse* (to abandon oneself), and *entregarse* (to surrender or hand oneself over).[27]

Examining Rafael's desire for holiness, Spanish commentators have noted that what Rafael possessed and many people lack is a deep and real desire coupled with a firm commitment to embrace whatever is necessary to be conformed to God in Christ. Many Christians desire holiness, and they pass through periods of real zeal for it, but they lack the willingness truly to die completely to what is false within themselves and to surrender completely to the divine will by embracing, in faith, whatever life throws at them. And so they fall short not for a lack of fervor or zeal, piety or devotion, or even the lack of a life of prayer and sincere love for God and neighbor, but rather because of a largely unconscious unwillingness to take the final step of authentic self-forgetfulness, blind faith, and surrender to God, whatever may come. Rafael,

---

25. See Rafael's letter to his novice master after his first departure (CW 203–5, #61) and his letter to the abbot asking for readmission as an oblate (CW 214–20, #64).

26. Cerro Chaves, *Silencio en los labios*, 337.

27. All three terms—whether as verbs or nouns—appear frequently in Rafael's writings. See Alberico Feliz Carbajal, *Escritos por temas*: "*abandonar*," 18–20; "*entregar*," 340–42; "*ofrecer*," 551–54.

over time and through his struggles, is a witness to what authentic holiness requires—even as he stops speaking explicitly of his desire to become a saint.

LONGING (*ANSIA*)

Longing/yearning (*ansia*) is a frequently used word in Rafael's vocabulary.[28] He experiences his desire for God as a profound hunger or thirst. It is a yearning totally different from the desire that many people experience for the superficial and passing things of this life.[29] The word *ansia* first appears in a letter Rafael wrote to his novice master as he prepared for his first entry to the monastery, describing himself as "eager [*ansia*] to fill myself with Him."[30] The word appears fourteen times in a later journal entry titled "As a Deer Longs for Flowing Streams" (Ps 42:1), in which Rafael reflects that his longing for God is like that of a desperate, thirsting deer, fleeing hunters, in search of hidden, flowing streams. He expresses his longing here too as a profound and aching thirst. The entry begins:

> Longing for eternal life . . . Longing to fly unto true life.
> The longings of a soul subject to the body, wailing to see
> God. It is a great suffering to live when all that remains in
> life is the hope of dying . . . the hope of death . . . the hope
> of an end, so that we might begin . . . Living is hard, but
> the hope that everything will come to an end does make it
> all easier. Longings for eternal life flutter about the choir in
> our church, even when the monastery is enveloped by the
> darkness of night.[31]

28. See some of the term's multiple occurrences in Feliz Carbajal, *Escritos por temas*, 1023.
29. CW 665–67, #196.
30. CW 51, #15.
31. CW 481, #137.

The passage above reflects a common spirit of classic love mysticism in which the soul longs for death in order to be fully united with Christ. Saint Paul expresses a similar sentiment when he writes, "For to me, living is Christ and dying is gain. . . . I am hard pressed between the two: my desire is to depart and be with Christ, for that is far better; but to remain in the flesh is more necessary for you" (Phil 1:21, 23-24). As the journal entry continues, Rafael quotes and reflects on the opening stanza of a poem by Saint Teresa of Ávila:[32]

> I live without living in myself,
> And in such a way I hope,
> I die because I do not die.[33]

Neither Saint Teresa nor Rafael is disparaging physical life, but they long for what lies beyond. Such fervent longing, says Rafael, is a grace. He writes later, in the same reflection on the deer that yearns,

> Great is divine mercy when it grants the soul a certain condition in which everything inspires it to lift its heart high above all created and earthly things. When the soul is in pain because it cannot see God, what does it care about the world? When the spirit loses itself in reflection on eternity,

32. Rafael had quoted the same stanza in an earlier journal entry. See CW 412, #108.

33. CF 483, #137. See *The Collected Works of St. Teresa of Ávila*, trans. Kieran Kavanaugh and Otilio Rodriguez (Washington, DC: ICS Publications, 1985), 3:375. The second line of this ICS translation does not coincide literally with the text that Rafael is quoting ("*y tan alta vida espero*"), which might literally be translated, "and such a high life I expect/hope for." This may reflect some differences in the Spanish manuscripts of Saint Teresa's poems—with ICS using one version ("*y de tal manera espero*") and Rafael using the other ("*y tan alta vida espero*"). Rafael's use is consistent with the poem as it appears in Santa Teresa de Jesús, *Obras Completas*, ed. Alberto Barrientos, 5th ed. (Madrid: Editorial de Espiritualidad, 2000), 1153.

what could it possibly care about the limited brevity of its own life? When the heart yearns for its homeland in heaven and union with the Eternal One, how could it not be indifferent toward this valley of tears in which it is exiled for a short time?[34]

Rafael also finds inspiration and vocabulary to express his experience in the work of Saint Teresa's contemporary, John of the Cross, alluding frequently to John's *Spiritual Canticle*, which was itself inspired by the biblical Song of Songs. Rafael resonates with the yearning of the bride seeking her Beloved.[35] A number of times, he quotes a line from the first stanza of John's *The Living Flame of Love*—"tear through the veil of this sweet encounter!"—in which the soul expresses its longing for that full union with God that surpasses any that can be attained in this life.[36]

In a journal entry written shortly before his third departure from the monastery, titled "Just God and Me," Rafael begins:

Silence on the lips, songs in the heart; a soul that lives on love, on dreams and hopes . . . a soul that lives for God. A soul that turns its gaze far away . . . so far from this world, spending this life in silence . . . singing in its heart. A monastery . . . a Trappist monastery . . . men. It's just God and me! The days pass quickly, and life with them . . . We dream about the past and hope for what is to come . . . The soul turns its gaze far away, seeking out true life, which is looking down from above a sea of hopes, and the soul hopes for better things. A Trappist monastery . . . songs for God. Who cares about human beings? Who cares whether it's

34. CF 482, #137.

35. See Rafael's citations of *The Spiritual Canticle*: CW ## 70, 75 (2x), 76, 78, 81, 99, 100, 145, 162 (2x).

36. See for example CW 526, #150. The full stanza reads, "O living flame of love / that tenderly wounds my soul / in its deepest center! Since / now you are not oppressive, / now consummate! if it be your will: / tear through the veil of this sweet encounter!" (*Collected Works of St. John of the Cross*, 52).

foggy or sunny? . . . Who cares about our surroundings? All of that is nothing, and nothingness is not worth our attention. The soul is looking for what it cannot find here . . . it is searching anxiously for God in the heights [*"Busca en las alturas sus ansias de Dios"*].[37]

Later in the same journal entry, Rafael continues:

The soul has no interest in anything but Christ. It is not moved by anything but God. It hides its longings [*ansias*], sorrows, crosses, and love deep within itself. Everything tires it out now. It no longer seeks in human beings what they can never give. For this soul there is no heaven or earth, no people or animals, no world at all, just mortal dust . . . The soul has only one occupation, and it fills its whole life: yearning [*ansia*] greatly for heaven, and adoring God.[38]

MADNESS OF LOVE (*LOCURA DE AMOR*)

Rafael's yearning for God is grounded in a profound sense of being loved by God and loving God in return. He often speaks of being "madly in love" with Christ and with God—of the madness of love: "I am thirsty for You . . . I weep for my exile, I dream of heaven; my soul longs for Jesus, in whom it finds its Treasure, its Life, its only Love; I expect nothing from human beings . . . My Jesus, I love You like crazy, and even so, I eat, laugh, sleep, talk, study, and live among human beings without doing anything crazy."[39] Indeed, he longs to love even more madly as he yearns to be with Christ: "You, Lord, whom I desire so much, whom I adore, whom I love above all things, for whom I long and pine and weep, and for whom, as You well know, my good Jesus, I want

---

37. CW 516, #147.
38. CW 517, #147.
39. CW 683, #202.

to lose my mind [*quisiera volverme loco*]."[40] Only three weeks before his death, he writes, "I want only to love You madly, with wild abandon [*amarte con frenesí, con locura*]."[41] One commentator has concluded that Rafael's "mad love" for Christ was an essential element in his embrace of his trials without reserve.[42] His attitude reflects a spirit that he shares with early Cistercian and Franciscan authors.

But the madness of love for God in Christ is not something that Rafael wanted only for himself. He wished that he could communicate it to all the world and fill everyone with the same frenzy of love. He writes to his uncle,

> I would so like to communicate to the whole world, so that the whole world would love God madly, and not think of anything else, and everyone would be very happy, as I am now, I who have nothing, not even my health, yet have everything . . . everything one can have in this life. I have God deep within my heart and want for nothing.[43]

But for the world to experience the same love for God would require people to turn their focus away from purely material and passing things. They would have to see that the apparent foolishness of loving God above things and in all things is not actually madness at all but the truest wisdom:

> Such is foolishness for Christ . . . with eyes fixed on Jesus, one forgets to eat and fails to fear the cold; neither humble poverty nor love of family can hold back lovers of Jesus . . . God alone . . . only Him . . . that is the only thought that holds power over them . . . the miracle of being madly in

---

40. CW 663, #195.

41. CW 673, #199.

42. Tomás Gallego Fernández, "Hermano Rafael, Loco por Cristo," *Cistercium* 254 (Jan.–June 2010): 60.

43. CW 567–68, #162.

love. The world and all who dwell in it come and go; people keep thinking about their businesses, the future of their estates, their illnesses. They cling to this earth, where they seek their rest. They suffer when they don't find it here, and weep when they have to leave . . . Those are the real fools, even though the world thinks it's foolish to love poverty, contempt, illness, and the cross.[44]

A mature love for God is not a matter of replacing the love of the things of this world with a love of the things that God can provide. Rafael sees that one must love God because of who God is, not in hopes of convincing God to fulfill one's personal dreams, allow attainment of one's spiritual aspirations, or spare one from life's trials—no matter how sincere and pious one's intentions. Rafael tells the abbot in the letter requesting readmission to the monastery as an oblate, "I love God just because, and that's it. Even though I love God very little, my love isn't mercenary. I know that He loves me, and that is enough for me."[45] One must love God madly—not madly seek after the things of the world or foolishly think that we can ultimately know better than God what is for our good.

Knowing How to Wait and to Hope

The Spanish verb *esperar*—used so often by Rafael—can be translated into English in various ways depending on its use in context. *Esperar* can translated as "to wait," "to expect," or "to hope." In Rafael's frequent use of the term, it often conveys the breadth of such meanings. When he calls his readers to *esperar*, he is inviting them to join him in trustful waiting on God, confidently expecting good things from God even when the present seems bleak, and serenely hoping in God whatever the present or future might hold.

44. CW 569–70, #162.
45. CW 217–18, #64.

Rafael longed for God. He was crazy with love. And yet his yearning was tempered by the recognition of the need to wait and to hope. He writes of himself during his final period in the monastery, "Only God and His will occupy my life. In His infinite mercy, He is *tempering* what was once vehement desire."[46] In the end, what matters is complete surrender to the divine will. If God determines that now is not the time for a deeper encounter, then the person must wait in humble trust. Whatever and whenever God wills is what is always best. Rafael, addressing himself, remarks, "Poor Brother Rafael! God has wounded you, but not yet killed you. Wait on . . . wait on with the sweet serenity of a certain hope."[47] It comes down to knowing how to wait: "It's all a matter of knowing how to wait, and in the end, up there, when our lives are over, our souls will quench their thirst at the one true stream, which is God."[48] This is the "science" [*ciencia*] or wisdom that everyone who truly loves and longs for God must learn: "the science to love and wait in hope."[49]

Learning to wait on God teaches and matures our surrender to the divine will. Our longing for God is a great good. Tempered by waiting, it forms us in humility and is the source of a deeper peace: "But I do believe that our longing to see God and our impatience in waiting for Him are made perfect in absolute submission to His will, with the serenity of those who desire nothing."[50] True peace comes with trust in God's mysterious but always loving will. So one must learn to yearn for God with a fervent love, and yet, at the same time, learn to wait on God's good pleasure: "Meanwhile, let us wait, and wait with faith, patience, peace, and love, detached from ourselves, free from our own desires, seeking out neither crosses nor paths. If we are docile, the Lord will point them out to

46. CW 651, #190.
47. CW 500, #141.
48. CW 482, #137.
49. CW 408, #106.
50. CW 572, #162.

us. He'll show us our path or road, and it's all the same so long as they lead us to Him."[51]

Authentic Christian hope is often forged through suffering. It is true that one can hope in God even in the best of times—hope is a divine gift poured out by God on all who walk in grace. But it is trial and suffering that can so often deepen and mature one's hope in God. It is in the darkness that hope is most needed; struggling and learning to hope in God in such difficult times deepen one's hope and endurance. Saint Paul reflected this truth when he wrote, "And not only that, but we also boast in our sufferings, knowing that suffering produces endurance, and endurance produces character, and character produces hope, and hope does not disappoint us, because God's love has been poured into our hearts through the Holy Spirit that has been given to us" (Rom 5:3-5). Rafael knew suffering; he learned endurance, which matured his character, all of it blossoming into an authentic and profoundly mature Christian hope.

Waiting to attain what one most loves and longs for, coupled with hope, puts our trials into their proper perspective. Knowing how to wait on God enables one to embrace life's difficulties as a divine instrument of God's loving, mysterious will:

> Blessed is that foolishness, which makes us live beyond the bonds of this earth, which helps us see the sorrows of our exile through the dazzling lens of hope, the certain hope of a splendid, resplendent day that *will not delay* . . . Blessed is that foolishness for Christ, which makes us realize how vain and small our suffering is, turning our bitter tears into the sweetest of songs, the pain and heartache of this life into the gentle fetters that bind us to Jesus.[52]

51. CW 402, #105.
52. CW 568–69, #162.

Even more than words, it is Rafael's witness of serenity in the midst of waiting and suffering that reveals the power of his insight.

Waiting and hoping, without lessening the depths of one's yearning, yields peace, serenity, and tranquility even in the midst of suffering. One learns to long for God without impatience, and one learns to surrender even in the face of darkness without fear:

> In La Trapa, the Trappist's most sublime moment, his *Te Deum* moment . . . is the moment of his death . . . Am I making sense? . . . Meanwhile, waiting is his life . . . Waiting with faith, with love, with holy peace . . . That is the only *joie de vivre* . . . to burn with love for God, and to know that our God is waiting for us. What does it matter if you're suffering or rejoicing? You have God, don't you? . . . Who are you, meanwhile? Don't worry about yourself, poor thing. You don't even *know* how to suffer, you aren't *capable* of rejoicing . . . Let God take you over, and then you will have neither suffering nor joy . . . you will have peace . . . Your heart will be still and rooted in God, and waiting will be your life . . . and waiting serenely, without being impatient or afraid . . . That is life, that is the only *joie de vivre*.[53]

In chapter seven of his Rule, having explained the arduous steps of humility—of learning to unseat the false self and to surrender to God's will—Saint Benedict declares that the monk will finally "arrive at the perfect love of God which casts out fear" (RB 7.67). Rafael Arnaiz, faithful son of Saint Benedict, fired with a yearning love for God, learned to wait on God's will even in suffering and so arrived at the goal held out by the great monastic teacher.

53. CW 329, #87.

CHAPTER 7

The Cross and Suffering

The monastic life is aimed at purity of heart as the doorway to eternal life. Saint Benedict lays out a path that assumes that his sons and daughters will arrive at this goal through the ordinary rhythms of prayer and work, realized in the midst of community. The daily routine of common and liturgical prayer, personal meditation on the Word of God, careful fidelity to everyday responsibilities, and the very human interactions among members of the community form the foundation of the monastic way. The life entails sacrifice and trials. But the principal sacrifices are not chosen methods of asceticism (fasting, penances, arduous vigils)—though such practices may have their place. Rather, they are the sacrifice of leaving behind the good things that life in the world has to offer, the discipline of remaining faithful one day after another, and the very real trials that arise when sinners live with other sinners. At a yet deeper level, Saint Benedict offers the triad of obedience, silence, and humility (RB 5–7) as tools for purifying the human heart. Each of them is an instrument of self-emptying, of overcoming self-centeredness, and of learning to surrender—ultimately to the mysterious but always loving will of God. This is the path that leads to purity of heart.

Suffering—trials and difficulties that pain us and thwart our plans—is common to every human life. Every human being knows suffering, but, as Rafael insists, not everyone knows how to accept and even embrace those trials in faith so that they can serve as an instrument for transformation. Suffering can simply happen to us, making us its victims, or, once it is inflicted on us, we can choose to embrace it and become not its victim, but its partner. Suffering embraced in faith can become a share in the suffering of Jesus on the cross—as his suffering was a sharing in ours. The cross in our lives can become the most powerful—if most often an unwelcome—tool for the self-emptying that leads to purity of heart in every Christian life. Human persons instinctively and fiercely feel the urge to reject suffering and overcome it, and this is exactly why embracing the suffering that cannot be changed and trusting in God in humble faith can bring us to the deepest surrender.

Rafael Arnaiz began his monastic life filled with enthusiasm and commitment to embrace its trials and sacrifices. Coming from his comfortable and loving background, with opportunities full of promise for a prosperous life in the world, the very fact of entering the monastery—and especially a Trappist monastery of the 1930s!—was already to embrace a substantial renunciation. Whatever further trials that life might bring, he was ready for it all. His writings during his first stay in the monastery manifest his zeal for every aspect of it. Obedience and humility, he presupposed, and the silence, though his sociable and fun-loving nature struggled at times, he affirmed whole-heartedly. It appeared that it was the "ordinary" path of monastic holiness that was to be his course—living life faithfully, praying and working, accepting the challenges of communal living, growing in obedience, silence, and humility. But then, unexpectedly, and as was quite unwelcome at first, he developed diabetes, and suddenly everything changed. Disappointment and suffering were added to—superimposed over—the general monastic tools of self-emptying. And because Rafael embraced in faith this share in the cross as he found it in his life, his trials and disappointments accelerated a process that for most of us takes a lifetime. Dying at a young age, without monastic profession, after having lived relatively little time in the monastery, unable to receive a deeper and broader formal monastic formation—nonetheless, Rafael attained that purity of heart that is at the authentic aim of the monastic life.

Rafael says of himself that he had entered the monastery thinking that the principal task involved taming his sinful human nature, and that he himself was the main agent of its achievement. Shortly after entering the monastery for the first time, he wrote, "Blasted nature, what a pain you are!! But I hope that with God's help I will conquer and master you, and for that, I need only one thing, persistence and prayer."[1] And a little later, he wrote, "The body is a creature of habit, and one must simply learn to master it."[2] There is truth in what the young novice wrote, as well as a long ascetical tradition to support him. But with time and with suffering, Rafael came to see that the journey was more about openness and surrendering to God's will and grace than about mastering his nature with God's help: "I used to think that I was the one who brought about virtue, and that if I did something good, I was the one doing that too . . . But no . . . O Lord! No, it's not like that. You bring about all that is good."[3] The true path is one of the deepest surrender of self:

> Lord, have mercy on me . . . Yes, I am suffering . . . but I wish my suffering weren't so self-centered. Lord, I want to suffer for the sake of your pain on the cross, for the forgetfulness of humanity, for my own sins and those of others . . . for everything, Lord, but not for my own sake . . . What is my significance among all creation? What am I in Your eyes? . . . What does my hidden life represent within infinite eternity? . . . If I could forget myself, it would be better, Lord.

1. CW 77, #27. (Document 27 in Saint Rafael Arnaiz, *The Collected Works* [CW], ed. María Gonzalo-García, trans. Catherine Addington, MW 162 [Collegeville, MN: Cistercian Publications, 2022]).
2. CW 97, #33.
3. CW 701–2, #210.

I have nothing but a refined sense of self-love and, I'll say it again, a great deal of selfishness.

With Mary's help, I will try to do better. I will endeavor to turn to You, Virgin Mary, whenever a memory from the world disturbs me, and offer You a *Salve* for the sake of all those in the world who offend You.

Instead of meditating upon my suffering . . . I will meditate upon gratitude, and love God in my misery.[4]

KENOSIS/SELF-EMPTYING

The greatest model of self-emptying is found in the incarnation and in the dying and the rising of Jesus. His cross and resurrection should be the pattern for every Christian life. This *kenosis* (self-emptying) of Jesus is expressed beautifully by Saint Paul in his famous hymn in Philippians (Phil 2:5-11). It begins with an exhortation to the reader to have the same attitude as Christ:

> Let the same mind be in you that was in Christ Jesus,
> who, though he was in the form of God,
> did not regard equality with God
> as something to be exploited,
> but emptied himself,
> taking the form of a slave,
> being born in human likeness.
> And being found in human form,
> he humbled himself
> and became obedient to the point of death—
> even death on a cross.
> Therefore God also highly exalted him
> and gave him the name
> that is above every name,
> so that at the name of Jesus
> every knee should bend,

---

4. CW 611, #173.

in heaven and on earth and under the earth,
and every tongue should confess
that Jesus Christ is Lord,
to the glory of God the Father.

This ancient Christian hymn celebrates the kenosis, self-emptying, of the Son of God in his incarnation and in his suffering and death. And it lays out the path for those who develop the "same mind that was in Christ Jesus." And, no less, it celebrates the new life that it can bring. In Rafael, we see both the self-emptying and the transformation that it brought in his life.

Saint Paul himself manifests this pattern as he reminds his readers that he once considered himself righteous—born of the right heritage, a Pharisee, observant and zealous for the Law. But he came to see that it was all for nothing:

> If anyone else has reason to be confident in the flesh, I have more: circumcised on the eighth day, a member of the people of Israel, of the tribe of Benjamin, a Hebrew born of Hebrews; as to the law, a Pharisee; as to zeal, a persecutor of the church; as to righteousness under the law, blameless. Yet whatever gains I had, these I have come to regard as loss because of Christ. More than that, I regard everything as loss because of the surpassing value of knowing Christ Jesus my Lord. For his sake I have suffered the loss of all things, and I regard them as rubbish, in order that I may gain Christ and be found in him, not having a righteousness of my own that comes from the law, but one that comes through faith in Christ, the righteousness from God based on faith. I want to know Christ and the power of his resurrection and the sharing of his sufferings by becoming like him in his death, if somehow I may attain the resurrection from the dead. (Phil 3:4-11)

We see in these words of Saint Paul the pattern manifest in the life of Rafael, who likewise "suffered the loss of all things" and who came to "regard them as rubbish" so that he might share in the sufferings of Christ and attain his resurrection. As the Letter to the Hebrews says of Christ, "He learned obedience from what he suffered" (Heb 5:8).

SUFFERING AS DE-CENTERING

The experience of suffering can be radically de-centering. When we are healthy and life is proceeding according to our plans and dreams, we can be tempted to think of ourselves as in control, safe, and even the center of the world around us. But suffering that cannot be changed or overcome is radically disruptive of that ultimately false construct. Trials and disappointment reveal the truth that we are not in control, that we are not the center, that we are powerless to realize our own plans and dreams as, when, and how we wanted. Suffering, then, can be de-centering, de-constructing, humbling, and in a deep way even humiliating—a tangible reminder of what we are and what we are not. And what we are is dependent, needy, and radically de-centered without God, while what we are *not* is in control and the authentic center of our own existence. Suffering is a powerful and indeed unique challenge or invitation to self-emptying because we instinctively resist it and, from our depths, long to rise to oppose it. But when we cannot overcome our trials, then we can truly experience the invitation to surrender to what we are not and to the God who can sustain and even transform us by means of the trials themselves.

Suffering and difficulties bring us to a crossroad, a moment of choice. We can become bitter, angry, and despairing. We can redouble our efforts to tough it out and keep a stiff upper lip. Or, if we respond with faith and with the model of Jesus before us, we can embrace the deep truth of our radical need as human beings and, with Jesus crucified, abandon ourselves into the mysterious but always loving and providential hands of God. God does not cause our suffering, but God does permit it, and God is at work in it to bring a greater good than we could imagine, as the resur-

rection of Jesus makes clear: "We know that all things work together for good for those who love God, who are called according
to his purpose" (Rom 8:28). Abandoned completely to God, we
can finally receive the inpouring of the divine life and love. Without that surrender, we are doomed to receive the divine outpouring,
at best, in dribs and drabs. God does not hold back, but we set up
obstacles as we subtly strive to maintain ourselves at the center of
our little worlds.

Rafael entered the monastery to give himself completely to
God, but the trials that arose because of his illness and the need
to leave the monastery revealed to him that he had not given
himself completely. Simply entering the monastery to fulfill his
beautiful, heartfelt dream and merely embracing the sacrifices that
could be seen and chosen had not exhausted his self-emptying.
He did not desire the many disappointments that came his way,
but he came to embrace them, welcome them, and even thank
God for them, because, in them, he saw the instruments for his
deeper self-emptying and for his radical abandonment to God.
He came to see each setback, each new disruption, and the progression of his disease as the tools by which he was more fully
united to Jesus on the cross. And thus he knew peace and even
joy as he suffered.

Beginning after the devastating disappointment of his first
departure from the monastery, Rafael developed a profound and
growing conviction that God was at work to enable him to surrender himself completely—as Rafael himself wished to do. This
perspective is apparent in his letter to the abbot of San Isidro,
requesting to return to the monastery as an oblate. The letter reflects a remarkable faith and spiritual maturity in a twenty-four-
year-old. He begins by reflecting on his previous entrance:

> I was searching for God, but I was also searching for His
> creatures, and I was searching for myself; and God wants
> me all to Himself . . . My vocation was from God, and is
> of God, but it needed to be purified, its rough edges needed

smoothing. I gave myself to the Lord generously, but I still wasn't giving Him *everything*; I gave Him my body, my soul, my career, my family . . . but I still held on to one thing: my dreams and desires, my hopes of being a Trappist and making my vows and singing the Mass. That kept me going at La Trapa, but God wants more, He always wants more. I needed to be transformed. He wanted His love alone to be enough for me.[5]

Even as he embraces his disappointments, Rafael sees that suffering is not only a tool for self-emptying. It is also the doorway to communion with the tremendous love of God. To be united with Jesus on the cross is to be joined with him in that amazing manifestation of the divine love for humanity that began with the incarnation of the Son of God and reached its crescendo in the cross and resurrection. To embrace one's own suffering, emptying oneself with Jesus on the cross, is at the same time to commune with the divine love, which is nowhere more manifest than in the death of the Christ. The cross of Jesus is at one and the same time the purest act of human surrender to God in humble trust as well as the clearest earthly manifestation of the unimaginable love of God for sinners. To unite oneself with the crucified—as Rafael did—is to join Christ in both his human surrender and in his divine loving. And it is to be joined in his radical love for every other human being—as we see in the transformation in loving that Rafael came to discover in himself in his final months.

MADE POSSIBLE BY LOVE

It is evident in all of his writings that Rafael had a strong sense of the Providence of God—that the divine hand is constantly at work in the world in order to bring about our true good. And Rafael saw in every new setback God's Providence at work, whether through

5. CW 214–15, #64.

what God might actively will or what God might merely permit. But Rafael was not writing academic theological reflections on divine Providence. He did not seek to understand or explain how exactly God works through the unfolding of the events of our lives, interacting with human freedom and with the advance of nature's processes. He simply believed that a loving God was always at hand, actively if mysteriously involved for each person's good. How that could be so was simply not his concern.

Ultimately, Rafael was able to surrender blindly to God at every turn because he felt himself profoundly loved by God. He was content to walk in dark faith, to allow himself to be led here and there, in and out, because he was confident that he was being guided by love. His writings are full of exclamations of his insight into God's love for humanity and of God's love for him personally.[6] He wrote to the monastery infirmarian before his final entrance, knowing the trials he would face: "Don't be jealous, brother, but God loves me very much."[7] In a journal entry written in the month before his death, he wrote,

> God is my friend . . . the God who could cast down the sun and make the sea draw back in awe . . . that God loves *me* so dearly that if the whole world had any idea, every creature on earth would go mad and howl with astonishment. But even all that . . . is nothing in comparison. God loves me so much that even the angels cannot fathom it. How great is the mercy of God! That He should love me . . . and be my friend . . . my brother . . . my father, my master . . . when He is God, and I am what I am![8]

6. See many of the citations identified in Alberico Feliz Carbajal, ed., *Hermano Rafael: Escritos por temas*, 2nd ed. (Burgos, Spain: Editorial Monte Carmelo, 2000), 91–98.

7. CW 592, #166.

8. CW 646–47, #188.

This is a love that Rafael discovers most profoundly in his experience of the cross: "All I can say is that I have found true happiness in loving the cross of Christ. I am happy, completely happy, more than anyone could ever imagine, when I embrace the blood-stained cross and realize that Jesus loves me despite my misery, my negligence, and my sins, as does Mary."[9]

With great emotion, Rafael told his brother, Luis Fernando—who was able to visit the monastery in the month before Rafael's death—that his greatest suffering was knowing himself so undeservedly and infinitely loved by God while finding himself unable to reciprocate the divine love as he so earnestly desired.[10] Raised in the heart of a loving family, Rafael was grounded in a profound sense that he was loved by God, which allowed him ultimately to welcome each new trial with peace and even with a sense of gratitude for his trials. They had become his "treasures."[11]

Being loved by God and loving God in return: both are necessary in order to truly embrace one's suffering. Rafael writes to his grandmother, "Have confidence that the Lord loves you, and if you have lived your life according to God's law, that is the law by which you must be judged, and that law is not severe. It doesn't demand great things. It comes down to just a little bit of love. . . . It doesn't consist of austerity or fasting or disciplines or suffering or sorrow . . . None of that is of any use if you don't have love for God."[12]

A PATH OF "HUMILIATION"

As we have seen, Saint Benedict presents obedience, silence, and humility as essential tools for the process of ongoing monastic conversion (*conversatio morum*) and for the graced attainment of

9. CW 642, #186.
10. OC 926–27, n. 1112.
11. CW 569, #162; 672, #199.
12. CW 334, #88.

purity of heart. Rafael enthusiastically embraced these three instruments from the very outset. With an authentic spirit of docility and trust, he placed himself under the obedience of the abbot and novice master. But in the unfolding of his own distinctive path of monastic conversion, his obedience became more deeply a radical obedience and surrender to the will of God in whatever form that might come. And this is the very purpose of monastic obedience. He also embraced the silence of the monastic life—and the strict silence of the Trappist life. His naturally outgoing nature may have rebelled at times in his early years, but he valued the silence and adhered to it faithfully. And as the normal monastic silence was joined by his sometimes painful physical isolation in the infirmary, Rafael came to embrace and willingly enter into the deeper silence that he encountered. But in a special way, it was humility that proved to be the divine tool for Rafael's conversion—humility especially in the form of what he experienced as "humiliations."

We have noted that Rafael's return to the monastery as an oblate rather than as a choir novice was seen by his superiors as a kind of humiliation. Rafael was well educated, from an upper-class family, and had all of the personal attributes that would have made him a candidate for monastic profession and ordination to the priesthood. It may be that the abbot wanted to soften this humiliation by putting Rafael on the path to ordination even as an oblate and later by giving him the black scapular of the professed monks. In his letter to the abbot requesting admission as an oblate, Rafael acknowledged the appearance of suffering a humiliation but professed that he felt none: "Your Reverence will speak of the humiliation this entails, the fact of being nothing and no one. But am I someone now? As for humiliation, I don't believe I will feel that way, because in order for a soul to be humbled it must first be up high and then be brought low, and I don't think I have to be brought low at all."[13] In any case, he continues, did not God

13. CW 216, #64.

suffer humiliation for us—in which case, who are we to complain? In a later reflection, Rafael writes: "Humiliation! What a poor understanding we have of that word. I have come to realize that in order to be humiliated, one must be *made low* . . . And could I possibly be made any lower? Am I high up in any way?"[14] As we will see below, he incorporated his status as oblate into his spiritual understanding of his vocation.

The struggle with humiliation for Rafael did not concern his status as an oblate in the monastery; rather, it was his inability to live the full rigors of the Trappist life, to feel useful in the life of the community, and to give good example to the monks around him. He acknowledges this form of struggle in his letter to the abbot: "I fear only one thing, and that is to fail to be a good example to the community in the observance of the holy Rule, but God wishes to take even that from me, which is a great consolation."[15] He already sees that it is this struggle that will be the more difficult: "It is a very great mortification to follow the Rule and observe the fasts, but perhaps it is an even greater one to have to take an indulgence."[16] The barbs thrown at him in the infirmary by Fr. Pío, the suggestion by monks that he was not cut out for the life because of the mitigations that his health required, and his obvious inability to join in the manual work of the monastery were a constant thorn for Rafael. The humiliation of not living up to his own high ideals of the monastic life remained a struggle and a trial for him. But he came to see that this trial too was a symptom of clinging to his own plan and ideals rather than simply surrendering to God's will for him. This too became a form of suffering and a share in the cross—together with his illness and the comings and goings by which God was at work bringing Rafael to a simple and complete surrender. He writes to his aunt,

14. CW 524, #150.
15. CW 217, #64.
16. CW 218, #64.

Truly, my dear sister, it is a great thing, a tremendous mercy from God, to realize that you are useless and to be humiliated because you are of no use whatsoever, because you can't follow the Rule, because you're sick. If only you knew how grateful I am to the Lord on that account. He has shown me my own self-love with such gentleness, and helped me see my many imperfections. It was necessary for the Lord to put me in this situation in order for my eyes to be properly opened, and for my desires to be uprooted, even my desire to be a Trappist; for me to abandon myself in His hands, and love Him more and more every day, as I realize that He alone can satisfy my soul . . . I needed my illness to show me that I was still attached to the world, to creatures, to my aches and pains and weaknesses. Living off alms and charity, holding God's hand tight . . . What a great mercy, Lord! I was so blind![17]

André Louf has argued that humility in the ancient monastic tradition of Cassian was not understood as one virtue among many, as later authors would view it. Rather, humility is a fundamental monastic attitude that seeks after a radical self-emptying and dependence on God, an active participation in the kenotic humility of Christ. Humility, then, has a character of humiliation—a process of embracing one's complete dependence on God.[18] It is the humiliation of accepting our humanity as it is, blessed but also broken and needy. Jane Foulcher, building on Louf's work, concludes that humility in the ancient monastic sense seeks to "destabilize the self, stripping away one's former socially constructed identity and exposing the monk to radical dependence on God."[19] This was the humility—the humiliation—that Rafael embraced

17. CW 400–401, #105.
18. André Louf, *The Way of Humility*, trans. Lawrence S. Cunningham, MW 11 (Kalamazoo, MI: Cistercian Publications, 2007).
19. Jane Foulcher, *Reclaiming Humility: Four Studies in the Monastic Tradition*, CS 255 (Collegeville, MN: Cistercian Publications, 2015), 85.

and pursued.[20] With each setback, each trial, each thwarting of
his plans and dreams, he was brought into closer communion with
the self-emptying humiliation of Jesus on the cross.

A SPIRITUALITY OF OBLATION

The word *oblate* comes from a Latin root that means "offering."
When Rafael entered the monastery for the second time, he not
only accepted his new canonical status as an oblate, but, more
deeply, he embraced its root meaning.[21] He became an oblation,
an offering to God in Christ. In a letter to his Aunt María as he
prepared for his second entry, he explained, "That's what 'oblate'
means . . . 'offering'. . . I offer myself to Him as I am, whether
good or bad, in good health or out of it; I offer Him my life, my
body, my soul, my heart, everything . . . absolutely everything."[22]
Having given up his dream of becoming a professed monk, Rafael
began to unfold a spirituality of oblation—of self-offering in love
for God, united with Christ on the cross, for himself and for the
good of others. In his final months, feeling that he had given all
that he had to offer, he gave all that remained—his life and, with
it, any final concern for his health:

> This morning, I offered my life to the Lord. It is no longer
> my own . . . May He be the one to take care of it, if He
> wants, because I'm not going to worry about it anymore. I

---

20. Saint Bernard wrote, "Humiliation is the only way to humility, just as
patience is the only way to peace, and reading to knowledge. If you want the
virtue of humility, you must not shun humiliations" (Letter 87, cited by Foulcher,
Reclaiming Humility, 233).

21. See Antonio María Martín Fernández-Gallardo, *El deseo de Dios y la
ciencia de la Cruz: aproximación a la experiencia religiosa del Hermano Rafael*, 2nd
ed., Biblioteca cisterciense, 5 (Burgos, Spain: Editorial Monte Carmelo, 2002),
101–13 (hereafter cited as Martín).

22. CW 318, #85.

will deal with it, yes, because He's the one who has lent it to me, but . . . that is all.

If He wishes, He will send me the remedies I need. If He does not wish it, I'll be just as content without them. I won't worry about my health at all whatsoever . . . I'll take whatever they give me, do whatever they tell me to do, be obedient in everything.[23]

And, as he does so, he understands it as his oblation:

I asked the Virgin Mary to intercede for me with Jesus, so that He will accept my offering. What a great joy it would be if God were to accept it! What a joy it would be to die for Jesus . . . and for Jesus to offer my life to the Eternal Father in reparation for the sins of the world, for wars, and unfaithful peoples, and priests, and the pope, and the church! I don't mind enduring suffering, so long as Jesus accepts my offering. I've already given Him my heart . . . I've given Him my will . . . Now I'm giving Him my life. I no longer have anything left, except to die whenever He wishes. May His will be done, not mine.[24]

In the month before his death, Rafael came to see that suffering was his call, his vocation—and not alone but with Jesus, and not for himself alone but for his family, for priests and missionaries, for the church and for the world.[25] His disappointments and his suffering, then, did not make him a passive victim. Rather, he freely chose to embrace his trials and offer them with the oblation of Jesus on the cross in his death for the world. His trials were transformed into his offering.[26] He did so without any self-conscious sense of heroism but with humility and in poverty of spirit.

23. CW 643–44, #187.
24. CW 644, #187.
25. CW 649, #189.
26. Martín, *Deseo de Dios*, 110.

The "School" of the Cross

Saint Benedict taught that the monastery is a "school of the Lord's service" that sets monks on "the road that leads to salvation" (RB Prol.). There, faithfully following the divine instruction, "we shall through patience share in the sufferings of Christ that we may deserve also to share in his Kingdom." Saint Bernard, together with the early Cistercians, thought of the monastery as a "school of charity" where monks learn to love God and to love others. And Rafael was an avid student both of the Lord's service and of charity. But for Rafael, the monastery was also essentially a "school of the cross."[27] For both Saint Benedict and Saint Bernard, the sacrifices, the trials, and the burdens of living together with other sinners in the monastery were the tools that teach charity and lead to salvation. And Rafael was no stranger to those. But Rafael's perspective also reflects both his own distinctive path of trial and sacrifice in the monastery (his comings and goings, embracing his status as an oblate, the lack of sympathy of some of his brother monks, the inability to receive optimal care in the monastery for his condition, and the like), but also the path of surrender and self-emptying that must mark every Christian life. This reality has led one commentator to conclude that the monastery also became for Rafael a "school of abandonment."[28] Rafael writes,

> What little I know, I have learned from the cross . . . I have always done my prayer and meditation at the cross . . . In truth, I don't know a better place, and I'm not going looking for one . . . so stay still, then. Therefore, Lord, as I consider the divine school of your cross, as I consider that it is only on Calvary, at Mary's side, where I can learn to be better, to

---

27. Victorino Blanco Mayo, *Rafael Arnáiz: modelo de entrega total (Descubriendo al Rafael profundo)* (Zamora, Spain: Ediciones Monte Casino, 2018), 60. See also Martín, *Deseo de Dios*, 257–68.

28. Martín, *Deseo de Dios*, 303.

love You, and to forget and disregard myself: "Do not permit me to be parted from You."[29]

It is by looking to and embracing the cross that one learns to dismantle what is false in oneself and thus truly to be able to offer oneself to God and to embrace the love offered by God in the crucified Jesus. And it is "at the foot of the cross," as Rafael writes, that one can learn, unite oneself, and be formed with the virtues and charity of Jesus: "it is only at the foot of Your cross, seeing You nailed to it, that we can learn forgiveness, humility, charity, and docility."[30] By being conformed to Jesus on the cross, one is formed to live the divine love that he lived—to *be* the divine love in the world in which we find ourselves. Rafael speaks of coming to this realization as the transformation that God worked in him through the cross.

THE "SCIENCE OF THE CROSS" AND KNOWING HOW TO SUFFER

In the monastery, Rafael found a wisdom that he had been seeking: "I sought wisdom, and I found it not in war, or in science, or in animals, or in human beings . . . I found it only in the love of God and contempt for the world."[31] But when speaking specifically of what one learns in the "school" of the Cross, Rafael speaks not of "wisdom" (*sabiduría*), but of "science" (*ciencia*). Suffering teaches a kind of knowledge that is learned experientially and by prayerful reflection on experience. Since it teaches the knowledge that is the most important, it is the truest form of science.[32] Christ is its teacher, and he proclaims his science, Rafael says, "to the

29. CW 630, #182.
30. CW 675, #200.
31. CW 587, #165.
32. CW 146, #45.

whole world from atop Calvary."[33] Like other sciences, it too has its method: it requires a particular discipline that includes solitude, recollection, and silence.[34] Ultimately, this is practical science that is learned through the experience of suffering.[35]

In what does this science consist, and why is it worth learning? The science of the cross teaches us how to suffer well because it consists of knowing how "to love and wait in hope."[36] It is only this form of knowledge that can penetrate the mystery of life and death, of suffering and love, hidden in Christ crucified and in the cross that each of us is called to bear.

In the "school" of the cross, says Rafael, one learns "how to suffer" [*saber sufrir*]. He was aware that every human being experiences suffering, but not everyone knows how to embrace it and to learn from it in faith. Not everyone learns to pass from being a victim of the suffering that cannot be changed into being a collaborator in God's mysterious action in the midst of one's trials: "all of humanity suffers, but there are so few who *know how* to suffer."[37] And so not everyone learns how to transform one's suffering into self-emptying and self-offering, together with that of Christ. Suffering can become a kind of "divine pedagogy" by which one learns consciously and freely to surrender to God—in and with Christ.[38] This is the difference between simply experiencing suffering and knowing how to suffer. Rafael quotes Saint Francis de Sales on poverty as a kind of parallel: "The virtue of poverty is not in being poor, but in loving one's poverty."[39]

Rafael's reflections on the cross are neither merely pious words nor abstract theological reflections. They flow from his own deeply

33. CW 676, #200.
34. CW 494, #140.
35. CW 623, #180.
36. CW 408, #106.
37. CW 352, #92.
38. Martín, *Deseo de Dios*, 180–81.
39. CW 401, #105.

prayerful reflection in faith on his own personal experience of suffering and disappointment. The cross for Rafael was the essential key to understanding God and the divine love for humanity as well as the necessary response of the human person. Ultimately, he declares that people can understand neither God nor themselves except through the lens of the cross: "If only the world knew how much one learns at the foot of the cross . . . If only the world knew that all theology, all mysticism and asceticism, even a thousand years' worth of philosophy is completely useless if one does not meditate and study at the foot of the cross of Christ."[40] Such knowledge cannot be learned from books or academic study but through meditating and more deeply immersing oneself in the self-giving love of Jesus "at the foot of the cross."

Rafael's "science" of the cross is not easily gained. It can be a hard-won knowledge that requires faith, trust, and love. Suffering remains suffering, and it is not always or even frequently accompanied by sweet assurances of the divine presence—as Jesus' cry from the cross makes clear. Rafael himself knew the experience of bearing the cross, at times without consolation, calling for perseverance in a kind of dark faith. He tells his Aunt María, "The hard thing is to stay on the Cross when Christ disappears before our eyes and the Cross remains, all dry and black and bloody . . . And neither Saint John nor the holy women nor Mary is on Calvary . . . We are all alone in darkness with the Cross. We neither know how to pray nor do we hear God, *nothing* . . . all we know is suffering . . . we look for Christ . . . and He is not there." [41] But, he continues, the only possible response is to hold on in faith, accepting that the present trial is part of the divine plan and that Jesus remains near though unseen and unfelt: "Let Him work, suffer . . . but love Him while you suffer. Love Him dearly through the darkness, despite the storm in which the Lord

40. CW 479, #136.
41. CW 240, #72.

has seemingly placed you, despite not being able to see Him. Love
the naked wood of the Cross."

Ultimately, it is only Jesus himself who can teach us the science
of the cross—a lesson that is learned in the midst of suffering and
in prayerful reflection in silence, in love, and in waiting:

> Christ Jesus, teach me to suffer . . . Teach me the science
> of loving scorn, injury, abjection . . . Teach me to suffer with
> the humble joy of the saints, never crying out . . . Teach me
> to be docile with those who do not love me, or who despise
> me . . . Teach me the science that You proclaim to the whole
> world from atop Calvary. But I already know it . . . a very
> gentle interior voice explains it all to me . . . something I
> feel inside me, something that comes from You and that I
> cannot explain, unravels such a great mystery that human
> beings cannot understand it . . . In my own way, Lord, I do
> understand it . . . it is love . . . it contains everything . . .
> I know now, Lord . . . I need nothing more, I need nothing
> else . . . it is love. Who can put the love of Christ into
> words? . . . May human beings fall silent, may creatures fall
> silent . . . May we all be silent, so that in that silence, we
> might hear those whispers of Love, of the humble, patient,
> infinite, boundless Love that Jesus is offering us with open
> arms from the cross.[42]

The wisdom that Jesus teaches on the cross is not purely an
intellectual insight or knowing. It is a loving knowledge, and, as
such, it is difficult to express or explain but is nonetheless a deep
and authentic truth:

> From time to time, I have felt the great, profound consolation
> of finding myself alone, having surrendered myself into God's
> arms. Solitude with God . . . nobody who has not experi-
> enced it can understand it, and I don't know how to describe

---

42. CW 676, #200.

it. All I can say is that it is a consolation one can only experience through suffering . . . and suffering alone . . . and with God, that is true joy. It is a desire for nothing but suffering. It is a very great longing to live and die ignored by everyone, unknown to the whole world . . . It is a great desire for everything that is God's will . . . It is not wanting anything but Him . . . It is wanting yet not wanting . . . I don't know, I can't explain it . . . only God understands me, but while I may not know the cause, I do know its effects.[43]

Perhaps most of us who read those words do indeed find it difficult to grasp the wisdom that Rafael had learned. But as we have seen, Rafael's confidence in God's love for him made him able to trust that God's hand was at work even in the midst of sudden disappointments and setbacks. And it is such abiding trust in God that makes it possible to embrace the cross, even without fully understanding or being able clearly to explain why.

LEARNING THE LANGUAGE OF THE CROSS

Rafael's mastery of the science of the cross was the fruit of his own experience, reflection, and prayer over time. And yet his reading provided him with language and concepts to understand and express what he was learning. In the long period after his first departure from the monastery, as he worked to come to grips with the reality of his diabetes and the seeming end of his dream of being a professed monk, Rafael began to read John of the Cross. He tells his aunt that he carries a text of John's writings in the glove compartment of his car as he goes out for long drives into the country so that he can read and meditate on his words.[44] And the great Spanish mystic offered him basic tools with which to begin to piece together a lasting and deepening perspective on

43. CW 626, #181.
44. CW 279, #77.

disappointment and trial.[45] Self-emptying, surrender, and walking in dark faith—a faith that believes without understanding or needing to understand the mysterious plans of God—are major themes in the works of Saint John.

Moreover, Rafael identified not only with the ideas of purification and letting go, but with the yearning love for God that so grounds and permeates the work of Saint John. In another letter to his aunt, Rafael quotes the opening and closing lines of stanza twenty-eight of Saint John's *Spiritual Canticle,* which expresses both longing and disinterested love in all that is less than God:

> Now I occupy my soul
> and all my energy in his service;
> I no longer tend the herd,
> Nor have I any other work
> Now that my every act is love.[46]

Rafael tells his aunt that he hopes that one day those words will more fully express the true dispositions of his heart.[47] As we have noted earlier, he frequently refers to the third stanza of the same poem to express both his yearning love and the necessity of letting go of all that holds one back or that is less than God: "I will not gather flowers."

Another of Rafael's companions along the way of learning the science of the cross was Thomas à Kempis, whom Rafael frequently cites. Thomas's *The Imitation of Christ* is a classic of Catholic spirituality. But one particular message that remained with Rafael was Thomas's exhortation to embrace the cross as we each find it in life, because in fact there is no escaping it: "wherever you go, you will find the cross."[48] In words probably based on his

---

45. Martín, *Deseo de Dios,* 208.

46. *The Collected Works of St. John of the Cross,* trans. Kieran Kavanaugh and Otilio Rodriguez, 3rd ed. (Washington, DC: ICS Publications, 2017), 78.

47. CW 266, #75.

48. CW 547, #158 (Thomas à Kempis, *Imitation of Christ,* trans. Ronald Knox and Michael Oakley [South Bend, IN: Greenlawn Press, 1990], 2.12).

reading of the *Imitation of Christ*,[49] Rafael writes, "The eternal life
for which the soul yearns day in and day out cannot be earned
except through surrender, sacrifice, and embracing the cross of
Christ . . . That is the only way."[50] Ultimately, as Thomas had
written, there is peace to be found in the cross: "It is a great consolation to have a cross . . . There is no greater peace than that
which is bestowed by suffering. Those who leave all things behind
suffer . . . those who leave all things behind for God's sake rejoice
in their suffering."[51]

For Rafael the wisdom of the cross was not learned and embraced all at once. He did not become a master of the science of
the cross in an instant. Instead, through remaining faithfully
present at the foot of the cross with his eyes on the crucified Jesus
and walking freely in dark faith, Rafael deepened his insight into
and grasp of this hidden wisdom with each new setback, worsening of his illness, exile from the monastery, deprivation, and trial.
And even in those instances of suffering, his complete acceptance
did not always come immediately but sometimes with waiting
and with prayer. Through it all, Rafael saw the providential hand
of a loving God who always wills, permits, and tolerates only what
is for our good.[52]

The Foolishness/Madness of the Cross

A profound and hidden wisdom it might be, but Rafael was quite
aware that the very idea of consciously and freely embracing the
cross could only seem like madness to the world. And it was a
form of madness in which he himself rejoiced. Rafael was a glad
herald of the foolishness of the cross.

49. Thomas à Kempis, *Imitation of Christ*, 2.12.

50. CW 457, #128. See also CW 496, #140.

51. CW 538, #154. Rafael is probably again recalling Thomas à Kempis, *Imitation of Christ*, 2.12.

52. Martín, *Deseo de Dios*, 215, 228.

As we saw in a previous chapter, Rafael was a young man with a passionate yearning love for God. He himself describes it as being "crazy for Christ" (*loco por Cristo*) and "crazy for God" (*loco por Dios*). His longing is a "foolishness/madness" of love (*locura de amor*) for Christ—a lunacy that he wished the whole world would experience.[53] And it was this yearning that kept him knocking over and over again at the door of the monastery where he firmly believed that God wanted him to be and where he could best find God. But as Rafael's gaze became more focused on the cross, his "foolishness for Christ" became increasingly a "foolishness of the cross" (*locura de la Cruz*). This new emphasis becomes evident, beginning in his writings before his final return to the monastery.[54]

Saint Paul had written of the "foolishness" of the cross. The "wise" people of this world cannot make sense of a Savior who freely chooses to suffer and die on the cross:

> For the message about the cross is foolishness to those who are perishing, but to us who are being saved it is the power of God. . . . For Jews demand signs and Greeks desire wisdom, but we proclaim Christ crucified, a stumbling block to Jews and foolishness to Gentiles, but to those who are called, both Jews and Greeks, Christ the power of God and the wisdom of God. For God's foolishness is wiser than human wisdom, and God's weakness is stronger than human strength. (1 Cor 1:18, 22-25)

In the same way, Rafael sees that freely choosing to embrace the cross through embracing one's suffering in union with Christ could only seem like madness to those who think according to the common sense of the world. To choose the sacrifices of the Trappist

---

53. See, for example, CW 566–67, #162.

54. See especially Rafael's letter to his Uncle Polín of September 25, 1937 (CW 566–73, #162), written before his final return, in which Rafael brings together these various terms and ideas. See also the journal entry titled "Living United to Your Cross" (CW 629–31, #182).

life was madness enough! But to return to that life, time and again, with a disease like diabetes was totally mad.

But Rafael was not simply accepting the reality of the cross, not really even "just" embracing it: he was clinging to it, rejoicing in it, savoring it. His love for Christ became a true love for Christ's cross. And this is a "madness" of entirely different degree, which he reveled in because, through these difficulties and trials, he was identified with Christ and Christ with him: "What great intimacy Jesus has with those who mourn! Blessed are our tears, sorrows, and illnesses, which are our treasures, all that we possess. They make us draw near to Jesus, since the love we have for Him is so little, so feeble, so weak that it is not enough on its own . . . !"[55] He was embraced by the love of Christ being poured out on the cross. His yearning love for Christ met the yearning love of Christ in his suffering and dying for sinners.

So intense was Rafael's identification with the suffering Jesus that he longed to share in those very trials and humiliations:

> I wish I could sleep on the stairs . . . I wish I could eat under Father Abbot's table . . . I wish I could walk around wearing a sack and a rope . . . I wish I could become mute for You, Lord . . . And sometimes I wish I could act the fool, shouting all through the monastery cloisters . . . throwing myself at the monks' feet . . . Lord, I don't know what I would do if they let me . . . perhaps nothing at all. . . . Who can think about prudence, when we see Jesus with the cloak and scepter of a *fool*? . . . Lord, Lord, I wish I could be that fool . . . and receive all the laughs and jeers You received.[56]

---

55. CW 569, #162.

56. CW 628, #181. One commentator reflects on Rafael's life as a type of the "fool for Christ"—saints who have identified themselves with the humility and humiliations of Christ by imitating them in radical ways (Tomás Gallego Fernández, "Hermano Rafael, 'Loco por Cristo,'" *Cistercium* 254 [Jan.–June 2010]: 49–69). Rafael himself refers to Saint Benedict Labre (1748–1783), who lived and died in freely chosen abject poverty. See the journal entry of March 19, 1938

But Rafael was quite aware that these feelings and convictions could only seem like madness to the world and that, in fact, it would be difficult even to try to explain it:

> I know only one thing, and it fills my soul with joy despite being so poor in virtue and so rich in misery . . . I know only this: I have a treasure I wouldn't trade for anything or anyone . . . my cross . . . the cross of Jesus. That cross is my only rest . . . how can I explain it! If you haven't experienced this . . . you can't even begin to imagine it. If only every human being loved the cross of Christ . . . Oh, if only the world knew what it was to embrace the cross of Christ *entirely*, for *real*, with *no reservations*, loving it *madly* . . . ![57]

The person madly in love with God in Christ must also learn to embrace the madness of loving the cross. To love God is to trust and surrender—which brings peace and serenity in trial without lessening the yearning:

> The world cannot and need not understand the foolishness of a lover of Christ . . . Foolishness, yes, there is no other word for it, the foolishness of the cross, which makes our souls go nuts and scrambles our words, which try to say so much and end up saying nothing at all. A foolishness tempered only by the "straitjacket" of conformity to God's will, which makes us quiet down when we want to cry out, which makes us prudent when our souls break loose and want to . . . I don't know . . . which makes our waiting calm, when longing for Christ beats impatiently in our hearts.[58]

(CW 660, #194). Rafael's mother recounts an instance during his third departure from the monastery when he joined a line of beggars seeking food from a Carthusian monastery in Burgos, seeking to share in the poverty of Christ. See Mercedes Barón, *Vida y escritos del Beato Fray María Rafael Arnáiz Barón, monje trapense*, 12th ed. (Madrid: Editorial Perpetuo Socorro, 2000), 443.

57. CW 671–72, #199.
58. CW 566–67, #162.

By entering a Trappist monastery, the young Raphael—of a wealthy family and with a promising future—had already embraced a wisdom different from that of "normal" secular and even church society. But he not only abandoned any worldly wisdom; he had embraced what could only seem like foolishness—the foolishness of the cross of Christ, and the foolishness of madly loving his own share in that cross.

"RELISHING/SAVORING" THE CROSS

About three weeks before Rafael's death, a bishop who was making a retreat of a few days at the abbey of San Isidro gave a conference to the community.[59] As the time was near the end of Lent, he reflected on the cross of Christ. One particular challenge of the bishop struck Rafael deeply, giving him words to express his own experience and his own frequent musings on the cross: the need to "relish" or "savor" the cross:

> Relishing the Cross . . . Oh, Lord Jesus! . . . How happy I am . . . I have found my soul's desire. It is not human beings, or creatures . . . it is not peace, or consolation . . . it is not what the world thinks it is . . . it is what no one could imagine it to be . . . it is the cross. How good it is to suffer! . . . At Your side, on Your cross . . . seeing Mary weep. If only I had the strength of a giant, to be able to suffer more! Relishing the cross . . . Living as a sick person, ignored and abandoned by everyone . . . Only You, and on the cross . . . How sweet is bitter sorrow, loneliness, pain, when devoured and consumed helplessly in silence. How sweet are the tears shed before Your cross. Oh, if only I could tell the world where true happiness is to be found! But the world does not and cannot understand this, for in order to understand the cross, you must love it, and in order to love the cross, you must suffer, and you must not

59. Rafael reflects on this conference in his journal entry of April 3, 1938, titled "Relishing the Cross" (CW 671–74, #199).

only suffer, but love suffering itself . . . and so few are willing
to follow You to Calvary in this way, Lord![60]

Rafael is not saying that one can love the *experience* of suffering.
Rather, he sees his suffering as a kind of doorway or path into
communion with the experience and the love of the crucified: "It's
so hard to explain why suffering can be loved! But I think it can
be explained, because it's not a question of loving suffering *itself*,
but rather what suffering is in Christ. Those who love Christ love
His cross. I don't know how to bring this to a conclusion, but I
do understand it."[61] Rafael is grateful for what requires him to
see his absolute need for God's love in Christ and for what enables
him to commune with that love manifest on the cross. And so he
clings to and savors his trials for what they are doing for him in
his radical poverty, humility, and surrender. He does not desire it
to be different: "I will not seek comfort or rest . . . I want only to
love the cross . . . to feel the cross . . . to relish the cross."[62]

Bernard—in a text probably not familiar to Rafael—identifies
three movements in a maturing encounter with the cross. His
words describe well Rafael's own advance:

> He that is yet but beginning in fear carries the cross of Christ
> with patience; he that has gone forward to hope, carries it
> with contentment; but he that is made perfect in love, em-
> braces the cross with the eagerness and the ardour of delight.
> For it is only the last who can say to the cross like blessed
> Andrew [the apostle], "I have always been thy lover and I
> have ardently longed to embrace thee." Far removed from
> such fervour is the disposition of him who bears his burden
> resignedly enough, yet would wish, if it could be so, that he
> had not "come to his hour."[63]

60. CW 672, #199.
61. CW 667, #196.
62. CW 674, #199.
63. Bernard of Clairvaux, "First Sermon for the Feast of St. Andrew," in *Saint Bernard's Sermons for the Seasons and Principal Feasts of the Year*, trans. by a Priest

And we see Rafael, the loyal son of Saint Bernard, embrace the cross in his life with just such "eagerness and ardor of delight."

A journal entry titled "How Good It Is to Live Close to the Cross of Christ!" is certainly written in the spirit of Saint Bernard:

> But those who truly love, those who experience what it is to unite themselves to Jesus on the cross . . . they can truly say that their suffering is delightful, that their pain is as sweet as honey, that it is a great consolation to suffer loneliness, boredom, and sadness at the hands of human beings. How good it is to live close to the cross of Christ![64]

The cross had become Rafael's true treasure.[65]

AN "OUTPOST OF HELL"

The walls and cloister of a monastery mark off a kind of holy ground. But it is not a separation between a wicked secular world on the outside and a heavenly existence within. One cannot enter the monastery with the hope of escaping the temptations and the trials by which we all must try to overcome sin and empty ourselves so that we can give ourselves to God and receive the divine self-giving. All of that is the common challenge of all Christians. But the walls of a monastery can be understood to demarcate—mark off—a kind of battleground, a fighting ring. By embracing the tools of the common monastic life, its residents seek to engage in a more focused way and more wholeheartedly in the struggle to overcome the false self and surrender to God. The walls of a monastery are not meant to protect from struggle, but rather to intensify it and to prevent facile escape from the battle.[66]

---

of Mount Melleray [Ailbe J. Luddy], 3 vols. (Westminster, MD: Carroll Press, 1950), 3:44–45.

64. CW 676, #200.

65. CW 672, #199.

66. Louf, *Way of Humility*, 59.

It is with this view of the monastery in mind that we can perhaps understand a surprising and even disturbing comment that Rafael made to his brother Leopoldo upon his final return to the monastery. Leopoldo had driven with Rafael from the family home to the Trapa. He reports that Rafael, the driver, pulled the car over within sight of the monastery and asked for a cigarette. Noticing that Rafael was crying, his younger brother asked him what was going on, and Rafael responded with the dark words, "Look, there, it is an outpost of hell" (*Mira, éso, es una sucursal del infierno*). After a time, calm once again, they drove the remaining distance, without any explanation of what those disturbing words might mean.[67]

Leopoldo himself attributed his brother's reaction to the knowledge and acceptance of the vocation that would lead rather soon to his death. Certainly Rafael knew quite well what awaited him: lack of adequate care for his illness and probably hunger and thirst, isolation in an infirmary cell, restrictions on his participation in common prayer and work, the constant presence of a mentally disturbed monk who had tormented him in the past, and the absence of a spiritual director to help him through his trials. We see in his first journal entries upon this return to the monastery that Rafael was passing through periods of desolation and even of a kind of dark night. He was a sensitive young man, and what he felt, he felt very deeply.[68] But at the same time, perhaps it can be said that Rafael, like Christ as described in the gospel of John, was mounting the wood of the cross. In a letter to Br. Tescelino, referring to his decision to return to the monastery for the last time, Rafael writes, "I

67. This story was recounted by Leopoldo in the context of his testimony during Rafael's subsequent beatification process. See OC 857, n. 1033, where the testimony is quoted at length.

68. For a consideration of this seemingly uncharacteristic remark of Rafael, see Tomás Gallego Fernandez, "El Hermano Rafael y 'su Trapa' a luz de un centenario," *Cistercium* 185 (April–June 1991): 439–64.

see La Trapa, I see a cross, and there I go. That's it."[69] Suffering became not just something that he passively endured; rather, he embraced it. Trials awaited him there, but the monastery was his battleground. In order to surrender completely to God with Christ, he was ready to face what lay ahead in order to do battle with what remained of what was false within himself.

The cross may have been Rafael's treasure. He may have been madly in love with the cross. He may have been grateful for the cross in his life. But it remained a cross, and the suffering remained suffering. But Rafael freely and gladly embraced it. The monastery had become "an outpost" or a kind of a gateway to his final, very real, trials, but it was a passage that he freely walked, confident that the victory of his final surrender awaited him on the other side of his struggles.

A Miracle of Transformation: "Indifference," Peace, and Love

The cross of Jesus only makes sense in light of the resurrection. His surrender was the gateway to his triumph. From his suffering and death, Jesus passed to unimaginable good. God the Father was present—though unseen—even in the darkest moments of Jesus' suffering, even as in his humanity he felt abandoned. But the Savior trusted even then and commended himself into the hands of his heavenly Father. And his hope was not disappointed. Now this is the promise to all who embrace their own cross in faith. Suffering and trial can be the gateway to unimaginable good. This was Rafael's own discovery as his earthly journey approached its end.

With a profound trust in the mysterious but providential work-ings of God, Rafael had begun to see, even with his first departure from the monastery and the discovery of his diabetes, that his trials

69. CW 599, #168.

were ultimately for his good. Each new trial and, with it, the renewed experience of struggle in coming to its acceptance in faith revealed to him that his complete abandonment to God was not yet complete. Each new suffering that God permitted for him opened his eyes in order to free him of his own self-derived plans and self-generated dreams. Rafael began to see the enormous grace and mercy of God at work through a path that humanly speaking so often ran contrary to what one would reasonably desire. God was uncovering for him a deeper, more authentic vision of reality and a truer path of surrender and self-offering. And so even while suffering in itself remained suffering, it could be, at the same time, for Rafael an invitation to gratitude and even joy—and thus, of peace.[70]

Rafael saw in himself that through the experience of suffering and his acceptance of it, God had worked a change within him. He found himself more able both to embrace others just as they were and to find peace in the midst of everything. In a letter to his Uncle Polín, written after his third departure from the monastery, he explained,

> On the path that the Lord is leading me down, this path that only God and I know, I have stumbled many times; I have endured deep, bitter sorrows; I have had to make continual renunciations; I have experienced disappointments; and the Lord has frustrated even the hopes I'd thought holiest. May He be blessed. Because, well, every part of that was necessary . . . My *solitude* was necessary. The renunciation of my will was necessary. My illness was, and is, necessary. But why? Because, look: as the Lord has led me from place to place, leaving me without a fixed abode, showing me what I am, and detaching me from His creatures, sometimes gently, other times roughing me up . . . along this whole path, which I see so clearly now, I've come to learn something, and my soul has changed . . . I don't know if this will make sense, but I've learned to love people as they are, and not as

70. CW 404, #105.

I wish they were. My soul—with or without a cross, whether good or bad, wherever it may be, wherever God places it, as God wishes it—has undergone a transformation . . . I can't explain it, I don't have the words . . . but I call it *serenity* . . . It is a very great peace that allows you to both suffer and rejoice . . . It is knowing you are loved by God, despite our littleness and misery.[71]

Later, in a journal entry written in the month before he died, Rafael did not hesitate to speak of the change that God had worked in him as a "great," "wonderful," "divine," and "tremendous" miracle.[72] He exclaims: "You are changing my soul so much! . . . What a wonderful miracle."[73] And a principal manifestation of this divine work was not only acceptance but an expansive love for others. Rafael had come to embrace both his own "wretchedness" as loved by God and his brother monks as they were.

Rafael's union with Christ in his sufferings had united him too with the Savior's love for the world: "*My vocation is to suffer*, to suffer in silence for the whole world; to immolate myself with Jesus for the sins of my brothers and sisters, for priests, for missionaries, for the needs of the church, for the sins of the world, and for the needs of my family, whom I do not want to see enjoying earthly abundance but rather very close to God."[74] Two weeks before his death, Rafael wrote:

I am filled with such tenderness when I think about these fathomless favors that Jesus grants me. My soul is filled with true love for human beings, for my weak, sick brothers and sisters . . . It is understanding now, and sweetly forgives the weaknesses that used to make it suffer when it would see them in its neighbor . . . Oh, if only the world loved God a

71. CW 551, #159.
72. CW 656–58, #193.
73. CW 655, #193.
74. CW 649, #189.

little, they would love their neighbor too. When you love
Jesus, when you love Christ, you also *necessarily* love what He
loves. Did Jesus not die of love for human beings? As our
hearts are transformed into the heart of Christ, then, we too
feel this and note its effects . . . and the greatest of them all
is *love . . . love for the Father's will . . . love for everyone* who
suffers and struggles, whether they're a father or a far-off
brother, whether they're English, Japanese, or Trappist.[75]

Again, only two weeks before his death, Rafael writes of the
marvelous work that God is accomplishing in him: "My soul loses
itself in this great wonder, and goes mute."[76] But here, he notes
that its manifestation is what he calls "indifference"—a term
drawn probably from early Jesuit training or perhaps in subsequent
reading: "Indifference is one of the transformations that Jesus has
brought about in my soul. I am amazed at this myself, because I'm
realizing that I've come to understand something I didn't before."[77]
By coming to accept, embrace, and even rejoice in his trials, Rafael
had arrived at an inner freedom, a peace that comes with having
abandoned oneself into the loving hands of a providential God.
Freed of attachments to things and to one's own plans, projects,
and priorities, he was at peace—even in the midst of his isolation
and the growing physical symptoms of his declining health due
to diabetes. He was not only at peace but happy: "Every day I am
happier to have completely abandoned myself in His hands."[78]

A Theologian of the Cross

Cardinal Antonio Innocenti, who was prefect of the Congregation
of the Clergy, is quoted upon studying Rafael's writings as con-

75. CW 684, #202.
76. CW 678, #201.
77. CW 679, #201.
78. CW 679, #201.

cluding that it was simply amazing that a young layman who had not studied philosophy, theology, biblical exegesis, patrology, or even Latin could have arrived at such a profound understanding of the mystery of the cross. Rafael's writings include page after page of deep reflections on the cross and suffering, and yet not one of the official censors or consultors who reviewed his writings could find anything of concern in his interpretations and explanations. Rafael, the cardinal concluded, had arrived at an exceptional clarity concerning the cross, the authentic spiritual path, and the contemplative life.[79] Rafael, the twenty-seven-year-old Trappist oblate, had become a true theologian of the cross—and, more important, his experience, reflection, and embrace of the cross in his own life had accelerated his own attainment of the purity of heart that is the goal of the monastic life.

79. Quoted by Tomás Gallego Fernández, "El hermano Rafael y su causa de beatificación," *Cistercium* 179 (Oct.–Dec. 1989): 422–23.

Conclusion

Anyone who sets out to live the gospel in its entirety is faced with the fact that embracing its message seems to be beyond our capacity. When we have this realization it is tempting to settle for less, telling ourselves, *This teaching is difficult; who can accept it?* (John 6:60). Saint Thomas Aquinas explains plainly why accepting some Gospel sayings can be as hard for us as it was for Jesus' first disciples when he spoke about their having to eat his flesh and drink his blood:[1] "a saying is hard either because it resists the intellect or because it resists the will, that is, when we cannot understand it with our mind, or when it does not please our will."[2]

The message that Christ preached from the cross is the hardest of Jesus' sayings. Mind and will resist it because it surpasses both our comprehension and the strength of our wills. But this is the science that Rafael went to learn at his Trapa. Rafael's attempt transformed his life into an extension of Christ's message, a hard saying, difficult for his contemporaries to accept and for us as well. When we read some of Rafael's words or consider his decision to return to the monastery despite the suffering that it involved for him, we may feel some resistance in our minds and wills, tempting us to dismiss his witness. However, if we dare to go beyond this

1. See John 6:22-69.

2. Thomas Aquinas, *Commentary on the Gospel of John Chapters 6–12*, trans. Fabian Larcher and James A. Weisheipl (Washington, DC: The Catholic University of America Press, 2010), 52.

initial response, we might be surprised to discover that Rafael himself knew this inner resistance well. But he fought against it, and as he gradually overcame his aversion through grace, he was able to identify it as the voice of his ego and self-will—the greatest obstacle for embracing the Gospel fully and living for God alone.

The Cistercian abbot Isaac of Stella spoke to his brothers of this battle within us in one of his sermons: "the son of man in me hates and persecutes the son of God, that is, the flesh persecutes the spirit."[3] But this persecution of the spirit by the flesh, he explains, is not manifest as overt hostility: rather, the flesh seeks to subvert the spirit not "by getting rid of it but by attracting it."[4] Rafael knew well what the Cistercian abbot meant: the flesh (the old man within) tries to entice the desires in us that come from the Spirit and redirect them toward worldly goals. Rafael had a strong spiritual desire to surrender his life completely to God through the monastic path, but many advised him to follow a more prudent course for his own good. Still, Rafael clung to his "God alone" to shield himself not only from the voices without, the spirit of the world, but above all from the enticing voice of the ego, the old man within, who Rafael knew still had some power over his flesh.

Eight centuries before Rafael, Isaac of Stella had told his monks regarding the old man, "he still needs to be crucified in each of us."[5] Moreover, he continued, "Why do we seek pleasure or rest? We are on the cross. Or rather, we used to be in the world; we are now in hell—but in a hell of mercy, not of anger—and we will be in heaven."[6] However, we can also apply here Saint Bernard's words, "Let self-will cease, and hell will be no more,"[7] pointing to the fact that it is our inner resistance to God's transformative

3. Isaac of Stella, *Sermons on the Christian Year*, trans. Lewis White, CF 66 (Collegeville, MN: Cistercian Publications, 2019), 4.

4. Isaac of Stella, *Sermons*, 4.

5. Isaac of Stella, *Sermons*, 2.

6. Isaac of Stella, *Sermons*, 6.

7. Bernard of Clairvaux, *Sermons for Lent and the Easter Season*, trans. Irene Edmonds, CF 52 (Collegeville, MN: Cistercian Publications, 2013), 170.

love and the fact that we are being stretched beyond our natural capacities that makes the process painful. If we surrender in trust, we will get to experience that God's *power is made perfect in weakness* (2 Cor 12:9). Even if suffering or confusion remains, God's grace will be sufficient so that we can press on following the Master. This was Rafael's experience.

When Jesus' invitation seemed to be beyond Rafael's powers, he refused to run away and abandon the Master. On the contrary, he persevered in faith, and through his fidelity in pursuing the monastic path, Rafael's heart and will were set in order so that he could become one with the Father's will: "the more we detach ourselves from disordered love for creatures and for ourselves, the closer and closer we get to the only love there is, the only wish, the only desire in this life . . . true sanctification, which is God."[8] The struggle ceased, and only mercy remained, only love and a single desire: God alone.

But why does God allow the struggle? Or, in the words of Saint Antony of Egypt, "Why did you not appear at the beginning so you could stop my suffering?"[9] Rafael acknowledged that when people are visited by suffering their natural reaction is to ask God, "Lord, why are you doing this?" But, Rafael continued, "It seems that God responds, 'Trust Me.'"[10] And he learned to trust more and more in response to the challenges and disappointments he encountered. He knew that Jesus had never been absent. When Rafael could not feel Jesus' presence, he believed that Christ looked at him from the cross, and little by little this became sufficient for him. Rafael wanted to acknowledge God as fully worthy of his trust, and in complete surrender he allowed the Father to do with him as he pleased. Remaining still under the hand of God, Rafael's heart was purified and made whole: he achieved the goal of the monastic way of life.

---

8. CW 680, #201.

9. Athanasius of Alexandria. *The Life of Antony: The Coptic Life and the Greek Life*, trans. Tim Vivian and Apostolos N. Athanassakis, with Rowan A Greer, CS 202 (Kalamazoo, MI: Cistercian Publications, 2003), 85.

10. CW 110, #36.

Blessed Guerric of Igny's depiction of the monk as one who is waiting in suspense for the Lord's return, one who hangs on the cross between heaven and earth,[11] matches Rafael perfectly. There is joy and hope in this kind of waiting, but there is also the pain of being stretched by desire. As he hung in suspense, Rafael was being called to exercise the virtues of faith, hope, and love given to him. Despite his apparent weakness, even helplessness, God was making him strong in his grace. Rafael learned in this way the science of the cross, which consists "of knowing how to wait."[12] He was learning how to suffer well, because in waiting for Christ and suffering in and for him there is no opposition between happiness and pain.

We can recognize in Rafael's life two essential forms of purification of his heart. At the beginning of his monastic journey, Rafael was prompt in selling all that hindered him from responding to Jesus' call to follow him. He kept up this active form of self-denial all his life, but later he realized that this was not enough. He had to temper his natural impulse to do more, to learn to simply be still, trusting in God's designs for him, even in the darkness of suffering. Waiting on the cross, Rafael was purified in a more passive way: "He sends me a cross, and draws me near to His own . . . and so all I have to do is wait, wait with faith and love, wait, embracing His cross."[13]

Toward the end of his life, Rafael became aware that the active and passive stripping that his heart had undergone was absolutely necessary, and he praised God for the work that divine grace had accomplished in him. Now, with a pure heart he could see God and recognize God's action. He was free. Free to live for God alone. Free to love God, and everyone in him. Rafael had become the saint he had always wanted to be, but without realizing it. He had also

---

11. See Guerric's First Sermon for Advent, in Guerric of Igny, *Liturgical Sermons I*, trans. a monk of Mount Saint Bernard Abbey, CF 8 (Shannon, Ireland: Cistercian Publications, 1970), 4–5.

12. CW 329, #87.

13. CW 630, #182.

become a prophet of his defining theme—"God alone"—which he repeated with his silent shouting, like the *voice of one crying out in the wilderness* (John 1:23). Like John the Baptist, Rafael was willing to decrease to let Christ increase.[14] And furthermore, because he no longer had a self to defend and had no need to conform himself to any expectations, Rafael could speak as a prophet, bringing God's message to his people: God alone, God alone!

Rafael himself acknowledged that it is difficult to capture the meaning of these two words.[15] They are full of awe before a God who is always greater, zeal for a God who deserves all glory, and love for a God who should be loved without measure. These two words are difficult to understand because they contain a wisdom that is foolishness in the eyes of the world. Ultimately, like the words of the prophets of old, they invite all Christians to make a choice: do you want to be a fool in the eyes of the world, or in the eyes of God? Loving God with an undivided heart and living for God alone implies letting ourselves be carried away by the foolishness of the cross. In this foolishness, we ourselves become fools for Christ, each one according to his or her vocation.

As Rafael silently preached this message, he was walking in the footsteps of the first Cistercian fathers. In their reform, they had followed the impulse they experienced in contemplating the excess and foolishness that God had shown in his incarnation and passion.[16] Bernard of Clairvaux called himself a jester, and Rafael compared himself with a clown, not because they did particularly strange things but because they were willing to follow a path of humiliation to proclaim, *Not to us, O Lord, not to us, but to your name give the glory, for the sake of your steadfast love and your faithfulness*

---

14. See John 3:30.

15. See CW 566, #162.

16. See John Saward's presentation of "Holy Madness" as the rationale for the Cistercian reform (John Saward, "God's Jesters: The Cistercians," in *Perfect Fools: Folly for Christ's Sake in Catholic and Orthodox Spirituality* [Oxford: Oxford University Press, 1980], 58–79).

(Ps 115:1 NRSV). To give God glory is to choose to love him above all things, no matter what.

Abba Pambo said, "If you have a heart, you can be saved."[17] Rafael had a heart, a big heart that experienced the struggle of clinging to people's affections and to his own desires and expectations, a heart that gradually became aware of all these weaknesses, and precisely for this reason opened itself wide to grace. And grace set in order what creation had given.[18] Rafael welcomed and cooperated with it, and he came to know the perfect love that casts out servile fear.[19] This is the transformation that Saint Benedict envisioned for those who dare to climb the steps of humility he described in chapter seven of his Rule (RB 7.67). Rafael ascended up to the last rung, descending into the depths of the Paschal mystery he embraced with his whole being.

Rafael's last words written in his journal read, "Only Jesus can fill the heart and soul."[20] His own heart and soul were full of the love he had discovered. As Rafael strove to live for God alone, deep within he knew that the God he loved also loved him, as if Rafael alone existed. But he did not believe that he was the exception. This love, hidden in the cross, is the treasure Christ offers to all. Who wouldn't go mad? We just need to try it, as Rafael wrote, "And then you'll start to say to yourself a bit, slowly at first, and then very quickly, 'God alone . . . God alone . . . God alone,' until suddenly you realize that you've gone crazy too, and your heart is overjoyed . . . because of how much you love God."[21]

17. *The Sayings of the Desert Fathers: The Alphabetical Collection*, trans. Benedicta Ward, rev. ed., CS 59 (London and Oxford: Mowbray; Kalamazoo, MI: Cistercian Publications, 1984), 197.

18. See Bernard of Clairvaux, *On Grace and Free Choice*, trans. Daniel O'Donovan, CF 19 (Kalamazoo, MI: Cistercian Publications, 1977), 72.

19. See 1 John 4:18.

20. CW 693, #206.

21. CW 567, #162.

APPENDIX

Excerpts from Rafael's Writings

CW 12. To Dom Félix Alonso García[1]

Ávila, November 19, 1933

Reverend Father,

I don't know if you will remember me, for it has been some time, about three years,[2] since I was last able to spend a few days at La Trapa. Even so, since that time, the Lord our God has been working within me in such a way that He has formed in me the firm intention to give myself to Him with all my heart and body and soul, and in order to fulfill my intention and resolution, and, moreover, trusting in God's help, it is my desire to enter the Cistercian Order. This is, in short, my Reverend Father, the reason that I am requesting an interview with you as soon as possible, so that your reverence might lend me your help and counsel.

---

1. Dom Félix Alonso García was the abbot of the monastery of San Isidro de Dueñas.

2. Rafael refers to the three years that had passed since his first visit to La Trapa, in September 1930, but he had in fact been to the monastery since then. He had done the Ignatian Spiritual Exercises there from June 17–26, 1932 (OC 88).

I believe that I can rely on God, and in Him alone I trust, but as I take my first steps, I also trust in the charity of your reverence, whom I already regard as a father, and whom I beg to admit me as his son.

I am in Ávila with my aunt and uncle, awaiting your reply with the natural anxiety of one who wishes to give everything to God.

On the other hand, I have only to add that I am not motivated to change my life in this way because of sadness or suffering or disappointment or disillusionment with the world . . . I have all that it can give me. God, in His infinite goodness, has given me such gifts in this life, many more than I deserve . . . As such, my reverend Father, if you receive me into your community alongside your sons, be assured that you will be receiving only a heart filled with joy and much love for God.

Awaiting your reply, and humbly asking your blessing, your son in Jesus and Mary,

Rafael Arnaiz

CW 64. To Dom Félix Alonso García

Ávila, October 9, 1935

J-H-S

Reverend and dear Father Abbot,

I have offered many prayers to the Most Blessed Virgin before beginning this letter, and spent a lot of time consulting Jesus by the tabernacle . . . The time has come for me to decide to open my heart to my superiors at once, in order to tell them my decision and the journey my soul has made.

Reverend Father, I want you to understand my words, which, though clumsy, are sincere; and for you to be merciful toward me. And so, I have asked God for this.

Reverend Father, I've been away from my beloved Trapa for nearly a year and a half now, and if only you knew, Reverend Father, how great a work the Lord has done in me! . . . And how

grateful I am to Him for the trial that He is making me endure
. . . I've often thought about how unworthy I am, that Jesus
should care for me, but how could He not? . . . Do I not care for
Him? God is so good, and He knows what He is doing, and
sometimes He uses the least and most miserable of all earthly
things in order to make known His majesty.

When I requested that you admit me into the community two
years ago, writing from this same Ávila, my desire was good and
holy; I was searching for God, and God gave Himself to me so
freely . . . I suffered, but when it's for His sake, it's not suffering
. . . I had hopes and dreams, I wanted to be holy, I thought with
delight about the choir, about being a real monk someday . . . There
was so much happening within me, Reverend Father . . . I was
searching for God, but I was also searching for His creatures, and
I was searching for myself; and God wants me all to Himself . . .
My vocation was from God, and is of God, but it needed to be purified, its rough edges needed smoothing. I gave myself to the Lord
generously, but I still wasn't giving Him *everything*; I gave Him my
body, my soul, my career, my family . . . but I still held on to one
thing: my dreams and desires, my hopes of being a Trappist and
making my vows and singing the Mass. That kept me going at La
Trapa, but God wants more, He always wants more. I needed to be
transformed. He wanted His love alone to be enough for me.

With a novice's zeal, I offered Him . . . I offered Him something, but I didn't know what. I thought I didn't have anything
left to give Him, that my life was the one thing I had left, and
that He already knew it was His.

Reverend Father, I have nothing else to tell you; God sent me
a trial, and at first I thought it meant that God didn't love me, that
His will was different, but He doesn't ask for our opinion or explain
Himself when He sends us something that's good for us. Weak
creatures, what do you know of God's designs! He'll handle doing
the work without consulting us. All we have to do is let ourselves
be shaped in His hands, and hold still, very still; later, the time and
light He has sent us will allow us to see His work clearly, and then
we will give Him infinite thanks for His loving care.

How many tears must be shed before one is willing to kiss the cross! First we ask for a cross, and then we cry when it is given to us; but once we are on it, how happy we are to find ourselves at Christ's side . . . Though He is a God, He died on the cross for us; so if we truly love Him, the cross ought to be and must be our delight. Isn't that so?

Forgive me, Reverend Father, I've gone astray from where I should be; I'll return to the purpose of my letter.

I was at the monastery about a year ago, and I shared how I was feeling at the time with Fr. Marcelo and with Your Reverence.[3] I asked Fr. Marcelo if it would be possible for me to one day enter as an oblate,[4] due to the diet I have to follow; he said yes, and Your Reverence told me to wait . . . I have waited, for the will of my superiors is the will of God . . . I have waited a year, which seemed like a century to me. The Most Blessed Virgin has upheld me in my vocation; the Lord has given me to understand that the world is not my place, that He wants me beside the tabernacle—and, Reverend Father, to the tabernacle I wish to go.

Once more, then, I ask the community to admit this poor man, who neither wants nor desires anything more than to dwell in the house of God.

I don't deserve to be a monk . . . Singing Holy Mass . . . Lord, if I am to see you so soon, what does it matter? . . . The vows . . . do I not love God with all my strength? Then what do vows matter? None of that prevents me from being at His side, dedicating my silence among men to Him, and loving Him quietly and humbly in the simplicity of the oblature.[5] Saint Benedict admitted oblates, and some of them became saints. Why should I not be among

---

3. Rafael spoke with the abbot alongside Fr. Marcelo León, master of novices, on the visit of November 21, 1934 (OC 392).

4. *Oblate*: A lay member of a monastery who does not take vows and observes a modified schedule (see CW 7, #13).

5. *Oblature*: The status of being an oblate (comparable to "the novitiate" for the status of being a novice).

them? . . . Of my own strength I cannot, but with Jesus and Mary at my side, I can do all things. When I fall, They will help me.

Your Reverence will speak of the humiliation this entails, the fact of being nothing and no one. But am I someone now? As for humiliation, I don't believe I will feel that way, because in order for a soul to be humbled it must first be up high and then be brought low; and I don't think I have to be brought low at all. Quite the contrary, the real humiliation is when a creature is exalted in the eyes of men, because when that person stands before God, so wretched and wicked in His divine eyes while so extolled by men . . . then he will know true humiliation.

Forgive me, and be merciful to me, Reverend Father—but surely the miter that the Lord has placed in your hands is more of a humiliation than being assigned the lowest place in a Trappist monastery. Did God not humble Himself? That can indeed be called humiliation, but when it comes to us? That word does not apply to us, insignificant dust that we are. Look what I'm saying, my good Father Abbot! Take all this as the ramblings of someone madly in love with God . . . and if I fail to show you the respect I owe you, forgive me; but I want you to know everything I am thinking and how I am feeling about it, and when I sat down to write, I promised to expose my soul completely.

There are so many things I'd say to you, if only I knew how to write. It gives me such joy to think of how God loves me, the path down which He is guiding me, the undeserved light He gives me . . . But of course, I have God, and God has hold of me; what more could I desire? I spoke to you of the cross before, but with Him I no longer have one. My sorrows and the tears I poured out for Him have turned into peace and calm. I have the Lord; let me live beside His tabernacle, eating the crumbs that fall from the convent's table, and I'll be happy . . . happy in my nothing, and joyous in my Everything, who is Jesus.

Your Reverence, do you see the work of God now? He has accomplished the greatest and most admirable work in me, a creature of His who—and I don't say this with insincerity or false modesty—has nothing and deserves nothing; I have only sins to offer such a good God . . . I possess neither virtue nor knowledge, but I do know what I am . . . and God knows it too. I might be able to fool human beings, but I can't fool Him.

Tell me, Reverend Father, if my vocation is not from God. Enlighten me if I am deceived; have no mercy. Jesus made use of a harsh blow to make me see clearly before. But if Your Reverence goes before God and considers my situation, you will see a man who, despite everything, is still thinking of his Trapa.

It has been two years (or it will be two in January) since I entered the novitiate. Even so, perhaps not in the eyes of men, but certainly in the eyes of God, I have not ceased for even a moment to be Brother Rafael, Cistercian novice. I assure you that, even if I were to spend the rest of my life in the world, in spirit I would continue to be a Trappist. I carry it deep within me, and the Virgin of La Trapa is always at my side. I am sure that She wants me there, and She wants me to inhabit the humility of which She is an example to us.

I fear only one thing, and that is to fail to be a good example to the community in the observance of the holy Rule, but God wishes to take even that from me, which is a great consolation. Of course, being despised and being no one is a consolation too, and a much greater one, but that is out of my hands and I am not seeking it either.

The other day, a very holy nun whom I went to consult about my decision told me that the Lord would give me so much more this way than if I continued to be a choir novice.[6] I also recall what Your Reverence told me when I entered the monastery, that God would repay me even in this world for the sacrifice I was making . . . Anyway, as God well knows, I don't follow God for any of that now . . . I love God just because, and that's it. Even though I love God very little, my love isn't mercenary. I know that He loves me, and that is enough for me.

---

6. *Choir novice*: When Rafael first entered the monastery, he was called a *choir novice* because he was in formation to become a choir monk, as distinct from a lay brother.

It is a very great mortification to follow the Rule and observe the fasts, but perhaps it is an even greater one to have to take an indulgence.[7]

I still haven't brought up my health, and well, it is the least of my concerns. I'm doing about the same, I carry on with my normal life other than when it comes to food. I could follow the Rule for many years, even. Diabetes is simply a matter of a particular type of diet: switching out some foods for others, maybe taking indulgences . . . Medication by way of injections from time to time, and that's it.

If what I am attempting were absurd on a practical level, I wouldn't have even dared to propose it to Your Reverence. I am merely holding onto Fr. Marcelo's words: that there are many cases like mine, or very similar to mine, in many of the monasteries in France.

If a donation is necessary in order to avoid burdening the community, I don't think my father would refuse me, but they don't know anything yet. I'm waiting for your reply before talking to them; I don't think they'd have or raise any objections.

In any case, I will wait for Your Reverence to decide and give me your answer about what I ought to do, or if I should come speak to you in person. Everything else can wait until afterwards. It's all in Mary's hands.

In Madrid, I went to see a doctor who is well known in this field, and he told me that I have a light form of pancreatic diabetes that would eventually correct itself, but in the meantime I should not consume excessive starch or sugar. I just have to be careful. I wouldn't have any trouble following this diet in the monastery, whether in the refectory in the infirmary, it's all the same to me, or in the guesthouse, if Your Reverence so instructs. Ultimately, when we go up to receive the Lord at Communion, He doesn't ask us if we have eaten this or that. He is the same for everyone in the community, isn't that so? He won't love me any less than

---

7. *Indulgence*: A reprieve from the usual monastic fare at mealtimes.

Br. Damián or Br. Bernardo because they eat bread and beans while I eat milk and eggs. God has arranged it thus, so He must know best. When we are all reunited in His presence, and the day is coming soon, such small differences will fade away. They are merely human differences, and we must dispense with all that is human, not just in heaven but also here on earth. For if we view everything supernaturally, everything brings us to God: both the rigorous fast of the one who can observe it, and the care taken by the one who is sick, amid all his miseries. Thus I return to my theme, Reverend Father: we who have God have everything. What does the rest of it matter?

I'm not writing to Fr. Marcelo because I know that he's sick and is not in the novitiate.[8] Please give him my kind regards, and the same to the whole community. My regards also to my confessor, Fr. Teófilo, who is often in my thoughts, for I have found myself so alone on so many occasions, and in such doubt, that I've had much to offer God, although it is all rather little.

Of course, I've also consulted souls who are very much of God, and they have enlightened me quite a bit. For most of the time that I've been away from La Trapa, however, I have been face to face only with God, and even that was only when He did not hide Himself from me. May He be blessed, for I certainly deserved that; my sins have not been few.

If only you knew, Reverend Father, how much the Virgin has helped me! She lifted me up when I fell, upheld me over all the threats I have faced in my vocation, and consoled me when I found myself struggling against the world, which is so clingy . . . Whether I'd been good, bad, or something in between, at seven in the evening when I united myself to my brothers in choir and prayed the *Salve* to her, I felt a seeming consolation at the thought of the Virgin uniting me to La Trapa; She was protecting us all, gazing upon us

---

8. Fr. Marcelo León died on October 1, 1935 (OC 396). He had been succeeded as master of novices by Fr. José Olmedo Arrieta on July 7, 1935 (OC 397).

all, both the Trappists in their monastery and me wherever I found myself. What would become of us were it not for Her?

Forgive me, Reverend Father, this letter is going on too long . . . this is an outlet for me. It's so difficult to speak of love for God and the Virgin in the world.

Tell Br. Ramón to pray for me, and that I think of him often. He has very much been on my mind, because he suffered, just as I did, in leaving it all behind, and that is very difficult . . . His prayers must be very pleasing to the Lord.

There are so many things I'd like to ask you to tell all my brothers, Fr. Francisco, Buenaventura, Br. Tescelino . . . everyone. They'll think I forgot, but souls who love one another for God's sake never forget, and in loving each other they love God. Loving Him in His creatures is a great consolation, and it takes nothing away from His glory; at least, if I am not mistaken.

Answer me, Reverend Father, I beg you for the sake of charity; it will bring consolation to my soul to learn that I may still, however unworthily, begin my name with the "Brother María" of the Cistercians.

Your Reverence can expect an oblate who wants only to give glory to God, to love Him, and to serve Him; a soul who wants nothing, and surrenders to Him even the desire to be professed, for He asks him to. And believe me, I surrender not with any violence to myself, but with pleasure and joy.

I will try to be a holy oblate with the aid of heaven, the counsel of my good superiors, and the help of my community, whom I ask to remember me in their prayers.

Humbly asking your blessing, your novice in Jesus and Mary,

Brother María Rafael
+O.C.R.[9]

---

9. *O.C.R.*: "*Orden Cisterciense Reformada*," or Reformed Cistercian Order (see CW 39, #12).

CW 72. To María Osorio[10]

Oviedo, November 16, 1935

J-H-S

My dearest sister,

First of all, I must say that as to "taking advantage" of writing me again . . . How could you say that! . . . Truly, I forgive you, because you don't know what you are saying. Now I'm the one who doesn't know what to say . . . It's very *beautiful* what's happening to you . . . I understand you perfectly, and I praise God for it.

I received your letter this morning. I was waiting for the mail to arrive at noon so that I could then go make my visit to the Lord . . . I read it with all the charity you need not ask of me . . . And after seeing in it your soul, which is so transparent to me, I went to see God at the Handmaids' convent.[11] On the one hand, I was very sad; I am human. On the other, I was very content . . . Overall, a bit overwhelmed by the *work of God* . . . I don't know what I said to Him. I talked to Him about you, and thinking of you, I prayed, though not for very long . . . a friend of mine was waiting for me. He "doesn't know what is happening to him," so perhaps he has a vocation. I didn't seek him out, but rather he sought me out, and if I can do something . . . Well, God will do it, just as He does everything. We are but His instruments . . .

Later, thinking of your letter, I hardly spoke to Him . . . I knew that you were suffering . . . I saw you at the foot of the cross on Calvary, all alone . . . on a stormy night, and the holy wood without Jesus . . . I saw you suffering. Do you remember what I drew that one night on a piece of paper when I saw you cry? . . . How good it is to be at the foot of the Lord's cross, when He is looking at us . . . The hard thing is to stay on the cross when Christ disappears before our eyes and the cross remains, all dry and black and

---

10. Rafael's aunt, married to Leopoldo Barón.
11. *Handmaids*: The Handmaids of the Sacred Heart of Jesus.

bloody . . . And neither Saint John nor the holy women nor Mary is on Calvary . . . We are all alone in darkness with the cross. We neither know how to pray nor do we hear God, *nothing* . . . all we know is suffering . . . we look for Christ . . . and He is not there.

What does that matter to us? . . . Is that not what the Lord wants? . . . Well then! . . .

Take heart, my dear sister; Jesus is on the other side of everything that you can't see. He is looking at you, He sees you cry for Him, and your tears wash away many things. How happy you will be! Mary did nothing but look at the Lord. What merit would she have had if the Lord had been there, and saw her, and spoke to her, and consoled her . . . ? There's no need for any of that.

Love God without seeing Him or feeling Him, although I know how hard it is not to feel Him, especially when one truly loves Him . . . And then you *feel Him without feeling Him.* Does that make sense? You believe yourself far from Him, but that's not true . . . You tell me of His justice, how He is punishing you . . . My poor sister . . . you are far from that. It's not that you don't deserve that . . . but rather that if the Lord were to allow His justice and punishment to fall upon us . . . who would survive?[12] No, there is no such punishment; His goodness toward you, on the other hand . . . Think about it, and you'll see: He loves you so! . . . He is cutting away your imperfections with the gentlest of chisels; He is *emptying* you out so that He might enter . . . don't you see? Without a doubt, this process requires tears, and many of them; but if they are His work, blessed be those tears . . .

Let Him work, suffer . . . but love Him while you suffer. Love Him dearly through the darkness, despite the storm in which the Lord has seemingly placed you, despite not being able to see Him. Love the naked wood of the cross . . . Your tears will dry, your suffering will pass, the night will come to an end. Such joy! . . .

12. Ps 130:3.

But love never ends.[13] It grows and expands, and when the Lord allows a small ray of light to reach us . . . we love and thank Him for it all the more. Is that not so, my dear little sister? Haven't you noticed that? . . . When it seems your suffering is at its worst, and God reveals something of Himself . . . What happens then? . . . Then it's as though water is "boiling" inside me, even if it's just for a moment.[14] When the cross returns, and it is bare once more . . . may that be blessed too!

Cry, cry as hard as you can, and suffer . . . but do so at the foot of the cross, and love God while you suffer. Such happiness! How God loves you . . . you'll see, someday very soon . . . What do you care about anything else? You have God's love. Even if you can't feel it, He is doing His work . . . let Him. . . .

I have such a great treasure, my dear sister . . . I should like to shout for joy and tell all of creation . . . "Bless the Lord . . . love the Lord . . . He is so good, He is so great . . . He is God." And instead, I have to keep quiet . . . quiet, always quiet, and love Him alone in silence. Do you understand? The world doesn't see, it's blind, and God needs love, so much love. I can't give Him enough, I'm small, I'm going crazy trying. I wish the world would love Him, but the world is His enemy.

Lord, what a great torture this is! I see this, but I cannot fix it . . . I am so small and insignificant. The love I have for You overwhelms me. I wish my family and friends, all of them, would love You very much, so that I could rest a little . . . But the world, which is so busy with its concerns and affairs and discussions, takes me for a madman . . .

Lord, what should I do? Love, love . . . I can't. The world spurns this treasure of mine, which is Your love. This makes me suffer, because You are suffering.

And then here you come, my dear little sister, a beggar for love . . . and you want me—of all people, me—to talk to you about

13. 1 Cor 13:8.
14. Quotation marks in the original.

God . . . It's enough to make one go crazy. How could I not talk to you? Of course I will . . . even though I have no words. I jump with joy as I see that your soul, like mine, wants nothing and yearns for nothing but love of God . . . That's when I don't know what to do or say. I can't even talk to you about the cross, or suffering, or anything at all, not about you, not about me. Love moves my pen, and the paper feels too small for it. I have no words. I get so worked up, sometimes I don't even know what I'm saying, but I pour my heart out, I can't help it . . .

What does it all matter? We're so little and insignificant. We obsess over the most irrelevant details . . . Love for God!!! There is no path, no route, no peak, no valley; it all disappears; love for God floods it all. Do you know what that means? Do you understand? Forgive me, I can't resist anymore, I'm weak and wretched and unprepared . . . I don't know what I am saying. When the water boils over, I have to let it.

Forgive me, again. I don't know if the same thing happens to you. Sometimes when I talked to you in the past—remember?—I'd get worked up a bit. The same thing happens when I write, I can't help it . . . I have to stop and light a cigarette. I don't know if that's the right thing to do. As you can see, I'm completely honest with you, too . . . But with this pen, I feel completely powerless to tell you everything I'd like to, and send you what I'd like to . . . Anyway, God sees, and you don't need me to explain. But this morning, when I saw that sentence in your letter where you said it was "just for me," I saw that clearly the same thing happens to you . . . Blessed be God, that He should permit such things in creatures as wretched as we are.

What I don't know is how we can live or reflect or think or do anything useful. Either we are foolish or we are oblivious. God forgive us.

It doesn't matter to me if you lack consolation or experience dryness or if your path goes one way or the other . . . It doesn't matter to me if you are suffering or rejoicing . . . What does matter to me is that *all this*, which is *nothing*, helps you to love Jesus as He was at Gethsemane, the Jesus of Nazareth who called mourners blessed.[15] What matters is that you follow Him wherever He goes, and that you see only the love with which He looks at you and draws you . . . Sometimes we are in the wheatfields of Judea, listening to Him speak on a calm afternoon; sometimes we follow Him into the courts of the temple and listen to Him there, awestruck. Sometimes we are on the Mount of Olives, wanting to help Him a little, wiping away His tears of blood . . . that is true suffering . . . We poor creatures know nothing of that.

Sometimes we walk the Way of Sorrows; sometimes He is on the cross, and we are at the Virgin's side . . .

But always with Jesus, at every moment, without giving any thought as to what we are to eat or drink or what we are to wear,[16] forgetting ourselves completely. Always with Him . . . Following Him quietly, without even the expectation that He will turn to look at us . . . Do we deserve that at all? . . . How good such a life is! If only you knew! Beggars for His love . . . when we follow in His footsteps with devotion, we forget about everything else, I promise you. There is nothing left on earth that could distract us.

How sad it is to see people remain indifferent when they see Jesus and his whole retinue of disciples pass by . . . How joyful the apostles and friends of Jesus must have been each time someone saw clearly, gave up everything, joined them, and followed the man of Nazareth. All He was asking for was a little bit of love.

Shall we go follow Him, my dear sister? . . . He sees our intentions. He looks at us, smiles, and helps us . . . We have nothing to fear. Let's go be the last in that retinue roving the lands of Judea. We'll keep quiet, but we'll be nourished with an immense, enormous love for Jesus . . . He doesn't even need us to speak, or for us to get up close so He can see us, or great deeds, or anything that would call attention to ourselves . . . Yes, let's go be the last of Jesus' friends, but the ones who love Him the most.

15. Matt 5:4.
16. Matt 6:25.

What does it matter if we don't hear Him or see Him, if we know He is close to us *one way or the other*?

We shall accompany the Virgin, and speak to Her of Her Son. We'll tell Her how much we love Him . . . so if people don't pay Him any mind, She needn't worry, we'll give Him all the love that is lacking in the rest of humanity, and if we had to give our lives for Jesus a hundred times over, we'd do it . . . We'll give Mary so much consolation, won't we? . . . With the tenderness of children toward such a good Mother . . . And what will She say to us then? . . .

Look, once I start writing like this, I never stop. I have a whole world inside me, and it is so vast, so great, you can't even imagine . . . And yet it is so simple . . . It consists of nothing more than a very great love for Jesus and infinite tenderness for Mary. What more could I desire?

You have one too, you just don't know it. Your whole life is Jesus, although you haven't realized it yet, and that's why you are suffer- ing . . . When you realize this . . . you'll see how good it is. Someday, I'm sure, you'll say, "How blind I was when I suffered for *my* sake rather than *His*." You'll get there, just let Him work.

There are so many things I wanted to share with you in this letter, and I don't know if I'll manage any of them. I wanted to send you consolation from God, but if there's human consolation here, take that too. Why not? . . . To me, you are my very beloved sister, to whom I owe so many things—in heaven, you'll see. The Lord used you and Uncle Polín to plant a seed in me, and it has taken a long time to grow . . . and I don't know whether it'll produce flowers or thorns, but either way, it comes from God.

If only I could repay you some of what I owe . . . I'll always remember our chats at Pedrosillo.[17] I'd tell you one trifle after another, and with such charity, that you'd help me to see the Lord. I learned so much from you. It's not that we are doing the opposite

17. *Pedrosillo*: María Osorio and Leopoldo Barón's former estate outside of Ávila.

now, because even if you don't realize it, you are still doing me just as much good now as you did then. I never suspected that I was going to be able to pay you back. Blessed be God who permits such things.

As for me, I don't have anything new to tell you. My life just takes me from home to church, and from church back home, and always at different times, depending on my father's schedule. He takes great consolation in being with me; he doesn't even go to the cinema, or the theater, or the club . . . He and I are more spiritually united now than ever before. How great is the work of God.

The other day I went to see my former confessor. He told me that my plan was absurd,[18] and that God seemed to have abandoned me. Those were his words . . . So I haven't gone back to see him. What he said didn't rattle me or trouble me in the least . . . I didn't make anything of it . . . God alone is enough for me. I've gotten used to that over the past two years . . . That's what the Lord wanted of me. May His will be done. . . .

You'll say I'm getting tiresome with all this talk about loving God . . . Forgive me, I don't know how to talk about anything else.

I'll leave you now. I didn't realize, but it's two in the morning, and I need to sleep a bit so that I can get up in the morning to receive the Lord. How fortunate we are! Don't you think? . . .

My dearest sister, I've picked up my pen once more in order to continue this letter, which I don't want to go on too much longer. If I allowed myself to keep going, I'd never finish.

I've just received the Lord. I went to Mass at eight o'clock with my father . . . I was thinking of you. I don't have anything else to say. How dull, right? But look, you have to understand, words are so clumsy. You know that it's when we are quiet that we speak the

---

18. That is, Rafael's plan to re-enter the monastery.

most . . . How sweet the Lord is! Isn't he? How He draws us, and the way He does it.

Look, it is so good to be at the door to the Cenacle, and to watch Him give the bread to each of His disciples . . . and there are always a few crumbs left over for you. Isn't that right? . . . He gives them to you, and they fill you up just so . . . How good is Jesus! With a tender gaze, He commands you to draw near, tell Him everything, let Him console you . . . You see His immense love for you . . . *Everything* disappears, the disciples, even your own self . . . He fills it all . . . How good is Jesus! Then there are no more sorrows or joys, and we don't know what to say . . . we can't speak. We stay there, lost in His embrace, and then He speaks to the soul with such great gentleness . . . My dearest little sister, how good is Jesus! And He loves us so . . . I'm telling you, it's enough to make you melt . . . Does this happen to you too?

Leave it to Him, and you'll see . . . I promise you, in one true Communion we'd receive enough to last us the rest of our lives, if only we knew how to make one . . . But instead, we are so wretched. What a tragedy! But let us not lose heart, even amid dryness . . . again, how good is Jesus!

Why do I speak to you like this? I don't know. I have this great tenderness . . . I want to be able to share it with you . . . I want to send you *everything* the Lord gives me so generously; I ask Him to share it for me.

I don't know how to keep going, I can't. Forgive me, little sister . . . but you understand, right? All I can say is that you were with me at the door to the Cenacle . . . and He gave you a crumb or two also, isn't that right? . . .

So, I'll leave it there for today. Don't stop writing this poor brother of yours, telling him every last one of your "trivialities." Don't doubt that if I could relieve you of a few splinters of your cross, even at the expense of what I love most, I would do it. For now, I settle for being able to send you this tiny ray of light, however dim, to scatter your darkness, and a few sparks of love for God, too.

All my love and affection, your beloved brother,

Brother María Rafael
O.C.R.

Don't you worry about your punctuation. I understand you perfectly . . . that's not important at all. I don't know how this letter went either; whether it's well written or not, the Virgin dictated it to me.

CW 138. My Notebook
Solitude

La Trapa, December 11, 1936

Solitude . . . that word brings so many things forth in my soul. It's so difficult to express the joy of solitude when it has caused you to shed so many tears in the past.

Nevertheless, how joyful it is to be alone with God . . . Such great peace prevails when we are alone . . . when God and the soul are alone. How different are the world's ways from those of Christ. The world seeks itself, and finds itself. The soul that does not look for God looks instead for other souls, and if it does not find them, it weeps for its loneliness . . . weeping sorrowful tears that embitter the heart and do not bring consolation.

But the heart that seeks Christ loves its solitude from everything and everyone, for it is in that very solitude that Jesus reveals Himself. It is in that solitude that He seeks souls. He leads them into that solitude, sometimes by means of sorrows and sacrifices.

God is selfish, and He doesn't let His friends seek any consolation outside of Himself . . . At the beginning, He pacifies them with consolation from other human beings, but there comes a time when human beings have nothing more to give, and what little they can offer cannot satisfy the soul . . . Tears may come, or disappointment, or heartbreak . . . but what does that matter? God is the one who is doing it. It's a question of perseverance, and if the soul perseveres, it will find itself alone . . . God's infinite mercy!!

Alone is exactly where God wants the soul. It's so hard to get up that little hill and leave behind all those hopes and affections. Sometimes it feels like leaving behind pieces of your soul . . . Oh, Lord! It's so hard sometimes to accompany You into the solitude of spirit and body where You want to take us! Day after day, Jesus accomplishes His work in the hearts of His friends . . . Little by little, sometimes gently, sometimes all at once, he goes about stripping away the many things that bind the soul to the earth and its creatures . . .

Let Him do it . . . He is the master of everything. And indeed, if God wants us for Himself, we can't stop Him from leading us into solitude, where He shall speak to our hearts, as Hosea says.[19] How great God is! How wonderfully He does things!

What was difficult for us at first and made us shed so many tears . . . that blessed solitude with Christ . . . becomes our greatest consolation on this earth!

In that solitude, the soul delights in the great consolation of knowing it is alone with God. In that solitude, it loves Jesus with all its strength, it laughs with Him and weeps with Him . . . What more could one want? . . . What could human beings have to offer? . . . Solitude is a divine school where one comes to know God and learns to stop expecting things from the world.

Blessed is the solitude that draws us closer to God and helps us detach ourselves from creatures. In it, we learn to accompany first Jesus on the cross, and then Mary, whose soul was more in heaven than on earth, and who reveals to us Her own loneliness in the wake of Her Son's death and invites us to accompany Her in it.

How great is the mercy of God!!

How deceived we were when we believed that solitude was a cross. How deeply blind we were to look for God in human consolation.

19. See Hos 2:14.

It is true that when He wills it, He reveals Himself to us in a thousand different ways . . . but it's also true that when this is by means of a consolation, it will always be like looking at a foggy landscape. Yes, it's true, God is there, but He is behind the fog . . . behind our senses, our feelings, our delusions . . . behind all those creatures we seek out first.

God reveals Himself to the soul through all these things, and essentially His image appears unfocused, hazy, imprecise . . . A foggy landscape . . . The landscape is there, but the fog makes it blurry, and all you can see at first is the fog.

God is in everything, but not everything is God. Souls who are accustomed to seeing the Creator in the smallest details of creation, in the wonders of nature, in the harmony of the introit to the Mass,[20] or in a human heart doubtlessly delight in God, and God often makes use of such things to awaken a sleeping soul.

There is no doubt that such a soul sees God, but it does so imperfectly, because before arriving at the landscape itself, its gaze has stopped to linger upon the fog . . . whether that be in the form of an insect, or the sun, or a piece of music, or the magnificence of someone's heart.

One comes to see so clearly that it is in solitude that one can truly encounter God. How great is His mercy, that He should help us leap over created things and place us in an immense plain without rocks or trees or sky or stars . . . An unending plain without any colors, without any human beings, without anything that could distract the soul from God.

This is the infinite goodness of the Eternal One, who without any merit on our part leads us into the realm of solitude in order to speak to our hearts there.

This is the infinite patience of God, who, day after day and night after night, remains in pursuit of souls, despite our faults, despite our ingratitude and selfishness, despite the obstacles we

---

20. *Introit*: the entrance antiphon at the beginning of the Mass.

constantly put between us, despite how often we hide from Him, hiding not from His wrath but rather . . . I'm ashamed to say . . . from His grace.

My soul stretches when I meditate upon those divine poems by Saint John of the Cross, who says in one of them,

She lived in solitude,

and now in solitude has built her nest.[21]

The mystical Doctor, in his commentary on the poem, says that the soul was already living in solitude when God, pleased with that solitude, built the nest in her. The Carmelite clearly had a generous soul, since he went looking for God in solitude; mine is not at all like that, for I do just the opposite. The Most High takes my hand and leads my soul from place to place, and often kicking and screaming against my will.

God's mercy is everlasting! What have I done to deserve such treatment from You?

But that's all over now. I will be generous. I will be docile. Wherever you lead me, I will love what You love, even life itself, if that is Your wish.

I will lose myself in solitude of spirit and body so that, as the poem said, we might build a nest of divine love within it, and there may You speak to me, instruct me, and guide me so that I don't get lost and go astray as I make my way through this world.

Lead me, Lord, down the path of solitude. It is a sure path, trod by no one else. With You for my guide, what is there to fear?

In the monastery of San Isidro, there is a little monk . . . no, even less than that, there is a simple oblate who is walking in the way of monastic life, his heart driven mad with joy in his solitude. His lips are sealed with silence, but nevertheless they are always

21. "She" refers to the soul, figured as a dove. This is from stanza thirty-five of the *Spiritual Canticle*. See *The Collected Works of St. John of the Cross*, trans. Kieran Kavanaugh and Otilio Rodriguez, 3rd ed. (Washington, DC: ICS Publications, 2017), 79.

whispering some prayer or song. Right now, they bear the poem of that monk from Hontiveros, Teresa's brother:[22]

> She lived in solitude,
> and now in solitude has built her nest;
> and in solitude he guides her,
> he alone, who also bears
> in solitude the wound of love.[23]

CW 162. To Leopoldo Barón[24]

Villasandino, September 25, 1937

Ave Maria

May the peace of the Lord be with you.

God alone . . . How difficult it is to understand and live these words, but once you do, even if just for a moment . . . once your soul has realized that it belongs to God, that it is His possession . . . that Jesus dwells within it, despite its wretchedness and weakness . . . once your eyes are opened to the light of faith and hope . . . Once you understand the purpose of life, which is to live for God and for Him alone, there is nothing in the world that can trouble your soul. And those who, possessing nothing, hope for everything, can wait serenely instead of anxiously. A great peace fills the hearts of those who live for God alone, and only those who desire God alone find peace . . .

God alone! How sweet it is to live like this!

My dear brother, I don't know why I have taken up the pen and begun to write . . . Really, I don't know; there's no need and I have nothing to say. There is only one reason, though a very small

---

22. Saint John of the Cross, born in Fontiveros, Spain, was the co-reformer of the Carmelite Order with Saint Teresa of Ávila.

23. *Spiritual Canticle* stanza 35, in *Collected Works of St. John of the Cross*, 79.

24. Rafael's maternal uncle, who lived in Ávila; addressed as "Uncle Polín" and "brother."

one, and that reason is a desire of mine (I still have some desires), which is the desire to speak of Him.

Nobody out in the world listens patiently to the crazy thoughts of someone who, upon glimpsing a small fraction of God's greatness, is stupefied . . . someone who, leaving behind the nothingness and vanity of worldly things, feels the urge to shout, "Senseless fools . . . what are you looking for? Make haste! . . . God alone, what else is there but Him?"

How could we possibly occupy ourselves with so many things—laughing, crying, talking, arguing—and meanwhile, God gets nothing?

The world cannot and need not understand the foolishness of a lover of Christ . . . Foolishness, yes, there is no other word for it, the foolishness of the cross,[25] which makes our souls go nuts and scrambles our words, which try to say so much and end up saying nothing at all. A foolishness tempered only by the "straitjacket" of conformity to God's will, which makes us quiet down when we want to cry out, which makes us prudent when our souls break loose and want to . . . I don't know . . . which makes our waiting calm, when longing for Christ beats impatiently in our hearts.

Foolishness for Christ . . . naturally, people don't understand it, so it must be hidden away . . . hidden within, deep within, so that only He may see it, and so that no one—if possible, not even we—realize that we are completely consumed by it . . .

Don't pay me any mind. I've already told you the reason behind all these clumsy words. As you can see, it's simple; I've gone crazy, that's all.

You are very busy with many things, which are all very appropriate, very good, and very necessary . . . Perhaps you suffer, perhaps not . . . But, seeing as we've agreed that I'm crazy, I'll tell you this: "So what! What about God?"

25. See 1 Cor 1:18.

And then you'll start to say to yourself a bit, slowly at first, and then very quickly, "God alone . . . God alone . . . God alone," until suddenly you realize that you've gone crazy too, and your heart is overjoyed and you don't know what to do or say, and you laugh a lot, so much, like an idiot, because of how much you love God, and you haven't a care in the world, and when someone says something to you, you'll answer "yes, yes, it's true, you're right," but within yourself, deep within, you'll be saying . . . "God alone, God alone."

And when someone makes you laugh, you'll laugh, and you'll also say, "God alone."

And when someone makes you suffer, you'll suffer, but you'll also say . . . "Well, all right . . . but God alone."

And then one day, you too will take up pen and paper and share all the foolish things that occur to you and you'll send them off wherever you like, or maybe you will lose so many of your marbles that you'll forget how to write at all.

I wouldn't want you to laugh at me, but it's all the same to me. Perhaps all these foolish things I'm writing to you will speak to you in some way. Perhaps they will communicate the state of my soul to you, which I would so like to communicate to the whole world, so that the whole world would love God madly, and not think of anything else, and everyone would be very happy, as I am now, I who have nothing, not even my health, yet have everything . . . everything one can have in this life. I have God deep within my heart and want for nothing. That, believe me, is perfect happiness, a happiness so hidden that of course no one thinks to envy it.

You love God too, don't you? And so perhaps you will enjoy knowing that not everything in the world is arguments and noise and material desires . . .

Since you love God, and want the whole world to love Him, you will be pleased to see that someone else loves Him very much too.

That's why I'm saying all these things to you . . . these things that hardly anyone cares about, or is interested in, and instead people laugh at them or twist my words . . . because only those who have some love for God can understand these things.

What do you see when you look around you? If you really examine it all closely, you'll find that none of it satisfies you completely, not at all. You'll find a great deal of frivolity, perhaps even paganism sprouting from the cracks in a poorly understood Christianity; efforts toward well-being, as if this life were eternal; fights, disputes . . . but very little of God.

If you're looking at yourself, it's best not to say anything. So, then, what's left? . . . God and God alone. He gives what the world and its creatures cannot. Our misery, forgetfulness, and ingratitude are covered with His infinite Mercy. The consolation that people so often deny us when we are in pain can be found in His cross, alone with Him on Calvary. The only Truth can be found in His Gospel, the words of eternal life.[26] And as if that weren't enough, everything else . . . can be found in His Mother Mary.

How joyfully one lives when one has God, and God alone.

How small life's problems prove, for their solution is in . . . God alone.

No, don't tell me what the luminaries of this age have to say about this . . . You know what they say. Why should I repeat it? . . . Didn't we decide that we wanted to be fools? Let's be fools, then, even if the world takes us for senseless idiots . . . Who cares? God sees it all, and there's more senselessness and idiocy in a single so-called luminary than there is in a million souls seized with foolishness for Christ.

Blessed is that foolishness, which makes us live beyond the bonds of this earth, which helps us see the sorrows of our exile through the dazzling lens of hope, the certain hope of a splendid, resplendent day that *will not delay* . . .

Blessed is that foolishness for Christ, which makes us realize how vain and small our suffering is, turning our bitter tears into

26. See John 6:68.

the sweetest of songs, the pain and heartache of this life into the gentle fetters that bind us to Jesus . . .

Blessed are those who mourn,[27] Jesus said on earth, by the water's edge, and a crowd made up of the sick, the lame, the poor, and sinners followed Him . . . I believe that after turning toward Jesus, their faces, once tear stained from all their weeping, were transformed with joyful laughter, blessing their afflictions and miseries, which united them to Jesus.

And Jesus looked at them with the tenderness that won over the world, and let Himself be loved by the poor, the afflicted, the sick, and sinners . . . And Jesus healed them, and Jesus consoled them . . . and Jesus, that loving Jesus, forgave them.

This scene is repeating itself now. Nothing has changed, except that Jesus is not walking by the Sea of Galilee . . . rather, Jesus is in the tabernacle. There, He receives His friends, consoles them, heals them, and forgives them . . .

What great intimacy Jesus has with those who mourn! Blessed are our tears, sorrows, and illnesses, which are our treasures, all that we possess. They make us draw near to Jesus, since the love we have for Him is so little, so feeble, so weak that it is not enough on its own . . . !

What a great joy it is to realize you are beloved of God! To be counted among His friends, to follow Him step by step in Jerusalem with your eyes fixed on His divine countenance, blessing our own misery for having inspired Jesus to attract our gaze, so that He might reach our hearts, heal us, forgive us . . . and love us enough to die for us on a cross.

Such is foolishness for Christ . . . with eyes fixed on Jesus, one forgets to eat and fails to fear the cold; neither humble poverty nor love of family can hold back lovers of Jesus . . . God alone . . . only Him . . . that is the only thought that holds power over them . . . the miracle of being madly in love.

27. Matt 5:4.

The world and all who dwell in it come and go; people keep thinking about their businesses, the future of their estates, their illnesses. They cling to this earth, where they seek their rest. They suffer when they don't find it here, and weep when they have to leave . . . Those are the real fools, even though the world thinks it's foolish to love poverty, contempt, illness, and the cross.

What is the world, in all its prudence, sense, and rationality, supposed to think of such utter nonsense? I don't bother to argue with it. It's useless and unnecessary.

There was a poor brother at La Trapa who often wept before the cross. The world was saying to him, "You're an idiot, weeping by choice is foolish, you're uselessly wasting your life with all that silence and penance. Why love the cross when life is so beautiful? Freedom is bright, not gloomy!"

But that Trappist kept on weeping and weeping, and his tears were sweet sighs in his heart, placed lovingly at the Virgin's feet. He wouldn't have traded a single one of his tears for all the gold in the world . . . That Trappist wept, but he wept for joy . . . What does the world know of love?

Blessed is foolishness for Christ, which turns tears into pearls and makes us love the cross. That is true joy, the joy of the one who lives for God alone, who trusts in God alone, who hopes in God alone. And it is not a raucous joy; it is the serene joy of a soul who might still live on this earth, but expects nothing from this world. It is the joy of one who lives for Christ and dreams of Mary, and so, my dear brother . . . what do you want me to say? I don't know how to speak, let alone write.

God alone, God alone . . . Seek nothing else, and you'll see: once you find yourself in Jesus's retinue across the fields of Galilee, your soul will be flooded with something I cannot explain.

You'll see, you'll remember neither your sorrows nor your joys, and you won't focus on yourself at all. You'll see, too, how foolishness comes over you. You won't mind walking around in the sun, or sleeping out in the open . . . Jesus is so sweet! It is so good to be in His presence!

If the path proves difficult, or arduous, or long, it won't matter . . . Jesus goes before us. We won't even look where we're going . . . for we have Jesus as our guide. We will be silent when He speaks, and treasure His words in our silence . . .

We'll press on, day or night, drunk with joy, utterly mad with it, not listening to the world or eating or sleeping or anything else. "God alone . . . God alone," our heart will *bellow*, because our lips cannot part to shout the name of Jesus through the streets and in the public square, to cry out the wonders of God, His greatness, His mercy . . . His love.

And that is how we shall keep our silence as we walk around in this world, which professes to be Christian but does not follow Christ. We will make up for what is lacking in others. We will love Him like nobody else. If anyone asks after your health, or your crosses or consolations, if anyone asks you anything about yourself at all, you can respond, "I don't know. I love Jesus so much that I don't have time to worry about that." That's when you'll have done it . . . your foolishness will be complete.

Oh, blessed Jesus, when will this farce come to an end?! When will the day come when we can leave behind this body and all its afflictions and miseries?! When will we leave behind this world and all its lies?!

How long, O Lord?[28] David said as his soul was bursting. "Must we live in so miserable a life?!" Saint Teresa of Jesus said. What else could we poor sinners say? For even if we have good desires, our works are so weak and feeble . . .

Oh, we can indeed weep and suffer, but not because of our own crosses and sorrows, which are very small indeed, but rather, because we do not love Jesus. We can indeed weep over how ungrateful we are toward Jesus, and how often we forget to turn to Mary . . . Mary. It wasn't enough for God to give us His Son on a cross;

28. Ps 13:1.

He gave us Mary, too. How is it possible, brother, that we aren't better than this?

I don't want to get lost in thought here. There's so much I want to say to you, but I'm so clumsy about it . . . as you can see.

All I can say is that what we can do, with Mary's help, is wait . . . Remember when we used to talk about that? I remember drawing you a Trappist looking straight at a wooden cross driven into the ground upon the place where one of his beloved brothers was at rest.

For the one who hopes, waiting is sweet . . . This thought comes over me often, and everything I have learned from it has helped me whenever I feel as though I've been waiting too long.

How sweet it is to wait with closed eyes and an open heart. Neither the body, our soul's prison, nor the world with all its creatures can damage the soul that hopes in God, no matter how harshly they chafe against it. We can conquer and disregard the body, and instead of fearing contact with creatures, love them, even searching them out in order to teach them the wisdom that Christ taught us . . . love.

How sweet it is to wait while doing good . . . How sweet it is to wait with a smile for our brothers and sisters as well as for our enemies . . . How sweet it is to wait when Jesus is the one we are waiting for . . .

How sweet it is to wait while thinking of God and dwelling under Mary's mantle.

But the waiting starts to feel slow and painful when we are afflicted with desires other than God, when our selfishness rejects the cross, when we confuse our longing for God with getting tired of living, *however subtly*. How often we deceive ourselves, thinking something is God that isn't. I don't want to pontificate about the definition of perfection, God forbid. But I do believe that our longing to see God and our impatience in waiting for Him are made perfect in absolute submission to His will, with the serenity of those who desire nothing.

But we are still imperfect, and we cannot help it when our souls cry out to Christ, saying, "Why do you fail to carry off what you have stolen?" as Saint John of the Cross wrote in his canticle, although he came to love Him "with a flame that is consuming and painless."

But I don't want to talk about myself, and I don't want to get involved in your business either . . . It's all of so little importance!

When I picked up my pen, I decided to talk to you about God alone, and now I can't think of anything, maybe because there's so much I want to say, and because I have such an intense desire to share the gentleness and peace that God has placed in my soul with another . . . As you can see, I can't do anything, but my intention is good, even if I don't know how to express myself. Perhaps the same thing has happened to you before, and thus you will understand what I mean.

Let nothing trouble you,[29] for He gives so much to the souls of His friends, only to have us shrug off the treasure that is Christ's gentle yoke[30] at every vain disturbance that life provides.

Let nothing trouble you, because everything is nothing . . . God alone. Let us not grow tired of repeating it. If we were to take the intensity of the effort we put into earthly matters and put it into love for God instead . . . things would be different.

Don't go looking for someone to talk to you about Him . . . you'll come away disappointed, and it isn't necessary, because "they cannot tell you what you want to hear."[31] When you hide the love you have for God, it's as though you love Him more . . . does that happen to you, too?

---

29. From a poem by Saint Teresa of Ávila. See *The Collected Works of St. Teresa of Ávila*, trans. Kieran Kavanaugh and Otilio Rodriguez (Washington, DC: ICS Publications, 1985), 3:386.

30. See Matt 11:29-30.

31. From stanza six of Saint John of the Cross's *Spiritual Canticle*. See *Collected Works of St. John of the Cross*, 4.

With silence, prayer, and a whole lot of inner madness, we can wait well for what is to come . . . and it will all come.

I don't know what else to say . . . I paused just now, and with my pen in my hand, looking up at this clear blue Castilian sky, I just ended up thinking . . . God alone . . . God alone . . . God alone.

Brother María Rafael

CW166. To Toribio Luis (Br. Tescelino) Arribas[32]

Villasandino, November 1, 1937

Ave Maria

My dearest brother in the Lord,

You've truly taken your time in sending me your address. Of course, if you'd done it earlier, I would've written you earlier, even though I wouldn't have had anything in particular to tell you, because you already know about my life. Even so, perhaps I would've sent you the diary I promised, if only I had written it. Although perhaps I wouldn't have sent it to you for the simple reason that I have so, so much boiling over inside me that I find silence to be more appropriate. Isn't that right?

My diary! . . . Woe is me . . . who could possibly be interested in that! A diary of mine! What do you want me to say, my dear brother? . . . The consolation you offer me is very great, in remembering this poor sick man . . . that's what my diary would say . . . sick, useless, nothing. What else do you want to know? Do you perhaps want me to send you a little piece of my cross? . . . You already know about it, why discuss it? May God reward your charity, and may the Virgin Mary bless you.

---

32. Br. Tescelino Luis was the second infirmarian at San Isidro, also known by his baptismal name, Toribio. After his conscription into the army, he was serving as a medic at the time of this letter.

Don't you worry about Brother Rafael, neither he nor anything that happens to him is of any importance whatsoever. The Lord wants to lead him down this path of insignificance; a path on which he is nothing and is good for nothing, where he seeks only to be forgotten by everyone and to pass through this world without anyone noticing.

Believe me, God alone is my desire. Realizing how empty creatures and earthly things leave the heart, I have learned that happiness does not come from seeing our desires fulfilled.

God alone, brother, God alone . . . That is the only diary I have, the only thing that can be said to satisfy this poor sinner's soul. This poor soul, in its pride, wanted to fly one day, and God, in His infinite goodness, clipped its wings, humiliated it, and showed it what it was . . . a piece of garbage with a great deal of vanity . . . that's all.

Don't worry about me, honestly . . . I'm embarrassed that you would. Besides, I can't tell you anything that you don't already know. I'll just give you the news you asked for.

I went to Burgos eight days ago.[33] I spent three of them hospitalized at San José. My urine glucose test came back 42/1000, and they declared me completely unfit. The first time they did so, as you know, I was frustrated that I could not serve God and Spain at the front . . . or perhaps take a bullet for them . . . Now, believe me, I couldn't care less, because I've realized that what I want is worth nothing in the eyes of God. The best thing to do is to place yourself in His hands, and nothing more . . . May He make of me, *and you*, whatever He wants. Don't you think so?

I know sometimes it's exhausting to suffer. But so what? . . . It's such a short time. I know that the desire to fly to God and cease to offend Him is strong. But so what? . . . We are so insignificant, and we know so little; the best thing to do is let Him work . . . It's clear that my time has not yet come.

---

33. The purpose of Rafael's trip to Burgos was to undergo a second medical exam for the military, to assess whether or not he was still unfit for service.

I know the anguish of having to keep kicking and screaming through this life as the world hurts us, our passions afflict our flesh, and creatures make us suffer, is very great at times . . . but what of Him? I'll stop here, perhaps I've said enough.

Jesus lived thirty-three years *knowing* that He was going to die on a cross, and all He asked of His Father was that His will be done.

Christ taught us to suffer, He taught us to keep quiet, He taught us to desire nothing but the Father's will. When will we ever learn?

How selfish we are! . . . How little love we have for God!

Anyway, I don't want to get off topic . . . they sent me home from the hospital, and now I'm here waiting . . . I don't know *what for.*

I wrote to Father Abbot saying that once I'd had my medical exam, I'd return to the monastery. Fr. José[34] wrote me back saying that I could come back whenever I wanted, the doors would always be open to me . . . *but* that I should think it over and not rush, because they don't have an infirmarian right now, and it would be a shame if the same thing happened to me as before. That's all.

Humanly speaking, this is very prudent, don't you think? But what should I do? Well, look, this is how I'm thinking about it, let's see what you think.

Imagine that you were sick at home, surrounded by care and attention, practically lame, useless . . . in a word, incapable of taking care of yourself. But one day, you see Jesus walk by outside your window . . . You see a crowd of sinners, lepers, the poor and the sick, all following behind Him. You see that Jesus is calling you, and He *offers* you a place in His retinue, and He looks at you with those divine eyes that radiate love, tenderness, and forgiveness, and He tells you, "Why aren't you following Me?" . . . What would you do? Would you tell Him . . . "Lord, I'd follow You if You gave me an infirmarian . . . if You gave me the means to follow You

---

34. Fr. José Olmedo, Rafael's second master of novices.

comfortably, without endangering my health . . . I'd follow You if I were healthy and strong enough to take care of myself . . ."

No, I'm sure that if you saw the tenderness in Jesus's eyes, you wouldn't say any of that. Rather, you'd get up from your bed without a care in the world, without thinking about yourself at all, and you'd join Jesus's retinue, even if you were the last one . . . you hear, the *last one* . . . and you'd tell Him, "I'm coming, Lord. I don't care about my illness, or death, or eating, or sleeping . . . If You'll have me, I will go. If You want, You can heal me . . . I don't mind if the path that You are leading me down is challenging and rugged and covered in thorns. I don't mind if You want me to die with You on a cross . . ."

I will go, Lord, because You are the one who is leading me. You are the one who promises me an eternal reward. You are the one who forgives, who saves . . . You are the only one who can satisfy my soul.

Begone, warnings about what might happen to me in the future. Begone, human fears. When Jesus of Nazareth is the one who guides you . . . what is there to fear?

Don't you think, brother, that you would have followed Him? And that nothing in the world, or in yourself, would have mattered? Because that's what is happening to me.

I feel Jesus' sweet gaze deep within my soul. I know that nothing in this world can satisfy me, just God alone . . . God alone, God alone . . .

And Jesus is saying to me, "*You can come whenever you want . . . Don't worry about having the last place. Would I love you any less for that? Perhaps even more.*"

Don't be jealous, brother, but God loves me very much.

On the other hand, my flesh is weighing me down; the world calls me crazy, senseless . . . I'm getting all kinds of prudent warnings . . . But what's all that compared to just one look from a God like Jesus of Galilee as He offers you a place in heaven and eternal love? Nothing, brother . . . even if it meant suffering until the end of the world, it would never be worth it to stop following Jesus.

I'm going to La Trapa very soon. I can't give you a date yet. My brother Fernando will be coming home from the front in the next couple of days, and I want to spend a few days with him. Then, my father wants to go to Oviedo . . . I don't know what plans he has. I'm sure he'll be getting everything out of the house. As soon as I have an opportunity to tell my parents (who still think I'll be spending the winter with them) that I have nothing left to do here and they should let me leave, I will go.

Believe me, all this is making me suffer greatly. You know where I'm going, and what I'm headed for. But I trust greatly in Mary, our Mother; She will help me, as She always has.

My cross is ever more difficult . . . it weighs ever more heavily on me, but my soul is also ever more filled with that . . . "God alone," who, as I've said, gives me strength. And that is the only account of my life that I could possibly give you.

Take heart, brother, and keep fighting. As you know, one need not be at the front, even if our selfishness would rather have us be there, where . . . perhaps a bullet might . . . Let us be generous. Are we agreed?

Do what they tell you to do, obey, and keep quiet . . . The bullets will come whenever the Lord decides it's the right time.

Am I wrong to say all this? I am ever less sure of myself, and I don't have anyone to ask. If only you knew how relieved I am to tell you all these things . . . You understand me so well. You've been so charitable toward me; only the Lord knows how much gratitude I have in my heart for you.

I'd appreciate it if you could write me back and tell me what you think, even if it's just a quick note.

When one is suffering, the sincere affection of a brother who can offer counsel is so encouraging. It helps us to embrace the cross of Christ, don't you think? . . . What else is love for?

If only I could do the same for you . . . But what good am I? If only I could help you in combat, at your side in the rear guard; if only I could help you with your family . . . I understand it all, even when you don't write about it.

If only I could make this sentiment penetrate your soul: that in God, in Him alone, is life, health . . . everything.

Believe me, brother, finding myself powerless to do anything I desire, the only thing I know how to do is humbly remember you in my prayers before the Most Blessed Virgin . . . I can do nothing more. But here, from His humble tabernacle, the Lord receives the words of your brother Rafael, who is thinking of you.

Do whatever you'd like with the books and all the other things. Let's not talk about it again, I have nothing more to say. My sister doesn't need them at the moment, and if she does, she'll find them elsewhere in Burgos, but I don't think she's all that keen on studying.

How was your family when you saw them last? My mother, in particular, thinks of you often.

How is your health? Any headaches recently? I want to hear everything. Don't you go thinking that I've ceased to be human, I am seemingly more and more so by the day . . . As you can see, everything contributes to an increase in . . . Well, nothing to be done about that.

Please do write me back. I truly need it right now, and welcome any help I can get. Please pray to the Virgin Mary for me especially; you know we can do all things with Her help . . . you'll pray for me, won't you?

I have nothing else to tell you. I know this letter is a total nuisance, forgive me; but please understand me and be merciful toward me as I pour out this soul you know so well. Sending you a big hug in Jesus and Mary,

Brother María Rafael

I was very pleased that Father Abbot gave you Aloysius Gonzaga's name . . . A very kindly saint . . . May he protect you.

¡¡VIVA ESPAÑA!!
Viva Cristo Rey[35]

---

35. "Long live Spain!! Long live Christ the King."

CW 202. God and My Soul
Holy Tuesday

La Trapa, April 12, 1938

I only find what I'm looking for in God, and I find it in such abundance that I no longer mind that I cannot find what I once dreamed of in human beings. That dream has come and gone . . .

I looked for truth and I didn't find it. I looked for love, and all I saw in human beings was a few drops that wouldn't satisfy my thirsty heart . . . I looked for peace, and I realized that there is no peace on earth.[36]

That dream came and went, but quietly, before I'd even realized . . . The Lord, who tricked me in order to draw me closer to Himself, is the one who made me realize it . . .

How happy I am now! "What are you looking for among human beings?" He says to me . . . "What are you looking for on this earth, where you are a pilgrim? What kind of peace do you want?" . . . How good is the Lord, who separates me from creatures and vanity!

I can see clearly now that true peace is to be found in God . . . that true love is to be found in Jesus . . . that the only Truth is Christ.

Today, at Holy Communion, while I had Jesus in my heart, my soul swam in the boundless, immense joy of having the Truth . . . I felt as if I possessed God, and God possessed me . . . I desired only to profoundly love the Lord who, in His great goodness, was consoling my heart, which was thirsty for something *I couldn't name* and searched for among creatures in vain. Without the noise of words, the Lord helped me to understand that He is what my soul desires . . . That He is Truth, Life, and Love . . . And that so long as I have Him . . . What am I looking for? What am I asking for? . . . What do I want?

36. Jer 6:14; 8:11.

Nothing, Lord . . . this world is too small to contain everything You give me. Who could explain what it's like to possess the ultimate Truth? Who could find the words to express what this means: "I desire nothing, for I have God"?

My soul almost weeps for joy . . . Who am I, Lord? Where can I put my treasure so it doesn't get tarnished? How could I possibly live in peace, without fear of getting robbed? What can my soul do to thank You?

Poor Brother Rafael, you'll have to answer to God for the great many blessings He has given you here! You must have a heart of stone not to weep for your great ingratitude and scorn for divine grace.

My Lord, I spend my life wallowing in my own misery, and at the same time I don't dream of anything but You, I don't live for anything but You. How does that make sense?

I am thirsty for You . . . I weep for my exile, I dream of heaven; my soul longs for Jesus, in whom it finds its Treasure, its Life, its only Love; I expect nothing from human beings . . . My Jesus, I love You like crazy, and even so, I eat, laugh, sleep, talk, study, and live among human beings without doing anything crazy. I'm ashamed to say I even . . . look for comfort. What explanation is there for this, Lord?

How is it possible that You have placed Your grace within me? If I made a return to You somehow . . . then maybe that would explain it.

Forgive me, my Jesus . . . I should be holy, and I'm not. And I'm the one who used to be scandalized by some of the miseries of human beings? Me? . . . Ridiculous.

You've already given me *light* so that I might see and understand, Lord; now give me a very, very big heart so that I can *love* human beings, who are Your children, and my brothers and sisters. My great pride saw flaws in them, while I was blind to my own.

And if You were to give the least of them what You have given me? But You do all things well . . . My soul weeps over its bad habits in the past, its old ways . . . It no longer looks for perfection in human beings . . . it no longer cries about not finding *a place to rest* . . . it has all of that now.

You, my God, are the one who fills my soul; You are my joy, my peace, and my calm. You, Lord, are my refuge, my strength, my life, my light, my consolation, my only Truth and my only Love.

I'm so happy. I have it all!

I am filled with such tenderness when I think about these fathomless favors that Jesus grants me. My soul is filled with true love for human beings, for my weak, sick brothers and sisters . . . It is understanding now, and sweetly forgives the weaknesses that used to make it suffer when it would see them in its neighbor . . . Oh, if only the world loved God a little, they would love their neighbor too.

When you love Jesus, when you love Christ, you also *necessarily* love what He loves. Did Jesus not die of love for human beings? As our hearts are transformed into the heart of Christ, then we too feel this and note its effects . . . and the greatest of them all is *love* . . . *love for the Father's will* . . . *love for everyone* who suffers and struggles, whether they're a father or a far-off brother, whether they're English, Japanese, or Trappist . . . *love for Mary* . . . In short, who can comprehend the heart of Christ? No one. But there are those who have tiny pieces of it . . . very hidden away . . . very much in silence, without letting the world notice.

My Jesus, how good You are. You do everything so wonderfully well. You show me the way; You show me the end.

The way is the sweet cross . . . it is sacrifice, renunciation, and sometimes the bloody battle that ends in tears on Calvary or in the Garden of Gethsemane; the way, Lord, is to be the last, to be the poor, sick, Trappist oblate who suffers by Your cross sometimes.

But it doesn't matter. To the contrary . . . one can only enjoy the gentleness of pain through humbly suffering for You. Tears shed at Your cross's side are a balm in this life of continual renunciation and sacrifice, and those sacrifices and renunciations are made pleasant and easy when the soul is alive with love, faith, and hope.

This is how You turn thorns into roses. So then, what is the end? . . . You are the end, and only You. The end is eternal possession of You in heaven with Jesus and Mary and all the angels and saints. But that will happen in heaven. And to encourage those of us who are weak, feeble, and fainthearted like me, sometimes You reveal Yourself to our hearts and say . . . "What are you looking for? What do you want? Who are you calling out for? . . . Take Me, consider who I am . . . I am the Truth and the Life."[37]

And then You flood the soul with delights that the world doesn't know about or understand. Then, Lord, You fill the souls of Your servants with ineffable sweetness, which they ponder in silence. Human beings hardly dare to begin to explain this . . .

My Jesus, I love You so much, in spite of what I am . . . and the worse and more miserable I am, the more I love You . . . and I will always love You, and I will cling to You and never let You go,[38] and . . . I don't know what else I was going to say.

Help me, Virgin Mary!

37. See John 14:6.
38. See Song 3:4.

Bibliography

The Writings of Rafael Arnaiz

The Collected Works. Edited by María Gonzalo-García. Translated by Catherine Addington. MW 61. Collegeville, MN: Cistercian Publications, 2022.

Hermano Rafael: Escritos por temas. 2nd ed. Edited by Alberico Feliz Carbajal. Burgos, Spain: Editorial Monte Carmelo, 2000.

San Rafael Arnaiz: Obras completas. Edited by Alberico Feliz Carbajal. 7th ed. Burgos, Spain: Grupo Editorial Fonte/Editorial Monte Carmelo, 2017.

Other Primary Sources

Aelred of Rievaulx. *The Liturgical Sermons: The First Clairvaux Collection.* Translated by Theodore Berkeley and Basil Pennington. CF 58. Kalamazoo, MI: Cistercian Publications, 2001.

Aquinas, Thomas. *Commentary on the Gospel of John Chapters 6–12.* Translated by Fabian Larcher and James A. Weisheipl. Washington, DC: The Catholic University of America Press, 2010.

Athanasius of Alexandria. *The Life of Antony: The Coptic Life and the Greek Life.* Translated by Tim Vivian and Apostolos N. Athanassakis. CS 202. Kalamazoo, MI: Cistercian Publications, 2003.

Benedict. *RB 1980: The Rule of St. Benedict.* Edited by Timothy Fry. Collegeville, MN: Liturgical Press, 1981.

Bernard of Clairvaux. *Homilies in Praise of the Blessed Virgin Mary.* Translated by Maria-Bernard Saïd. CF 18. Kalamazoo, MI: Cistercian Publications, 1993.

Bernard of Clairvaux. *On Grace and Free Choice.* Translated by Daniel O'Donovan. CF 19. Kalamazoo, MI: Cistercian Publications, 1977.

Bernard of Clairvaux. *On Loving God, with an Analytical Commentary by Emero Stiegman.* Translated by Robert Walton. CF 13B. Kalamazoo, MI: Cistercian Publications, 1995.

Bernard of Clairvaux. *On Precept and Dispensation.* Translated by Martinus Cawley. CF 1. Shannon, Ireland: Irish University Press, 1970.

Bernard of Clairvaux, *On the Song of Songs I.* Translated by Kilian Walsh. CF 4. Spencer, MA: Cistercian Publications, 1971.

Bernard of Clairvaux. *On the Song of Songs II.* Translated by Kilian Walsh. CF 7. Kalamazoo, MI: Cistercian Publications, 1976.

Bernard of Clairvaux. *On the Song of Songs IV.* Translated by Irene Edmonds. CF 40. Kalamazoo, MI: Cistercian Publications, 1980.

Bernard of Clairvaux. *Sermons for Advent and the Christmas Season.* Translated by Irene Edmonds, Wendy Mary Beckett, and Conrad Greenia. CF 51. Kalamazoo, MI: Cistercian Publications, 2007.

Bernard of Clairvaux. *Sermons for Lent and the Easter Season.* Translated by Irene Edmonds. Edited and revised by Mark A. Scott. CF 52. Collegeville, MN: Cistercian Publications, 2013.

Bernard of Clairvaux. *St. Bernard's Sermons for the Seasons and Principal Feasts of the Year.* Translated by a Priest of Mount Melleray [Ailbe J. Luddy]. 3 vols. Westminster, MD: Carroll Press, 1950.

Bernard of Clairvaux. *The Steps of Humility and Pride.* Translated by M. Ambrose Conway, CF 13A. Kalamazoo, MI: Cistercian Publications, 1989.

Cassian, John. *The Conferences.* Translated by Boniface Ramsey. Ancient Writers Series 57. New York: Paulist Press, 1997.

Gilbert of Hoyland. *Sermons on the Song of Songs, I.* Translated by Lawrence C. Braceland. CF 14. Kalamazoo, MI: Cistercian Publications, 1978.

Gilbert of Hoyland. *Sermons on the Song of Songs, III.* Translated by Lawrence Braceland. CF 26. Kalamazoo, MI: Cistercian Publications, 1979.

Guerric of Igny. *Liturgical Sermons, I.* Translated by Monks of Mount Saint Bernard Abbey. CF 8. Shannon, Ireland: Cistercian Publications, 1970.

Isaac of Stella. *Sermons on the Christian Year.* Translated by Lewis White. CF 66. Collegeville, MN: Cistercian Publications, 2019.

John of the Cross. *The Collected Works of St. John of the Cross*. Translated by Kieran Kavanaugh and Otilio Rodriguez. 3rd ed. Washington, DC: ICS Publications, 2017.

John of Ford. *Sermons on the Song of Songs, II*. Translated by Wendy Mary Beckett. CF 39. Kalamazoo, MI: Cistercian Publications, 1982.

Regulations of the Order of Cistercians of the Strict Observance. Published by the General Chapter of 1926. Dublin: M. H. Gill and Son, 1926.

The Sayings of the Desert Fathers: The Alphabetical Collection. Translated by Benedicta Ward. CS 59. London and Oxford: Mowbray. Rev. ed. Kalamazoo, MI: Cistercian Publications, 1984.

Santa Teresa de Jesús. *Obras Completas*. Edited by Alberto Barrientos. 5th ed. Madrid: Editorial de Espiritualidad, 2000.

Teresa of Ávila. *The Collected Works of St. Teresa of Ávila*. Translated by Kieran Kavanaugh and Otilio Rodriguez. Washington, DC: ICS Publications, 1985.

Thérèse of Lisieux. *The Story of a Soul: The Autobiography of Saint Thérèse of Lisieux*. 3rd ed. Translated by John Clarke. Washington, DC: ICS Publications, 1996.

Thomas à Kempis. *The Imitation of Christ*. Translated by Ronald Knox and Michael Oakley. South Bend, IN: Greenlawn Press, 1990.

Works about Rafael

Álvarez, Tomás. "El hermano Rafael, escritor espiritual." *Cistercium* 179 (Oct.–Dec. 1989): 409–17.

Barón, Mercedes. *Vida y escritos de Fray María Rafael Arnáiz Barón, monje trapense*. 12th ed. Madrid: PS [Perpétuo Socorro] Editorial, 2000.

Beltrame Quattrocchi, Paulino. *Fascinado por el Absoluto: Hermano Rafael*. Translated by Tomás Gallego Fernández. Madrid: Ediciones Paulinas, 1991.

Blanco Mayo, Victorino. *Rafael Arnáiz, modelo de entrega total (Descubriendo al Rafael profundo)*. Zamora, Spain: Ediciones Monte Casino, 2018.

Cerro Chaves, Francisco. *Silencio en los labios, cantares en el corazón: vida y espiritualidad del Hermano Rafael*. BAC estudios y ensayos, 4. Madrid: Biblioteca de Autores Cristianos, 2000.

De Pascual, Francisco Rafael. "Son tus Santos, nuestros amigos." *Cistercium* 254 (Jan.–June 2010): 7–28.

Feliz Carbajal, Alberico. "Dios y el Hermano Rafael." *Cistercium* 174 (1988): 99–126.

Fernández, Gonzalo María. *El Beato Hermano Rafael: Biografía Espiritual.* 2nd ed. Venta de Baños, Spain: Abadía Cisterciense de San Isidro de Dueñas, 1993.

Fernández, Gonzalo María. *God Alone: A Spiritual Autobiography of Blessed Rafael Arnáiz Barón.* Translated by Hugh McCaffery. Edited by Kathleen O'Neill. MW 14. Kalamazoo, MI: Cistercian Publications, 2008.

Gallego Fernández, Tomás. "El Hermano Rafael, testigo de la trascendencia de Dios." *Cistercium* 174 (1988): 27–68.

Gallego Fernández, Tomás. "El hermano Rafael y su causa de beatificación." *Cistercium* 179 (Oct.–Dec. 1989): 419–24.

Gallego Fernández, Tomás. "El hermano Rafael y 'su Trapa' a luz de un centenario." *Cistercium* 185 (April–June 1991): 439–64.

Gallego Fernández, Tomás. "Hermano Rafael, 'Loco por Cristo.'" *Cistercium* 254 (Jan.–June 2010): 49–69.

Gil de Muro, Eduardo T. *Rafael Arnáiz: Sin mirar a los lados.* Burgos, Spain: Editorial Monte Carmelo, 1989.

Jiménez Duque, Baldomero. "La experiencia del Hermano Rafael a la luz de las enseñanzas de San Juan de la Cruz." In *Espiritualidad del Hermano Rafael.* Venta de Baños, Spain: Abadía de San Isidro de Dueñas, 1984. 63–85.

Maqueda, Duque de [Leopoldo Barón Torres]. *Un secreto de la Trapa (Beato Hermano Rafael).* 6th ed. Burgos, Spain: Editorial Monte Carmelo, 1998.

Martín Fernández-Gallardo, Antonio María. "Beato Rafael Arnáiz: algunas claves de su experiencia espiritual." *Cistercium* 241 (Oct.–Dec. 2005): 1045–92.

Martín Fernández-Gallardo, Antonio María. *El deseo de Dios y la ciencia de la Cruz: Aproximación a la experiencia religiosa del Hermano Rafael.* 2nd ed. Biblioteca cisterciense, 5. Burgos, Spain: Editorial Monte Carmelo, 2002.

Martín Fernández-Gallardo, Antonio María. *San Rafael Arnáiz Barón: Vida y mensaje del Hermano Rafael.* 2nd ed. Madrid: Edibesa, 2009.

Martínez Camino, Juan Antonio. *Mi Rafael: San Rafael Arnáiz, según el Padre Teófilo Sandoval, su confesor, intérprete y editor.* 2nd ed. Bilbao, Spain: Editorial Desclée de Brouwer, 2009.

Palmero Ramos, Rafael. *El hombre más feliz de la tierra.* 2nd ed. Burgos, Spain: Editorial Monte Carmelo, 1996.

Palmero Ramos, Rafael. "Teología del dolor en la enfermedad en el Hermano Rafael." In *Espiritualidad del Hermano Rafael.* Venta de Baños, Spain: Abadía de San Isidro de Dueñas, 1984. 481–500.

Sánchez Monge, Manuel. *La pasión de sólo Dios: el hermano Rafael.* Burgos, Spain: Editorial Monte Carmelo, 2000.

Sánchez Monge, Manuel. *Una santidad muy humana: espiritualidad del Hermano Rafael.* Madrid: Editorial Edapor, 1992.

Vilariño Periáñez, Almudena. "El hermano Rafael, modelo de fidelidad y constancia." *Cistercium* 254 (Jan.–June 2010): 35–47.

Yáñez Neira, Damián. "Cistercienses españoles escritores: Arnáiz Barón, San Rafael (1911–1939[8]), OCSO." *Cistercium* 262 (Jan.–June 2014): 172–80.

Yáñez Neira, Damián. "Como al hermano Rafael hace ahora cincuenta años." In *Espiritualidad del Hermano Rafael.* Venta de Baños, Spain: Abadía de San Isidro de Dueñas, 1984. 25–42.

Yáñez Neira, Damián. "Recordando al Padre Teófilo Sandoval: Maestro spiritual." *Cistercium* 221 (Oct.–Dec. 2000): 1127–40.

Other Works

Casey, Michael. *The Undivided Heart: The Western Monastic Approach to Contemplation.* Petersham, MA: St. Bede's Publications, 1994.

Connor, Elizabeth. *Charles Dumont, Monk-Poet: A Spiritual Biography.* MW 10. Kalamazoo, MI: Cistercian Publications, 2007.

Crisógono de Jesús Sacramentado. *San Juan de la Cruz: el hombre, el doctor, el poeta.* Barcelona, Spain: Editorial Labor, 1935.

Foulcher, Jane. *Reclaiming Humility: Four Studies in the Monastic Tradition.* CS 255. Collegeville, MN: Cistercian Publications, 2015.

Freeman, Brendan. *Come and See: The Monastic Way for Today.* MW 52. Collegeville, MN: Cistercian Publications, 2010.

Gorman, Michael J. *Cruciformity: Paul's Narrative Spirituality of the Cross.* Grand Rapids, MI: William B. Eerdmans Publishing Company, 2001.

Harmless, William. *Desert Christians: An Introduction to the Literature of Early Monasticism.* New York: Oxford University Press, 2004.

Jamison, Christopher. *Finding Happiness: Monastic Steps for a Fulfilling Life*. London: Weidenfeld and Nicolson, 2008.

La Vida Cisterciense en el Monasterio de San Isidro de Dueñas. Burgos, Spain: Editorial Monte Carmelo, 1928.

Louf, André. *The Cistercian Way*. Translated by Nivard Kinsella. CS 76. Kalamazoo, MI: Cistercian Publications, 1983.

Louf, André. *In the School of Contemplation*. Translated by Paul Rowe. MW 48. Collegeville, MN: Cistercian Publications, 2015.

Louf, André. *The Way of Humility*. Translated by Lawrence S. Cunningham. MW 11. Kalamazoo, MI: Cistercian Publications, 2007.

Luckman, Harriet A., and Linda Kulzer, eds. *Purity of Heart in Early Ascetic and Monastic Literature: Essays in Honor of Juana Raasch, O.S.B.* Collegeville, MN: Liturgical Press, 1999.

Merton, Thomas. *Cassian and the Fathers: Initiation into the Monastic Tradition, One*. Edited by Patrick F. O'Connell. MW 1. Kalamazoo, MI: Cistercian Publications, 2005.

Merton, Thomas. *The Climate of Monastic Prayer*. CS 1. Kalamazoo, MI: Cistercian Publications, 2018.

Merton, Thomas. *The Monastic Journey*. Edited by Patrick Hart. Mission, KS: Sheed Andrews and McMeel, 1977.

Merton, Thomas. *The Silent Life*. New York: Farrar, Straus and Giroux, 1957.

Nguyen, Joseph H. *Apatheia in the Christian Tradition: An Ancient Spirituality and Its Contemporary Relevance*. Eugene, OR: Cascade, 2018.

Raasch, Juana. "The Monastic Concept of Purity of Heart and Its Sources." *Studia Monastica* 8–12 (1966–1970): 8:7–33, 183–213; 10:7–55; 11:269–314; 12:7–41.

Saward, John. "The Fool for Christ's Sake." In *One Yet Two: Monastic Tradition East and West*. Edited by M. Basil Pennington. CS 29. Kalamazoo, MI: Cistercian Publications, 1976. 48–80.

Saward, John. *Perfect Fools: Folly for Christ's Sake in Catholic and Orthodox Spirituality*. Oxford: Oxford University Press, 1980.

Scholl, Edith. *Words for the Journey, A Monastic Vocabulary*. MW 21. Collegeville, MN: Cistercian Publications, 2009.

Sheridan, Mark. "The Controversy over Apatheia: Cassian's Sources and His Use of Them." *Studia Monastica* 39 (1997): 287–310.

Stewart, Columba. *Cassian the Monk*. Oxford Studies in Historical Theology. New York: Oxford University Press, 1998.

Stewart, Columba. Introduction to *Purity of Heart in Early Ascetic and Monastic Literature: Essays in Honor of Juan Raasch, O.S.B.* Edited by Harriet A. Luckman and Linda Kulzer. Collegeville, MN: Liturgical Press, 1999. 1–15.

Thomas, Robert. *Passing from Self to God: A Cistercian Retreat*. Translated by Martha F. Krieg. MW 6. Kalamazoo, MI: Cistercian Publications, 2006.